The CAR Book

1988 Edition

*An Indispensable Guide
to the Safest,
Most Economical New Cars*

Jack Gillis

with
Karen Fierst

Foreword by
Clarence Ditlow
Center for Auto Safety

PERENNIAL LIBRARY

Harper & Row Publishers, New York
Cambridge, Philadelphia, San Francisco, Washington
London, Mexico City, São Paulo, Singapore, Sydney

Publisher's Note

The ratings, statistics, and other data found in this book were current when this book went to press. Because of occasional changes by automobile manufacturers in their cars' design and performance, however, some of this data may change during the current model year.

THE CAR BOOK *(1988 edition)*. Copyright © 1987, 1986, 1985, 1984, 1983, 1982, 1981 by Jack Gillis. All rights reserved. Printed in the United States of America. No part of this book may be used or reproduced in any manner whatsoever without written permission except in the case of brief quotations embodied in critical articles and reviews. For information, address Harper & Row, Publishers, Inc., 10 East 53rd Street, New York, N.Y. 10022. Published simultaneously in Canada by Fitzhenry & Whiteside Limited, Toronto.

ISSN: 0893-1208

ISBN: 0-06-096223-2

87 88 CW 5 4 3 2 1

Contents

Acknowledgments

In each of the eight years that we have been preparing *The Car Book*, we have tried to improve upon and add to each subsequent edition. Some of the most significant changes have been made during the past three years. During that time, Karen Fierst, whose name now appears on the title page, has had the primary responsibility for compiling and organizing the thousands of items that need to be reviewed, analyzed and digested in order to make the car buying process easier for the American car buyer. As in the 1986 and 1987 editions, her hard work, management ability and long hours were the primary reasons we were able to meet this year's early deadline.

The compilation of such massive amounts of information is possible only with the assistance of a number of people including: Graphic artist Susan Cole, a talented and creative designer and Jennifer Barrett, a gifted artist and true friend; Teresa Wooten-Talley, a speedy, skillful and hard working word processing professional; Researchers Christina Mendoza, Barbara Tracy, Tanny Southerland and Sheri Soderberg Pittman; Barry Fierst and his creative and tireless work on the computer; Clarence Ditlow and the staff of the Center for Auto Safety, especially Evan Johnson, Esq., for his exhaustive review of the state lemon laws and Russell Shew, one of America's foremost automobile experts; John Michel, whose whose four years of patient and expert editorial supervision of this publication for Harper & Row will be greatly missed; John Noettl, president of Vehicle Support Systems and his staff including James Marshall, Jennifer Cook Mirabito, Steven N. Noettl, Christopher Lank, and Matthew P. Figueroa; Karen Steinke and Steve Smith of Chronicle Type & Design; Jim Armstrong and Harriet Rubin of Harper & Row; Ed Lewis of the Tire Industry Safety Council; Nancy Green of the National Association of Governor's Highway Safety Representatives; and, Ann Lavie and Torryn Phelps, Insurance Service Organization.

Special thanks and much appreciation also go to superagent Stuart Krichevsky and publicist Lisa Kitei and, most especially, to my wife, Marilyn Mohrman-Gillis.

As always,
For Marilyn, Katie, and John

When *The Car Book* was first published by the U.S. Department of Transportation in 1980, the Federal Government was committed to helping consumers buy better and safer cars. If consumers ended up with lemons or defective cars, the government worked to get the cars fixed or the consumers reimbursed. Now, instead of protecting consumers from shoddy quality and safety hazards, the government is protecting car companies. As a result, the unsuspecting consumer pays more for less when buying a 1988 model.

From its first days in January 1981, the Reagan Administration has kept its political promise to get the government off the backs of the car companies. The result — the car companies have jumped on the backs of consumers. The U.S. Department of Transportation (DOT) has refused to require the popular minivans and pickups to meet all safety standards, so families riding in these vehicles are at greater risk than those riding in cars and station wagons. School children take 8 million rides every day in school buses that have failed DOT safety compliance tests. DOT has terminated vital consumer information programs ranging from safety ratings on cars to tread life on tires. It has also stalled standards for side impact crashes which account for one-third of all occupant fatalities. The Federal Trade Commission has virtually eliminated its consumer protection programs which required auto companies to publicize secret warranties and reimburse consumers victimized by known defects in cars.

Under this adminstration, despite a sharp rise in consumer complaints over defects in cars, federal investigations and remedial programs for defective cars have fallen off. Safety recalls are at a record low. Hundreds of investigations into serious safety defects have been closed or suspended—despite evidence showing the need for a recall. In over 40 cases involving millions of vehicles, where the DOT has found such serious safety defects that it asked for voluntary recalls, the manufacturers have refused — and DOT will not order mandatory recalls. Investigations now take so long that 5 million vehicles under investigation are beyond the recall limit of 8 years from date of sale.

Even the biggest economic lemon ever produced by the auto industry, 1978-85 GM diesels, has brought no direct help from the Federal government. Instead, the FTC (with Chairman James A. Miller, III, a former $1500-a-day GM consultant, casting the deciding vote) dropped its lawsuit to help consumers. The FTC abdicated to an arbitration program run by the Better Business Bureau and funded by GM. Yet these cars and trucks are so bad that consumers can scarcely sell or trade them. If they do, they find they lose $3,000 to $6,000 in excess depreciation on a car for which they paid a $1,000 premium. This is often on top of repair expenses for the diesel engine itself, which was nothing more than a converted gasoline engine.

The Department of Transportation has taken no action to protect consumers from the most lethal safety defect ever — automatic transmissions in 1966-80 Fords that fail to hold or engage in park. From January 1981 through April 1985, when DOT decided not to take responsible actions, over 100 people were killed when these Ford vehicles jumped out of park and ran over them. The total known fatality toll is over 400, far more than for any other defect (including the infamous Firestone 500 steel belted radial tires and the Ford Pinto with the exploding gas tank). Yet DOT has tried to help Ford cover up the defect by blaming the driver—even though this incidence happens five to ten times more often in Fords than in other cars.

To help consumers victimized by the auto companies and ignored by the government, the Center for Auto Safety has instituted a class action program. Already we have organized class actions on over 20 million defective vehicles, including: 1978-85 GM diesels, 1976-80 GM cars and trucks with defective Type 200 automatic transmissions, 1976-80 Fords with automatic transmissions that jump from Park to Reverse, 1980 GM X-cars with brakes that lock-up, and 81-84 Chevettes with defective crankshaft bolts. So far, the class actions on 1978-80 GM diesels 1976-80 GM vehicles with THM 200 transmissions and 1981-

84 Chevettes have been settled for $22.5 million, $19.5 million, and $20 million respectively.

In relaxing and seeking to relax over 60 present or proposed safety standards, the Reagan Administration has ignored the costs to consumers for needless accidents and injuries. One of the worst examples of ignoring consumer costs is the rollback of the bumper standard. All 1980-82 cars have bumpers that prevent damage to the car and bumper in crashes up to 10 mph with another car or 5 mph into a concrete wall. Yet the Department of Transportation (DOT) reduced this standard to only 2.5 mph into a wall for 1983-86 models, scarcely faster than a toddler walks. As a result, automobiles now suffer hundreds of dollars of damage in minor parking lot accidents that would have previously caused no damage. For example, in a series of low speed accidents, the 1983 Honda Accord with 2.5 mph bumpers sustained an incredible $2,320 more in damage costs than a similar 1982 Honda with 5 mph bumpers. Despite a congressional mandate to provide information on poor bumpers to consumers, DOT is once again cooperating with the car companies and refusing to tell the public which cars have shoddy bumpers.

The Center for Auto Safety has repeatedly challenged the government's actions over the years with many major successes. We won a lawsuit forcing the Department of Transportation to reinstate its tire treadwear rating program in 1985. Another legal victory required the Environmental Protection Agency to recall polluting cars rather than accepting car companies' promises to make cleaner cars in the future, thus forcing consumers to breathe dirtier air now. Yet another lawsuit forced DOT to keep giant trucks off heavily traveled, two-lane roads.

Federal gas mileage standards are one of the most successful government programs ever adopted, with 1988 cars getting more than twice the fuel economy of 1974 cars. These standards saved consumers $3,000 in gas costs on a 1988 model and reduced oil imports by $16 billion. Yet Transportation Secretary Elizabeth Dole played into the hands of the oil exporting countries by relaxing these standards, beginning with 1986 cars and 1985 trucks. The Center for Auto Safety has filed suit to overturn this relaxation and get higher gas mileage vehicles for consumers.

Rather than let the auto companies foist unsafe, inefficient, and defective automobiles on the American public while the government turns its back on consumers, the Center for Auto Safety has increased its efforts to improve *The Car Book* for 1988. With the information on 1988 models at their fingertips in this book, consumers can select those cars that are safer, more economical and efficient. The continued publication of *The Car Book* ensures that if manufacturers take advantage of the Federal Government's relaxation of auto regulations and produce less safe and poorer quality vehicles, the American public will know the difference.
—*Clarence M. Ditlow   Executive Director,   Center for Auto Safety*

The price of the average new car this year will reach $14,000! This astonishing statistic is one reason why we are making this year's edition of *The Car Book* available earlier than ever before. With nearly across-the-board price increases, the need for important information about this expensive purchase has never been greater. Nevertheless, we stand by our advice that it's best to buy cars made later during the production schedule in order to increase your chances of buying a model free from manufacturing defects.

One of the most dramatic innovations to be introduced with the 1988 models is four-wheel steering. Initially available on only one Japanese model, (Honda Prelude), this remarkable feature will improve highway handling as well as low speed maneuverability. Otherwise, the most widespread change in the 1988 models is the larger selection of cars with built-in automatic crash protection. This year, at least 25 percent of all new models will be designed to automatically protect passengers in crashes of at least 30 mph.

While American car buyers are finally getting safer cars, only a short time ago automakers were convinced that consumers didn't care about safety. Actually, we did care, but because we could not compare safety in the showroom, we were not able to demonstrate our desires by buying the safer cars.

That's why, eight years ago, we began to publish *The Car Book*. Our hope is that this information will help consumers to cast their vote in the market place for safer and better performing cars.

Even though there are few truly new models on the market this year, we are excited about many of the 1988 cars because manufacturers are striving to attain higher quality. As we reviewed the 1988 models, we continue to notice dramatic improvements in the design and assembly of American cars. The U.S.-built Japanese cars (Chevrolet Nova, Honda Accord and Civic, Nissan Sentra) are every bit as well assembled as their Japanese counterparts.

Manufacturers are listening to our demands. A few years ago, when the benchmark for domestic cars was poor quality and design, we responded by buying Japanese cars in record numbers. We were even willing to pay surcharges for these high-quality, well-designed, economical cars. Unfortunately, during those early years of our infatuation with small Japanese cars, we were trading off high quality and economy for safety. The Japanese cars performed poorly in the crash tests.

Still believing that the American public didn't care about safety, the U.S. car makers failed to take advantage of the clear advantage they had over these early Japanese competitors - safer cars. On the other hand, the Japanese, sensing Americans' underlying concern about safety and dismayed by their own poor performance in crash tests, went back to the drawing boards, redesigned their cars, and are now producing very good scores in the crash test program.

It is easy to understand why more and more car buyers are factoring safety into their purchase decision. While you, no doubt, consider yourself a safe driver and feel little immediate threat of an automobile accident, the odds are against you. Every year, over 45,000 people are killed and 4 million more are injured in car accidents. An auto-related death occurs every ten minutes and an injury every nine seconds. While these statistics are hard for most of us to imagine, picture this: a major airline crash with no survivors, every day of the year. On average, each of us can expect to be in a serious automobile accident once every ten years.

But how does today's consumer buy safety? There are two factors often mentioned in determining the safety of a car—handling and the ability of the car to protect you in the event of collision.

First, a word about handling. A lot of misconceptions exist about the ability of a high-performance car to protect you from being in an accident. You often hear people say that they bought a small or high-performance car in order to avoid potential accidents. The fact is, while a very, very unresponsive car could be the cause of an accident, most new cars are relatively good at meeting basic handling requirements. In fact, many consumers feel uncomfortable driving so-called "high performance" cars because their highly responsive steering, acceleration and suspension systems can be difficult to control. But the most important reason good handling is over-rated as safety protection is that nearly every automobile collision is, by its nature, an "accident": a totally unpredictable event happening so fast that it is beyond human capacity to prevent it once it has begun, no matter how well your car handles.

Because accidents are impossible to predict and, unfortunately, statistically inevitable, the key to protecting yourself is to purchase a car that offers a high degree of crash protection. But how do you know which cars will have the best chance of protecting you in the event of a collision?

Then there are the owning and operating costs to consider. Our financial commitment to the car industry is staggering. The average new car now costs nearly $14,000. The over $350 billion we spend to own and operate our cars includes various "hidden costs"—fuel, maintenance, and insurance—seldom considered in the showroom, but rarely forgotten after the purchase is made.

Along with these mounting expenses, we are witnessing the development of a product so complex that few of us can adequately compare one car to another. We need help in this complex marketplace, which is what The Car Book is all about: information on one of the most difficult and expensive purchases you will ever make.

"The Safety Chapter" will help you include safety in your new car decision and help you decide which of the new automatic crash protection systems is best for you.

"The Fuel Economy" chapter will guide you to the money saving gas misers and offers advice on some products to avoid.

As we keep our cars longer, we are becoming more concerned about repair costs after the warranty expires. "The Maintenance Chapter" compares those all important costs to help you save money.

If your new or used car is not living up to your expectations, "The Warranty Chapter" can help you understand what you are entitled to. This year, for the first time, we compared warranty coverage to let you know the best and worst.

"The Insurance Chapter" can help you save money on an expense that is often forgotten in the showroom.

"The Complaint Chapter" gives you step-by-step help in resolving those inevitable problems quickly and efficiently.

While most of us can't tell one tire from another, there are crucial differences. "The Tire Chapter" provides you with information to help you select the best tires.

There is no question that buying a new car is difficult. But consumers are learning that one way to get better performing and safer cars is by buying the cars with good safety records, low maintenance costs and insurance discounts. The The Car Book is designed to help you get a good buy for your hard-earned dollars. Use "The Purchasing Guide" to compare the cars you are considering, and read the chapters to learn more about each model. Then review "The Shopping Guide" for tips on successfully negotiating your way out of a showroom.

While, no single car excels in every category, there are some great new cars for 1988. Use The Car Book to guide you through the trade-offs, claims, promises, facts, and myths to the car that will best meet your needs.

The information in The Car Book is based on data collected and developed by private automobile engineering firms, the U.S. Department of Transportation, and the Center for Auto Safety.

THE PURCHASING GUIDE

How to Use the Guide

The "Purchasing Guide" will provide you with an overall comparison of the cars in terms of safety, fuel economy, maintenance, and insurance costs. The cars are put into size classes based on weight. We used weight because currently the relative safety of automobiles is dependent on weight. The U.S.

Environmental Protection Agency (EPA) uses interior volume to categorize automobiles. Because of this, our list of subcompacts may not exactly match the EPA's list. For example, the EPA lists the Mercedes as a compact car.

To fully understand these summary charts, it is important to read the appropriate section

in the book. You will note that here and throughout the book some of the charts contain empty boxes. Empty boxes appear where the data were unavailable at the time of printing. We will be updating this information in later printings as it becomes available.

Good Choices			
Subcompacts	**Compacts**	**Intermediates**	**Large**
Chevrolet Nova	Dodge Aries	Buick Century	Chevrolet Caprice
Dodge Colt	Plymouth Reliant	Chevrolet Celebrity	Ford LTD Crown Victoria
Ford Escort	Chevrolet Cavalier	Dodge 600	Mercury Grand Marquis
Plymouth Colt	Oldsmobile Firenza	Oldsmobile Cutlass Ciera	
Mazda 323	Pontiac Sunbird	Plymouth Caravelle	
Toyota MR-2		Pontiac 6000	
Volkswagen Golf		Volvo DL	

Based on information in the Purchasing Guide, this list shows the highest-rated cars in each of the four size categories. Ratings are based on expected performance in five important categories (crash test, fuel economy, warranties, repair costs, and insurance costs), with the heaviest emphasis on crash test performance. Only those cars for which information in all five categories was available are included.

Car	Crash Test Performance[1]	Fuel Economy mpg[2]	Repair Cost[4]	Warranty Rating	Insurance Rate[5]
Acura Integra	Good		High	Poor	Surcharge
Chevrolet Nova	Good	30/37	Low	Average	Regular
Chevrolet Spectrum	Poor	37/41	Medium	Average	Regular
Chevrolet Sprint	Poor	44/49	Medium	Average	Regular
Dodge/Ply. Colt	Good	34/38	Medium	Good	Surcharge
Dodge Omni/Ply. Horizon	Poor	25/34	Low	Good	Regular
Ford Escort	Good	26/34	Medium	Average	Regular
Ford Festiva		39/43	Medium	Average	Surcharge
Honda Civic		33/37	Medium	Poor	Regular
Honda CRX-Si		34/39	Medium	Poor	Surcharge
Honda Prelude		23/27	Medium	Poor	Surcharge
Hyundai Excel	Moderate	28/37	High	Poor	Regular
Isuzu I-Mark	Poor	33/39	High	Poor	Regular
Mazda 323	Moderate	26/30	Low	Average	Surcharge
Mercury Tracer		28/35	Low	Average	Regular
Mitsubishi Cordia	Good	24/31	High	Poor	Surcharge
Mitsubishi Mirage	Good	34/38	High	Poor	Surcharge
Mitsubishi Precis	Moderate	28/37	High	Poor	Surcharge
Mitsubishi Tredia	Poor	24/31	High	Poor	Surcharge
Nissan Pulsar		23/29	High	Poor	Surcharge
Nissan Sentra	Poor	29/36	High	Poor	Surcharge
Nissan Stanza		22/28	High	Poor	Regular
Pontiac LeMans		31/40	Medium	Average	Regular
Subaru DL/GL	Poor	25/32	High	Poor	Surcharge
Subaru Justy	Good	37/39	High	Poor	Surcharge
Toyota Corolla/FX16		25/29	High	Average	Regular
Toyota MR-2	Good	24/30	High	Average	Surcharge
Toyota Tercel		31/35	High	Average	Regular
Volkswagen Fox		25/30	High	Poor	Regular
Volkswagen Golf	Good	25/33	Medium	Poor	Surcharge
VW Jetta/Scirocco	Moderate	25/34	High	Poor	Surcharge
Yugo GV	Poor	27/32	Medium	Poor	Surcharge

Car	Crash Test Performance[1]	Fuel Economy mpg[2]	Repair Cost[4]	Warranty Rating	Insurance Rate[5]
BMW 325i		17/29	High	Average	Regular
Buick Skyhawk	Good	25/36	Medium	Average	Regular
Buick Skylark	2 dr. Good 4 dr. Poor	19/27	Medium	Average	Discount
Cadillac Cimarron	Good	20/27	Medium	Average	Discount
Chevy Cav./Pont. Sunbird	Good	25/36	Low	Average	Regular
Chevrolet Beretta		25/35	Low	Average	Regular
Chevrolet Corsica		25/35	Low	Average	Discount
Chrysler Conquest	Good	18/22	Medium	Good	Surcharge
Chrysler LeBaron	Poor	20/25	Low	Good	Discount
Chr. LeB. GTS/Dod. Lncr.	Poor	25/34	Low	Good	Discount
Dodge Aries	Good	25/30	Low	Good	Discount
Dodge Daytona	Good	21/29	Low	Good	Surcharge
Dod. Shad./Ply. Sundance	Poor	25/33	Low	Good	Regular
Ford Mustang	Good	25/30	Low	Average	Surcharge
Ford Tempo	Poor	22/27	Low	Average	Discount
Honda Accord	Good	25/30	High	Poor	Regular
Isuzu Impulse	Poor	21/27	Low	Poor	Surcharge
Mazda RX-7		17/24	Low	Good	Surcharge
Mazda 626		21/28	Low	Average	Regular
Mercury Topaz	Poor	22/27	Low	Average	Discount
Mitsubishi Starion	Good	18/22	High	Poor	Surcharge
Nissan 200 SX	Poor	23/28	High	Poor	Surcharge
Olds Cutlass Calais	2 dr. Good 4 dr. Poor	19/27	Medium	Average	Regular
Oldsmobile Firenza	Good	25/36	Low	Average	Regular
Plymouth Reliant	Good	25/30	Low	Good	Discount
Pontiac Fiero	Good	24/35	Low	Average	Surcharge
Pontiac Grand Am	2 dr. Good 4 dr. Poor	20/27	Medium	Average	Surcharge
Renault Medallion		25/33	Low	Average	Discount
Toyota Camry	Good	22/27	High	Average	Discount
Toyota Celica	Good	22/28	High	Average	Surcharge
VW Quantum	Poor	19/24	High	Poor	Regular

Car	Crash Test Performance[1]	Fuel Economy mpg[2]	Repair Cost[4]	Warranty Rating	Insurance Rate[5]
Acura Legend		19/24	High	Poor	Regular
Audi 5000S	Poor	24/31	High	Good	Surcharge
Buick Century	Good	24/31	Low	Average	Discount
Buick LeSabre	Good	19/29	High	Average	Discount
Buick Regal		20/29	High	Average	Regular
Buick Riviera	Good	19/29	Medium	Average	Regular
Cadillac Eldorado	Good	17/24	Medium	Good	Regular
Cadillac Seville		17/24	High	Good	Regular
Chevrolet Camaro	Good	17/27	Medium	Average	Surcharge
Chevrolet Celebrity	Good	24/31	Low	Average	Discount
Chevrolet Monte Carlo	Moderate	19/27	Low	Average	Surcharge
Chrysler New Yorker		19/26	Low	Good	Discount
Dodge Dynasty		19/26	Low	Good	Regular
Dodge 600	Good	20/25	Low	Good	Discount
Ford Taurus		21/29	Low	Average	Discount
Ford Thunderbird	Poor	21/27	Medium	Average	Surcharge
Mercedes 190 E		21/24	High	Average	Regular
Mercury Cougar	Good	21/27	Medium	Average	Surcharge
Mercury Merkur	Poor	18/21	Medium	Good	Surcharge
Mercury Sable		21/29	Low	Average	Discount

Car	Crash Test Performance[1]	Fuel Economy mpg[2]	Repair Cost[4]	Warranty Rating	Insurance Rate[5]
Mitsubishi Galant	Good	18/22	High	Poor	Discount
Nissan Maxima	Poor	18/26	High	Poor	Regular
Nissan 300 ZX T	Moderate	17/25	High	Poor	Surcharge
Oldsmobile Cutlass Ciera	Good	24/31	Low	Average	Discount
Olds Cut. Supreme Classic	Moderate	18/25	High	Average	Regular
Oldsmobile Delta 88	Good	19/29	High	Average	Discount
Oldsmobile Toronado	Good	19/29	Medium	Average	Regular
Peugeot 505 T	Poor	18/24	High	Poor	Regular
Plymouth Caravelle	Good	20/25	Low	Good	Discount
Plymouth Colt Vista Wag.	Poor	21/27	Medium	Good	Discount
Pontiac Bonneville	Good	19/29	High	Average	Discount
Pontiac Firebird	Good	17/27	Medium	Average	Surcharge
Pontiac Grand Prix		20/29	High	Average	Regular
Pontiac 6000	Good	24/31	Low	Average	Discount
Saab 9000 T	Good	19/26	High	Average	Regular
Sterling		18/23	High	Average	Regular
Toyota Cressida	Good	18/24	High	Average	Regular
Volvo DL	Good	22/27	Medium	Good	Discount
Volvo 760	Good	17/20	High	Good	Discount

Large

Car	Crash Test Performance [1]	Fuel Economy mpg [2]	Repair Cost [4]	Warranty Rating	Insurance Rate [5]
Buick Electra	Poor	19/29	High	Average	Discount
Cadillac Brougham		17/24	High	Good	Discount
Cad. Fleetwd Sixty Spec	Poor	17/24	High	Good	Discount
Chevrolet Caprice	Moderate	19/27	Low	Average	Discount
Chrysler 5th Ave		17/23	Low	Good	Discount
Dodge Diplomat		17/23	Low	Good	Discount
Ford LTD Crown Victoria	Moderate	17/24	High	Average	Discount
Lincoln Continental		17/24	High	Good	Discount
Lincoln Mark VII		17/24	High	Good	Regular
Lincoln Town Car		17/24	High	Good	Regular
Mercury Grand Marquis	Moderate	17/24	High	Average	Discount
Oldsmobile 98	Poor	19/29	High	Average	Discount
Plymouth Gran Fury		17/23	Low	Good	Discount
Pontiac Safari Wagon		17/24	High	Average	Discount

Pickups, Minivans & 4x4s

Car	Crash Test Performance[1]	Fuel Economy mpg[2]	Repair Cost[4]	Warranty Rating	Insurance Rate[5]
Chevrolet Astro	Poor	20/25	Medium	Average	Discount
Chevrolet C-10 Pickup		17/22	Medium	Average	Regular
Chevrolet S-10 Blazer 4x4	Poor	20/25	Medium	Average	Regular
Chevrolet Suburban	Poor	13/16	Medium	Average	Discount
Dodge B 150 Van	Poor	13/14	Low	Good	Discount
Dodge Caravan	Good	18/23	Low	Good	Discount
Dodge Dakota	Good	17/22	Low	Good	Regular
Dodge Raider	Poor	17/19	Medium	Good	Regular
Ford Aerostar	Poor	17/23	Low	Average	Discount
Ford Bronco II	Moderate	17/21	Low	Average	Regular
Ford E-150 Club Wagon	Poor	14/17	Low	Average	Discount
Ford F-150 Pickup	Poor	16/20	Low	Average	Regular
Ford Ranger	Good	22/27	Low	Average	Surcharge
Isuzu Spacecab Pickup	Poor		Medium	Poor	Regular
Isuzu Trooper II 4x4	Poor	16/18	Low	Poor	Regular
Jeep Cherokee 4x4	Poor	22/25	High	Poor	Regular
Jeep Comanche	Poor	22/25	Medium	Poor	Regular
Jeep Wrangler	Poor	18/20	Medium	Poor	Regular
Mazda B-2000 Pick-up	Poor	21/26	Low	Average	Regular
Mitsubushi Montero	Poor	17/19	High	Poor	Regular
Nissan Pickup	Poor	20/26	Low	Poor	Surcharge
Nissan Van		18/22	Low	Poor	Discount
Plymouth Voyager	Good	18/23	Low	Good	Discount
Suzuki Samurai	Good	28/29	Medium	Poor	Regular
Toyota Van Wagon	Moderate	20/22	Medium	Average	Discount
Toyota 4-Runner 4x4	Poor	19/22	Medium	Average	Surcharge
Volkswagen Vanagon	Poor	16/18	High	Poor	Discount

The **SAFETY** Chapter

In 1979, the U.S. Department of Transportation began an experimental crash test program to find a way to compare the occupant protection offered by one car versus another. The results of these tests show that there are significant differences in the ability of various automobiles to protect belted occupants during frontal crashes.

The test consists of crashing an automobile into a concrete barrier at 35 mph; this is similar to two identical cars crashing head-on, traveling at 35 mph. In the test, each automobile contains electronically monitored dummies in the driver and passenger seats.

In releasing the results, the government presents a confusing array of numbers that most consumers find very difficult to understand and almost impossible to use in comparing the results of one car with another.

We have analyzed the data and presented the results using the Crash Test Rating Index. The index provides a general means of comparing the results of one car to another. The tables on the following pages allow you to compare the crash test performance of today's cars.

It is best to compare the test results of cars within weight classes, such as compacts with compacts; they should not be used to compare cars with vastly different weights. For example, you should not conclude that a subcompact that did well is as safe as a large car that did well.

The results evaluate performance in frontal crashes only. About 50 percent of deaths and serious injuries occur in frontal crashes. Remember that the results only measure protection for belted occupants. Using safety belts is the single most effective means of protecting yourself in an accident.

The Best and the Worst

The following table provides the best and worst crash test rating index among the cars tested to date. Lower numbers indicate better performance. The tables on the following pages provide more information and the results for other cars.

Subcompacts	Compacts	Intermediates	Large*
BEST			
Toyota MR-2 (1636)	Pontiac Fiero (1284)	Volvo DL (1549)	Buick Estate Wagon (2394)
Acura Integra (1732)	Ford Mustang (1674)	Saab 9000 (1597)	Chevrolet Caprice (2394)
Ford Escort (1838)	Buick Skyhawk (1692)	Buick Century (1940)	Olds Custom Cruiser (2394)
Subaru Justy (1901)	Cadillac Cimarron (1692)	Chevy Celebrity (1940)	Pontiac Safari (2394)
	Chevrolet Cavalier (1692)	Olds Cutlass Ciera (1940)	
	Olds Firenza (1692)	Pontiac 6000 (1940)	
	Pontiac Sunbird (1692)		
WORST			
Chevrolet Sprint (3828)	Fd. Temp./Merc. Tpz. (3782)	Peugeot 505 (3921)	Buick Electra (3017)
Mitsubishi Tredia (3783)	Chrysler LeBaron (3390)	Audi 5000 S (3179)	Cadillac DeVille (3017)
Isuzu I-Mark (3655)	Dodge Lancer (3320)	Nissan Maxima (3085)	Cadillac Fleetwood (3017)
Chevrolet Spectrum (3655)	Chry. LeBaron GTS (3320)	Plymouth Colt Vista (3051)	Oldsmobile 98 (3017)

*There are relatively few large cars so the "Best and Worst" comprise nearly all of the cars for which there are crash test results.

Crash Tests: How the Cars Are Rated

A car's ability to protect you in a crash depends on its ability to absorb the force of the impact rather than transfer it back to you, the occupant. This is a function of the car's size, weight, and, most important, design. In the crash tests, engineers measure how much of the crash force was transferred to the head, chest, and thighs of the occupants.

The tables that follow provide information on seven crash test categories.

The first column provides an *overall crash test rating index*. The *index* is a single number that describes all of the forces measured by the test.

The index number is based on a formula that includes all the measured forces in proportion to their likelihood of causing an injury and compensates for the fact that passengers are less likely to be in the car.

In using the index, keep in mind that lower numbers indicate better performance. The index is best used to compare cars within the same size and weight class.

The second two columns indicate *driver protection* and *passenger protection*. The tests indicate how much force the head, chest, and upper legs would experience in a frontal collision and whether that force would severely injure or kill the occupants. The results are presented as Good, *Moderate*, and **Poor**.

Occupant Protection

Good = Occupant would survive impact without serious injury or death.

Moderate = Automobile did not quite meet government criteria for passing test. Questionable whether injuries would be serious.

Poor = Automobile failed to meet minimum criteria for protecting passengers. Crash would seriously injure or kill occupants.

The remaining tests are presented on a Pass/Fail basis. These results indicate whether that car passed the test at 35 mph, which is 5 mph faster than government regulations require. (At 35 mph, a crash is considered to be 36 percent more severe than at 30 mph.)

Windshield Retention

Pass = Most of the windshield would remain attached to the car after a crash.

Fail = The windshield would not remain attached to the car after a crash.

Windshield Passenger Protection

Pass = Parts of the car would not come through the windshield after a frontal crash.

Fail = Car parts would come through the windshield after a frontal crash.

Fuel Leakage

Pass = The fuel system would not leak after a crash.

Fail = The fuel system would probably leak after a crash.

Note: Not all cars are tested and variations among identical cars are not considered since only one of each model was crashed. Crash test results may vary due to differences in the way cars are manufactured, how models are equipped, and test conditions. There is no absolute guarantee that a car that passed will adequately protect you in an accident. "Corporate twins" that are structurally the same, such as the Dodge Omni and Plymouth Horizon, can be expected to perform similarly. Some two-door models may not perform exactly like their four-door counterparts.

The results presented on the following pages provide an indication of how this year's cars can be expected to perform in the tests. They are included here only where it is believed that the design of the automobile has not changed enough to produce a change in the results.

Crash Test Performance
Subcompact

Car	Index Lower Numbers Better	Occupant Protection		Windshield		Fuel Leak
		Driver	Passenger	Stays in Place	Protects Passenger	Front
Acura Integra 2 dr.	1732	Good	Good			
Chevrolet Nova 4 dr.	2027	Good	Good	Pass	Pass	Pass
Chevy Spectrum (I-Mark 2) dr.	3655	Poor	*Moderate*	Pass	Pass	Pass
Chevy Spectrum (I-Mark 4) dr.	3466	Poor	*Moderate*			
Chevrolet Sprint 2 dr.	3828	Poor	Poor	Pass	Pass	Pass
Dodge Colt 4 dr.	2068	Good	Good	Pass	Pass	Pass
Dodge Omni 4 dr.	2741	Good	Poor	Pass	Pass	Pass
Ford Escort 2 dr.	1838	Good	Good			
Hyundai Excel 2 dr.	2418	Good	*Moderate*			
Hyundai Excel 4 dr.	2477	*Moderate*	Good			
Isuzu I-Mark 2 dr.	3655	Poor	*Moderate*	Pass	Pass	Pass
Isuzu I-Mark 4 dr.	3466	Poor	*Moderate*			
Mazda 323 LX 2 dr.	2494	*Moderate*	Good	Pass	Pass	Pass
Mitsubishi Cordia 2 dr.	2213	Good	Good	Pass	Pass	Pass
Mitsubishi Mirage (Colt) 4 dr.	2068	Good	Good	Pass	Pass	Pass
Mitsubishi Tredia 4 dr.	3783	Poor	Poor	Pass		Pass
Plymouth Colt (Dodge) 4 dr.	2068	Good	Good	Pass	Pass	Pass
Plymouth Horizon (Omni) 4 dr.	2741	Good	Poor	Pass	Pass	Pass
Subaru GL 4 dr.	3015	Poor	Good			
Subaru Justy 2 dr.	1901	Good	Good			
Subaru XT 2 dr.	1914	Good	Good	Pass	Pass	Pass
Toyota MR-2 2 dr.	1636	Good	Good	Pass	Pass	Pass
VW Cabriolet Rabbit Conv. 2 dr.	2893	Poor	Good	Pass	Pass	Pass
Volkswagen Golf* 4 dr.	2631	Good	Good	Pass	Pass	Pass
Volkswagen Jetta 4 dr.	2499	Good	*Moderate*	Pass	Pass	Pass
VW Scirocco 2 dr.	†	Good	*Moderate*	Pass	Pass	Pass
Yugo GV	†	Poor	Good			

* Model tested had automatic crash protection.
†Data incomplete, unable to calculate index.
Empty box means data unavailable.
Parenthesis indicate actual model tested.

Crash Test Performance
Compact

Car	Index Lower Numbers Better	Occupant Protection Driver	Occupant Protection Passenger	Windshield Stays in Place	Windshield Protects Passenger	Fuel Leak Front
Buick Skyhawk (Cavalier) 2 dr.	1981	Good	Good	Pass	Pass	Pass
Buick Skyhawk (Sunbird) 4 dr.	1692	Good	Good			
Buick Skylark (Grand Am*) 2 dr.	2311	Good	Good			
Buick Skylark (Calais*) 4 dr.	2116	Poor	Good			
Cad. Cimarron (Sunbird) 4 dr.	1692	Good	Good			
Chevrolet Cavalier 2 dr.	1981	Good	Good	Pass	Pass	Pass
Chevy Cavalier (Sunbird) 4 dr.	1692	Good	Good			
Chevrolet Cavalier Conv.	2030	Good	Good	Pass		Pass
Chry. Conquest (Starion*) 2 dr.	2509	Good	Good			
Chrysler LeBaron 2 dr.	3390	Moderate	Poor			
Chrys. LeBaron GTS (Lancer) 4 dr.	3320	Poor	Good	Pass	Pass	Pass
Dodge Aries (Reliant) 4 dr.	2504	Good	Good	Fail	Pass	Pass
Dodge Daytona 2 dr.	1762	Good	Good	Pass		Pass
Dodge Lancer 4 dr.	3320	Poor	Good	Pass	Pass	Pass
Dodge Shadow 2 dr.	2902	Poor	Good			
Dodge Shadow (Sundance) 4 dr.	†	Good				
Ford Mustang 2 dr.	1674	Good	Good			
Ford Mustang Conv.	2731	Good	Moderate	Fail		Pass
Ford Tempo 2 dr.	3782	Poor	Poor	Pass	Pass	Pass
Ford Tempo 4 dr.	2776	Poor	Good	Pass	Pass	Pass
Ford Tempo* (Topaz) 4 dr.	2391	Moderate	Good			
Honda Accord* 2 dr.	2032	Good	Good			

Crash Test Performance
Compact

Car	Index Lower Numbers Better	Occupant Protection Driver	Occupant Protection Passenger	Windshield Stays in Place	Windshield Protects Passenger	Fuel Leak Front
Isuzu Impulse 2 dr.	†	Poor	Poor	Pass		Pass
Mercury Topaz (Tempo) 2 dr.	3782	Poor	Poor	Pass	Pass	Pass
Mercury Topaz (Tempo) 4 dr.	2776	Poor	Good	Pass	Pass	Pass
Mercury Topaz* 4 dr.	2391	*Moderate*	Good			
Mitsubishi Starion* 2 dr.	2509	Good	Good			
Olds Cut. Calais (Gnd. Am*) 2 dr.	2311	Good	Good			
Olds Cut. Calais* 4 dr.	2116	Poor	Good			
Olds Firenza (Sunbird) 2 dr.	1692	Good	Good			
Plymouth Reliant 4dr.	2504	Good	Good	Fail	Pass	Pass
Plymouth Sundance 4 dr.	†	Good				
Ply. Sundance (Shadow) 2 dr.	2902	Poor	Good			
Pontiac Fiero 2 dr.	1284	Good	Good	Pass		Pass
Pont. Gnd. Am* 2 dr.	2311	Good	Good			
Pont. Gnd. Am (Calais*) 4 dr.	2116	Poor	Good			
Pont. Sunbird (Cavalier) 2 dr.	1981	Good	Good	Pass	Pass	Pass
Pontiac Sunbird 4 dr.	1692	Good	Good			
Toyota Camry* 4 dr.	2696	Good	Good			
Toyota Celica 2 dr.	1797	Good	Good	Pass	Pass	Pass
VW Quantum 4 dr.	2992	Poor	Poor	Pass	Pass	Pass

* Model tested had automatic crash protection.
†Data incomplete, unable to calculate index.
Empty box means data unavailable.
Parenthesis indicate actual model tested.

Crash Test Performance
Intermediate

Car	Index Lower Numbers Better	Occupant Protection Driver	Passenger	Windshield Stays in Place	Protects Passenger	Fuel Leak Front
Audi 5000S 4 dr.	3179	Poor	Good	Pass	Pass	Pass
Buick Century 2 & 4 dr.	1940‡	Good	Good	Pass	Pass	Pass
Buick LeSabre 2 dr.	2302	Good	Good	Pass	Pass	Pass
Buick LeSabre (Olds 88) 4 dr.	2082	Good	Good	Pass	Pass	Pass
Buick Riviera (Toronado) 2 dr.	2268	Good	Good	Pass	Pass	Pass
Cad. Eldorado (Toronado) 2 dr.	2268	Good	Good	Pass	Pass	Pass
Chevrolet Camaro 2 dr.	2010	Good	Good			
Chevy Celebrity (Century) 2 & 4 dr.	1940‡	Good	Good	Pass	Pass	Pass
Chev. Monte Carlo (Cut. Sup.) 2 dr.	2344	Good	*Moderate*	Pass		Pass
Dodge 600 ES (Caravelle) 4 dr.	2230	Good	Good	Pass	Pass	Pass
Ford Thunderbird 2 dr.	2452	Poor	Good	Pass	Pass	Pass
Mercury Cougar 2 dr.	2217	Good	Good	Pass		Fail
Mercury Merkur 2 dr.	2968	*Moderate*	Poor	Pass	Pass	Pass
Nissan Maxima Wagon 4 dr.	3085	*Moderate*	Poor	Fail	Pass	Pass
Nissan 300 ZX 2 dr.	2608	Good	*Moderate*	Pass		Pass
Olds Cut. Ciera (Century) 2 & 4 dr.	1940‡	Good	Good	Pass	Pass	Pass
Olds Cut. Sup. Classic 2 dr.	2344	Good	*Moderate*	Pass		Pass
Oldsmobile Delta 88 4 dr.	2082	Good	Good	Pass	Pass	Pass
Oldsmobile Toronado 2 dr.	2268	Good	Good	Pass	Pass	Pass
Peugeot 505 4 dr.	3921	Poor	Poor			
Plymouth Caravelle 4 dr.	2230	Good	Good	Pass	Pass	Pass
Plymouth Colt Vista 4 dr.	3051	Poor	Poor	Pass	Pass	Pass
Pont. Bonneville (LeSabre) 2 dr.	2302	Good	Good	Pass	Pass	Pass
Pont. Firebird (Camaro) 2 dr.	2010	Good	Good			
Pont. Grand Prix (Cut. Sup.) 2 dr.						
Pontiac 6000 (Century) 2 & 4 dr.	1940‡	Good	Good	Pass	Pass	Pass
Saab 9000 4 dr.	1597	Good	Good			
Toyota Cressida 4 dr.	2894	Good	Good	Pass	Pass	Pass
Volvo DL Wagon 4 dr.	1549	Good	Good	Pass	Pass	Pass
Volvo DL 4 dr.	†	Good				
Volvo 760 4 dr.	2247	Good	Good	Pass	Pass	Pass

* Model tested had automatic crash protection.
†Data incomplete, unable to calculate index.
‡Index for 2 dr. model was 2143.
Empty box means data unavailable.
Parenthesis indicate actual model tested.

Crash Test Performance
Large

Car	Index Lower Numbers Better	Occupant Protection Driver	Occupant Protection Passenger	Windshield Stays in Place	Windshield Protects Passenger	Fuel Leak Front
Buick Electra 4 dr.	3017	**Poor**	Good	Pass		Pass
Buick Estate Wagon (Caprice)	2394	Good	*Moderate*	Pass	Pass	Pass
Cadillac DeVille (Electra) 4 dr.	3017	**Poor**	Good	Pass		Pass
Cadillac Fleetwood (Electra) 4 dr.	3017	**Poor**	Good	Pass		Pass
Chevrolet Caprice 4 dr.	2394	Good	*Moderate*	Pass	Pass	Pass
Ford LTD Crown Vic (Gr.Marq.) 4 dr.	2717	*Moderate*	*Moderate*	Fail		Pass
Mercury Grand Marquis 4 dr.	2717	*Moderate*	*Moderate*	Fail		Pass
Olds Custom Cruiser (Caprice)	2394	Good	*Moderate*	Pass	Pass	Pass
Oldsmobile 98 Electra 4 dr.	3017	**Poor**	Good	Pass		Pass
Pontiac Safari (Caprice) 4 dr.	2394	Good	*Moderate*	Pass	Pass	Pass

* Model tested had automatic crash protection.
†Data incomplete, unable to calculate index.
Empty box means data unavailable.
Parenthesis indicate actual model tested.

Crash Test Performance
Pickups, Minivans & 4x4s

Car	Index Lower Numbers Better	Occupant Protection Driver	Passenger	Windshield Stays in Place	Protects Passenger	Fuel Leak Front
Chevrolet Astro	4669	Poor	Poor	Pass	Pass	Pass
Chevrolet S-10 Blazer 4x4	2998	*Moderate*	Poor	Pass	Pass	Pass
Dodge B-150 Van	3024	Poor	Good			Pass
Dodge Caravan (Voyager)	2287	Good	Good			
Dodge Dakota	2279	Good	Good			
Ford Aerostar	3200	Poor	*Moderate*			
Ford Bronco II 4x4	2349	Good	*Moderate*	Pass	Pass	Pass
Ford E-150 Club Wagon	4111	Poor	Poor	Pass	Pass	Pass
Ford F-150 Pickup	3233	Poor	Poor	Pass	Pass	Pass
Isuzu Spacecab Pickup	3589	Poor	*Moderate*			
Isuzu Trooper II 4x4 2 dr.	†	Good	Poor	Pass	Pass	Pass
Jeep Cherokee 4x4	2547	Good	Poor	Pass	Pass	Pass
Jeep Comanche P-up	3742	*Moderate*	Poor			
Jeep Wrangler YJ	2477	Good	Poor			
Mazda B-2000 Pickup	3565	Poor	Poor	Pass	Pass	Pass
Plymouth Voyager	2287	Good	Good			
Suzuki Samurai 4x4 2 dr.	2454	Good	Good	Pass	Fail	Pass
Toyota Tercel Wagon 4x4	1996	Good	Good	Pass	Pass	Pass
Toyota Van	2930	*Moderate*	*Moderate*	Pass	Pass	Pass
Toyota 4-Runner 4x4 2 dr.	3309	Poor	Good	Pass	Pass	Pass
Volkswagen Vanagon	3966	Poor	*Moderate*			Pass

* Model tested had automatic crash protection.
†Data incomplete, unable to calculate index.
Empty box means data unavailable.
Parenthesis indicate actual model tested.

On impact, the car begins to crush and slow down. The person inside continues to move forward at 35 mph.

The Second Collision

As the diagram to the left demonstrates, a car crash actually involves *two* collisions. The first is when the car hits another object and the second is when the occupant collides with the inside of the car. While using your safety belt is your greatest defense against the injuries caused by the *second collision*, most of us do not use safety belts. As a result, even low-speed crashes can cause serious injuries because of the car's inside design. According to the National Highway Traffic Safety Administration, the following are the major causes of injury to the occupant in the *second collision*:

Steering wheel	27%
Instrument panel	11%
Side (doors)	10%
Windshield	5%
Front roof pillar	4%
Glove box area	3%
Roof edges	3%
Roof	2%

Within 1/10 of a second, the car comes to a stop, but the person keeps moving forward at 35 mph.

When taking a car for a test drive, you should look for the following protective features:
- Are the knobs and controls recessed below the dash?
- Does the steering wheel have a large padded hub?
- Are the dash, sun visors, and roof pillars well padded?
- Are the doors free of sharp and protruding objects?
- Will and air cushion inflate in the event of a collision?

1/50 of a second after the car has stopped, the unbelted person slams into the dashboard or windshield. This is the human collision.

Only with *effective* seat belts will the person stop before his or her head or chest hits the steering wheel, dash, or windshield.

Automatic Crash Protection

The concept of automatic protection is not new—automatic fire sprinklers in public buildings, automatic release of oxygen masks in airplanes, purification of city water and the pasteurization of milk are all commonly accepted forms of automatic safety protection. Ironically, of all the products we buy today, the one most likely to kill us is not equipped with automatic safety protection. Advocates of automatic protection technology are ready to point out that we incorporate better technology in safely transporting electronic equipment, eggs and china than we do in packaging humans in automobiles.

Over a decade ago, in cooperation with the federal government, the automobile industry developed two basic types of automatic crash protection: air bags and automatic safety belts. While these devices will not prevent all deaths, they will cut in half your chances of being killed or seriously injured in a car.

Never before has such a simple concept generated such heartfelt controversy. The idea behind automatic crash protection is to design cars to protect people from the "second collision." The "second collision" occurs after impact when the passenger comes forward and collides with the car. Because the "second collision" occurs within milliseconds and because most people (70 percent) do not use seat belts, providing automatic, rather than manual, protection dramatically improves the chances of escaping injury.

The U.S. Department of Transportation has been "studying" automatic crash protection for 20 years. Finally, in 1984, the Supreme Court issued a strong remand to the U.S. government to make a decision.

The new rule requires 25 percent of 1988 model cars to be equipped with some form of automatic crash protection that will protect the driver and front-seat passenger in a 30 mph collision into a fixed barrier. To meet the standard, car manufacturers may use air bags, automatic seat belts or new automatic protection technology. The requirement is to be phased in over time and by the 1990 model year every new car sold in the United States will be required to have automatic crash protection. The rule encourages the use of air bags rather than automatic belts.

On the following pages, we have described how air bags and automatic safety belts work. We have also provided a list of what the automakers plan to offer this year in the way of automatic crash protection devices.

Automatic Safety Belts

The majority of people do not wear safety belts. The fact is most people find safety belts inconvenient and uncomfortable. In contrast, automatic safety belts offer protection with little or no effort. As their name implies, they move automatically into place when you enter the car and are automatically released when you leave.

There are several types of automatic belts. Some have an automatic lap belt as well as shoulder belt and some move out of the way more completely than others. Cars with automatic belts often come with extra padding under the dash to protect the occupant's knees and lower body in a collision. Generally, automatic belts are less complicated and

less expensive than air bags. However, an air bag will offer more protection in a high-speed frontal collision.

There are many different automatic belt systems being offered this year. The easiest to use are the motorized belts offered in such cars as the Toyota Cressida and Camry, Ford Escort and Subaru XT-Coupe. (See the table for a complete list.) The belt moves forward, out of your way, when you open the door. When you close the door it moves back, securing the belt over your chest. The Toyota system is illustrated below and has been a unique selling point on the Cressida for a number of years.

Non-motorized belts are generally attached to the door. When the door is opened, the

attached belt pulls away to let you in. The Volkswagen non-motorized system is a simple and easy-to-use belt. On the other hand, the General Motors system is a complicated web of belts that looks rather intimidating and will probably turn many consumers off to the concept of automatic crash protection. Many people who want GM cars with automatic crash protection may choose another brand when they see how cumbersome the GM system is.

Because of the many different types of automatic belts, make sure you try the system out a number of times before you finalize your purchase.

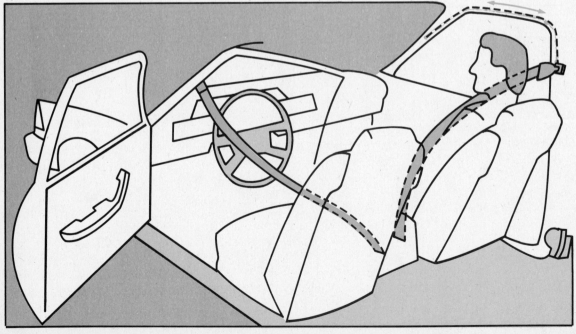

The Toyota system: When the door is opened a small electric motor pulls the belt forward and out of the way for an easy exit and entry.

Air Bags

Hidden in the steering wheel hub and the right side of the dashboard, air bags provide unobtrusive and effective protection in frontal crashes. When needed, they inflate instantly to cushion the driver and front seat occupants. By spreading the crash forces over the occupant's head and chest, air bags protect fragile parts of the body from violently hitting the hard surfaces of the car. Manual seat belts are also provided in cars with air bags to protect occupants in nonfrontal crashes. However, air bags offer protection in frontal crashes even if the safety belt is not fastened.

General Motors installed air bags in over 10,000 cars from 1974 to 1976. These cars traveled over 600 million miles and the death and injury rate of the occupants was 50 percent lower than for non-air bag cars. Studies on the actual operation of the air bags reported no cases where they failed to deploy or the inflator malfunctioned. This reliability rate (99.995 percent) is far higher than such safety features as brakes, tires, steering, and lights, which have shown failure rates of up to 10 percent. Many consumers who have questions about air bags are finding that dealers often do not know the facts about these safety devices. The following are some answers to typical questions about air bags. This information is based on a publication prepared by the Insurance Information Institute

entitled *About Air Bags*.

Will air bags work in multiple crashes? While air bags reach peak inflation and begin to deflate quickly, they are designed to remain inflated long enough to protect occupants in multiple collisions. If, after hitting another vehicle or object, your car is involved in a second or third impact, the bags are designed to protect the front-seat occupants throughout the crash sequence.

Will air bags protect children? Studies of actual crashes indicate that children have been protected by air bags. In fact, air bags protect virtually all occupants in the front seat, because they will fill most of the front seating area. Of course, using a child safety seat is the best way to ensure that your child gets the best protection possible.

Is the gas that inflates air bags dangerous? Nitrogen, which comprises 78 percent of the air we breathe, is the gas that inflates the bags. A solid chemical, sodium azide, generates the nitrogen to inflate the bag. Sodium azide does not present a safety hazard in normal driving, in crashes, or in disposal. In fact, occupants of the car will never even contact the sodium azide.

Will air bags inflate by mistake? Air bags are designed to inflate only in frontal impacts equivalent to hitting a

solid wall at 12 mph or higher. They will not inflate when you go over bumps or potholes or hit something at low speed. Even slamming on your brakes will not inflate your air bags, unless you hit something. In the unlikely event of an inadvertent air bag deployment, you would not lose control of the car. General Motors tested driver reaction by inflating air bags without warning at speeds of up to 45 mph. GM reported that "without exception, the drivers retained control of the automobile."

Will air bag systems last very long? Air bags are reliable and require no maintenance. Because they have no moving parts, there is nothing to wear out. They are designed to work for the life of the car in which they are installed.

In a study of 228 cars in which air bags deployed, 40 had traveled more than 40,000 miles. One car had traveled almost 115,000 miles at the time of the crash. In every case, the air bags worked as designed.

Will air bags protect occupants without seat belts? Air bags are designed to protect unbelted, front-seat occupants in frontal crashes of at least 30 mph into a wall. Equipping cars with airbags reduced the average injury severity in serious frontal crashes by 64 percent, even though more than 80 percent of the occupants were unbelted.

What Happens in an Air-Bag Crash?

The following are true stories about people whose lives have been saved by air bags:

Milwaukee, Wisconsin, April 1986

On rural highway 175 near Milwaukee, Wisconsin, state trooper John Leitner clocked a motorcyclist hurtling by him at 99 mph. Quickly climbing into his cruiser, he took off in pursuit at speeds of up to 115 mph. Suddenly, the cruiser skidded out of control and slammed into an embankment at 35 mph.

"I saw the crash coming," Leitner recalls, "so I threw up my arms to protect my face. The next thing I felt was the soft silver bag in my face. It happened so fast that I didn't even remember that my cruiser had an air bag." Leitner climbed out of the car with only a few minor cuts and bruises. His boss reported that Leitner's wife doesn't want him on patrol again, unless he has another air bag-equipped cruiser.

Detroit, Michigan, March 1986

When Tim Rancour's company car turned out to be a 1985 Ford Tempo, equipped with an air bag, he wasn't particularly thrilled. The 31-year-old Aetna auditor had become part of an experiment to see if air bag company cars would lower injury rates.

Early one March morning, Rancour was driving to work when a 1982 Chrysler Cordoba suddenly crossed the yellow line and came straight at him.

In less than a tenth of a second after the crash, the electronic sensor on the front of Rancour's car relayed a signal to inflate the air bag stored in his steering wheel. Instantly, a pillow of air formed to cushion Rancour's face and belted chest. After the accident Rancour got out of his Tempo, which weighed a thousand pounds less than the Cordoba, and went over to see if the other driver was all right. The unbelted Cordoba driver was hospitalized.

Satellite Beach, Florida, July 1977

A grandmother, with her six-year-old granddaughter sitting on an arm rest next to her and her four-year-old grandson standing on the front seat, crashed into the side of a panel truck while traveling 46 mph. The air bag activated "so quickly that I was not even aware at the time what was happening," she recalled after the crash. The impact with the bag "was just like putting your head in a soft pillow," she said. "There's no feeling of hurt." Although her car was destroyed, she and her grandchildren, all unbelted, walked away from the crash.

Irwinton, Georgia, July 1985

A local pulpwood worker, taking a short cut home on a quiet two-lane road southwest of Irwinton, missed a sharp right turn and plowed into a solid dirt embankment at over

50 mph. After the accident, the driver, who had no idea his used 1974 Oldsmobile had airbags, was able to walk away with only minor injuries.

The first people at the accident scene didn't know what to make of the air bags. A deputy sheriff first thought the bags were clothing and that there was a body in the car. The next day when the driver came back to look at the wreck, he said, "I hope I can buy another car with bags."

Kansas City, Missouri, October 1975

A prominent doctor was involved in a head-on collision after a heavy work day. He said he dozed off for a few seconds while driving and "awakened just an instant or two before I struck the city transport bus." The doctor's car was estimated to be traveling 30 to 40 mph; the bus was stopped. The doctor, who was unbelted, reported that as the air bag deployed, "I felt nothing except a slight jar." He walked away from the "almost total" wreckage of the car, "much to the amazement of a policeman who was nearby and saw the crash." He commented that, as a doctor, "I felt quite certain that the air bags prevented me from having severe lacerations of my face, and possibly chest, from flying glass. These bags sustained me in one position. Without this, I certainly would have been forced forward and maybe would have gone out the front windshield."

The doctor was so impressed with the performance of the air bag that he attempted to buy another air-bag car. After a three-state search of GM dealers failed to turn up such a car, he attempted to special order one. General Motors refused to fill his request.

Mahopac, New York, September 1974 and January 1977

In this case a young woman was involved in two air-bag crashes. In September 1974, traveling at 31 mph, she struck a car that was pulling out from an intersection. Her only injuries were some minor bruises. In January 1977, her car was damaged beyond repair when it skidded off an icy road and smashed into a tree at 15 to 20 mph. Ex-pressing her gratitude for the air bags, she said, "This is our security blanket…"

Her seat belts were unfastened in both crashes. "I know it seems foolish, particularly after the first accident, for me not to use seat belts, but the fact is they make me uncomfortable. The beauty of the air bags is that they are not subject to the driver's negligence or carelessness."

Pittsburgh, Pennsylvania, March 1982

A 1974 Oldsmobile equipped with an air bag was sideswiped and forced into the opposing traffic lane where it collided head-on with a Ford Pinto. The Oldsmobile driver bruised his shoulder and received a minor cut under his eye and a bump on the forehead. The driver of the Pinto was killed instantly and the passenger was hospitalized for many weeks.

St. Louis, Missouri, June 1973

This case demonstrates that an air bag can even offer protection when more than one impact takes place. Two teenage girls were attempting to cross an inclined triple-track railroad crossing when the driver lost control of the car. They were traveling at 28 mph when the car bottomed out on the tracks, causing the air bag to inflate. After the air bag inflated, the car continued, out of control, until it struck a utility pole. The passenger was unharmed and the driver received a bloody nose.

Automatic Crash Protection Systems - 1988

Car	Type of System	Availability
Acura Legend Coupe LS	Driver Air Bags	Standard
Acura Legend Sedan LS	Driver Air Bags	Standard
BMW L6, M6, 735i, 750iL	Driver Air Bags	Standard
Buick LeSabre	Belts	Standard
Buick Regal	Belts	Standard
Buick Skylark	Belts	Standard
Chrysler Conquest	Motorized Belts	Standard
Chrysler Fifth Avenue	Driver Air Bags	Optional[1]
Chrysler LeBaron Coupe	Belts	Standard
Dodge Daytona	Belts	Standard
Dodge Diplomat	Driver Air Bags	Optional[1]
Ford Escort	Motorized Belts	Standard
Ford Tempo [4]	Driver Air Bags	Optional
Honda Accord Hatchback	Belts	Standard
Honda Prelude	Belts	Standard
Hyundai Excel	Belts	Optional
Isuzu Impulse	Motorized Belts	Standard
Jaguar XJ-S, XJ-SC	Motorized Belts	Standard
Mazda MX6	Motorized Belts	Standard
Mazda 626 LX Sedan	Motorized Belts	Standard
Mercedes-Benz All Models	Driver Air Bags	Standard
Mercury Topaz [4]	Driver Air Bags	Optional
Mitsubishi Precis	Belts	Optional
Mitsubishi Starion	Motorized Belts	Standard

1. Introduction date to be determined.
2. Optional Driver Air Bags to be introduced mid-year.
3. Mid to late year introduction.
4. Motorized belts standard.

Automatic Crash Protection Systems - 1988

Car	Type of System	Availability
Nissan Maxima	Motorized Belts	Standard
Oldsmobile Calais	Belts	Standard
Oldsmobile Cutlass Supreme	Belts	Standard
Oldsmobile 88	Belts	Standard[2]
Peugeot 505 GLS Sedan	Belts	Standard
Peugeot 505 STI Sedan	Belts	Standard
Plymouth Grand Fury	Driver Air Bags	Optional[1]
Pontiac Bonneville	Belts	Standard
Pontiac Gran Am	Belts	Standard
Pontiac Grand Prix	Belts	Standard
Porsche 944 Turbo, 944S	Dual Air Bags	Standard
Porsche 944	Dual Air Bags	Optional
Saab 900S 3 dr.	Motorized Belts	Standard
Saab 900 Turbo 3dr.	Motorized Belts	Standard[3]
Saab 9000 Turbo	Driver Air Bags	Optional[3]
Sterling 825SL	Motorized Belts	Optional
Subaru XT Coupe [5]	Motorized Belts	Standard
Toyota Camry	Motorized Belts	Standard
Toyota Cressida	Motorized Belts	Standard
Volkswagen Golf GL	Belts	Standard
Volkswagen Jetta GL	Belts	Standard
Volvo 780	Driver Air Bags	Standard
Volvo 740 GLE [6]	Driver Air Bags	Optional
Volvo 760	Driver Air Bags	Standard
Yugo GVS	Belts	Optional

5. Selected DL/GLs also have standard motorized belts.

6. Turbo model has standard driver air bags.

Note: Chevrolet Beretta may offer belts as standard equipment.

RSV (Research Safety Vehicle)

For most consumers the ultimate safety car conjures up the image of an armored tank. This need not be the case. In 1975 the federal government set out to dispel the notion that building a safe car means sacrificing styling, comfort, performance, or fuel economy. The result of their work, pictured below, was an attractive, fuel efficient, compact four-passenger car—not unlike many of the popular cars on the road today. But that's where the comparison ends.

The RSV, or Research Safety Vehicle, is capable of protecting occupants in crashes up to 50 mph. It can take front and rear collisions of up to 10 mph with no damage. In addition to being equipped with air bags, the car is made of sheet metal filled with foam. The foam-filled sections provide protection by dramatically reducing crash forces and keeping other cars from penetrating the interior.

Even with these lifesaving features, the RSV can accelerate from 0 to 55 in less than 17 seconds and has a fuel economy rating of nearly 29 mpg. One of the design criteria that the government imposed on this U.S.-built car was that the safety features be composed of readily available systems and designs, not futuristic technology that would be impossible to produce economically. The government estimated that this car could have been mass-produced and sold for $7,000 to $8,000.

Most safety experts are very concerned about the RSV. Their concern, however, rests not with the car but with the auto manufacturers. Although the car was developed years ago, using technology available at that time, manufacturers have yet to incorporate any of the major lifesaving features into today's cars. It has been estimated that if every car were equipped with the features of the RSV, we could reduce our national consumption of gasoline by 40 percent and save more than 10,000 lives annually.

For a detailed description of the car, write to the National Highway Safety Administration (the address is in "The Complaint Chapter" under Federal Agencies) and ask for the report entitled "The Safe, Fuel Efficient Car—A report on its producibility and marketing," dated October 1980.

Research Safety Vehicle:
The Car of the Future

About 60 percent of those killed or injured in car crashes would have been saved from serious harm had they been wearing safety belts. Yet only three out of every ten Americans currently uses these lifesaving devices.

Safety belts are particularly important in subcompact cars.

If you are riding in a subcompact, your chances of being killed or seriously injured in a collision with a large car are eight times greater than for the occupants of the large car. Wearing your belt will greatly improve your odds for survival.

Why don't people wear their belts? Sometimes it is because

they don't know how safety belts work or simply don't know the facts about safety belts. Following are some of the myths many people hold about safety belts.

Once you know the facts, you should be willing to buckle up.

How a Safety Belt Works

Have you ever wondered if your safety belt will actually hold you back in the event of a crash? The illustration shows how most safety belts work. Your belt is designed to move freely while you are driving, enabling you to easily reach all of the dashboard controls and remain comfortable. In an accident or sudden stop, your belt is designed to lock immediately and prevent your body from moving forward.

Today's cars have two types of locking systems. "Belt sensitive" systems lock in response to a sudden movement of the occupant's body. If your safety belt locks in response to a sharp jerk on the belt, you have a "belt sensitive" system.

If your belt does not grab when you pull on it, then you probably have a "vehicle sensitive" system. The diagram to the right illustrates how a "vehicle sensitive" system works. To test a "vehicle sensitive" belt system, apply the brakes suddenly (where it is safe to do so) and pull on the belt. It should lock up.

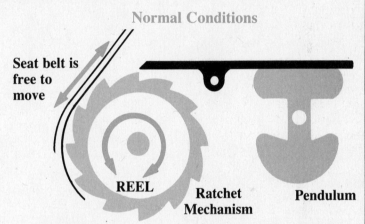

Normal Conditions

Seat belt is free to move

REEL Ratchet Mechanism Pendulum

Under normal conditions, the pendulum and bar remain horizontal. The reel, which holds the belt, is free to rotate, allowing the occupant to move freely.

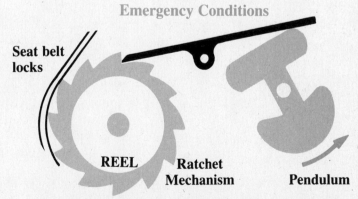

Emergency Conditions

Seat belt locks

REEL Ratchet Mechanism Pendulum

In a collision or sudden stop, the pendulum moves forward causing the bar to engage the ratchet. The reel and seat belt lock in place, keeping the occupant from moving forward.

Safety Belt Myths and Facts

MYTH

"I don't need a safety belt when I'm traveling at low speeds or going on a short trip."

"I don't want to be trapped by a seat belt. It's better to be thrown free in an accident."

"Pregnant women should not wear safety belts."

"I don't need seat belts because I'm a really good driver. I have excellent reactions."

"I just don't believe it will ever happen to me."

"I can touch my head to the dashboard when I'm wearing my seat belt so there's no way it can help me in a car accident."

"I don't need it. In case of an accident, I can brace myself with my hands."

"Most people would be offended if I asked them to put on a seat belt in my car."

FACT

Three out of four accidents happen within 25 miles of home. Accident rates are much higher on city streets than on highways. Eighty percent of deaths and serious injuries occur at speeds under 40 mph.

The chance of being killed is 25 times greater if you're ejected. A safety belt will keep you from plunging through the windshield; smashing into trees, rocks, or other cars; scraping along the ground; or getting run over by your own or another car. If you are wearing your belt, you're far more likely to be conscious after an accident to free yourself and other passengers.

According to the American Medical Association, "Both the pregnant mother and the fetus are safer, provided the lap belt is worn as low on the pelvis as possible."

No matter how good a driver you are, you can't control the other car. When another car comes at you, it may be the result of mechanical failure and there's no way to protect yourself against someone else's poor judgment and bad driving.

Every one of us can expect to be in a crash once every 10 years. For one out of 20 of us, it will be a serious crash. For one out of every 60 born today, it will be fatal.

Safety belts are designed to allow you to move freely in your car. They also have a latching device that locks the safety belt if your car should come to a sudden halt. This latching device keeps you from hitting the inside of the car or being ejected. It's there when you need it.

At 35 mph, the impact on you or your passengers is brutal. There's no way your arms and legs can brace you against that kind of collision. The speed and force are just too great. The force of impact at just 10 mph is equivalent to the force of catching a 200-pound bag of cement from a first-floor window.

Polls show that the majority of people would willingly use their belts if you, the driver, would ask them.

It has been over twenty years since the U.S. government required automakers to install safety belts. During that time, manufacturers have rarely acknowledged belts, paid little attention to their design and have successfully prevented the government from imposing any type of dynamic crash-test standard to determine if they really work. They have, however, included them in their regular tally of the costs imposed on them by government regulation. Why then, after decades of neglect, are automakers suddenly spending millions of dollars to enact state seat belt laws?

The automakers became interested in safety belt laws last year when the U.S. Department of Transportation issued a requirement that automatic crash protection must be phased into all cars beginning with the 1987 models. Secretary of Transportation Elizabeth Dole included in the rule an escape clause that will allow manufacturers to get out of the requirement if states representing two-thirds of the population pass laws requiring adults to buckle up by April 1, 1989. The automakers failed to achieve their goal and consumers will now be able to buy cars with automatic crash protection.

While most safety advocates welcome the laws, the ones passed to date are weak and not being enforced. In addition, most of the laws are based on secondary enforcement— meaning you cannot be stopped for failing to wear your belt. If you are stopped for some other reason and the officer notices you don't have your belt on by the time he or she reaches the car, you may be fined. In many cases the fines are less than a parking ticket.

Another unusual feature of these laws is that most of them allow drivers to avoid buckling up with a doctor's permission. This loophole was inserted to appease those who were not really in favor of the law. However, many doctors are wondering if they will be responsible for the injuries of unbuckled patients. In fact, the State of New York Medical Society cautions doctors not to give medical dispensation from the law because "No medical condition has yet been found to warrant a medical exemption for seat belt use."

Even though most laws are weak, they have heightened awareness and are generally raising the level of usage. Belt use in states that have passed the laws tends to rise sharply after the law is enacted, but then drops after the law has been on the books for a few months.

The following table describes the laws in those states that now require safety belt use.

State	Safety Belt Law
California	**Law applies to:** All occupants over 4 years old in private passenger vehicles under 6001 lbs. and front seat occupants over 4 years old in taxi cabs. **Who is responsible:** Driver responsible for 4-16 year olds, passengers over 16 responsible for themselves. **Enforcement:** Secondary, you *cannot* be stopped for not wearing a safety belt. **Fine:** $20 or traffic school; $50, subsequent offense. **Exemptions:** Written medical, certain delivery vehicles.
Colorado	**Law applies to:** Front seat occupants. **Who is responsible:** Not specified. **Enforcement:** Secondary, you *cannot* be stopped for not wearing a safety belt. **Fine:** $10. **Exemptions:** Written medical.

State	Safety Belt Law:
Connecticut	**Law applies to:** Front seat occupants in passenger vehicles without air bags. **Who is responsible:** Driver responsible for 0-16 year olds, passengers over 16 responsible for themselves. **Enforcement:** Primary, you *can* be stopped for not wearing a safety belt. **Fine:** $15, no points. **Exemptions:** Written medical, certain delivery vehicles, motor vehicles equipped with air bags.
District of Columbia	**Law applies to:** Front seat occupants. **Who is responsible:** Driver responsible for 0-16 year olds, passengers over 16 responsible for themselves. **Enforcement:** Secondary, you *cannot* be stopped for not wearing a safety belt. **Fine:** $15.
Florida	**Law applies to:** Front seat occupants. **Who is responsible:** Driver responsible for 0-16 year olds, passengers over 16 responsible for themselves. **Enforcement:** Secondary, you *cannot* be stopped for not wearing a safety belt. **Fine:** $20. **Exemptions:** Written medical, certain delivery vehicles.
Hawaii	**Law applies to:** Front seat occupants in passenger cars and vehicles required to have seat belts. **Who is responsible:** Driver responsible for 0-15 year olds, passengers over 15 responsible for themselves. **Enforcement:** Primary, you *can* be stopped for not wearing a safety belt. **Fine:** Maximum $15 (note: 10% insurance reduction for no-fault/medical part of policy). **Exemptions:** Written medical or number of passengers exceeds number of belts.
Idaho	**Law applies to:** Front seat occupants. **Who is responsible:** Occupants responsible for themselves. **Enforcement:** Secondary, you *cannot* be stopped for not wearing a safety belt. **Fine:** $5, no points. **Exemptions:** Written medical, if number of front seat passengers exceeds number of belts.
Illinois	**Law applies to:** Front seat occupants in all motor vehicles traveling more than 15 mph which are required to have seat belts themselves. **Who is responsible:** Driver responsible for 0-16 year olds, passengers over 16 responsible for themselves. **Enforcement:** Primary, you *can* be stopped for not wearing a safety belt. **Fine:** Maximum $25. **Exemptions:** Written medical, letter carriers.
Indiana	**Law applies to:** Front seat occupants in passenger cars. **Who is responsible:** Occupants responsible for themselves. **Enforcement:** Secondary, you *cannot* be stopped for not wearing a safety belt. **Fine:** Maximum $25. **Exemptions:** Written medical, certain delivery vehicles.
Iowa	**Law applies to:** Front seat occupants. **Who is responsible:** Driver and passenger can both be cited. **Enforcement:** Primary, you *can* be stopped for not wearing a safety belt. **Fine:** $10. **Exemptions:** Written medical, certain delivery vehicles.
Kansas	**Law applies to:** Front seat occupants. **Who is responsible:** Occupants responsible for themselves. **Enforcement:** Secondary, you *cannot* be stopped for not wearing a safety belt. **Fine:** $10. **Exemptions:** Written medical, certain delivery vehicles.

State	Safety Belt Law:
Louisiana	**Law applies to:** Front seat occupants in passenger cars. **Who is responsible:** Occupants responsible for themselves. **Enforcement:** Primary, you *can* be stopped for not wearing a safety belt. **Fine:** $25†‡. **Exemptions:** Written medical, letter carriers.
Maryland	**Law applies to:** Outboard front seat occupants. **Who is responsible:** Driver responsible for 0-16 year olds, passengers over 16 responsible for themselves. **Enforcement:** Secondary, you *cannot* be stopped for not wearing a safety belt. **Fine:** $25. **Exemptions:** Written medical, certain delivery vehicles.
Michigan	**Law applies to:** Front seat occupants. **Who is responsible:** Driver responsible for 0-16 year olds, passengers over 16 responsible for themselves. **Enforcement:** Secondary, you *cannot* be stopped for not wearing a safety belt. **Fine:** $25†‡. **Exemptions:** Written medical.
Minnesota	**Law applies to:** Front seat occupants and all children under age 11. **Who is responsible:** Driver or passenger can be cited. **Enforcement:** Primary, you *can* be stopped for not wearing a safety belt. **Fine:** No fine, safety warning only. **Exemptions:** Written medical, certain delivery vehicles, if number of passengers exceeds number of belts.
Missouri	**Law applies to:** Front seat occupants. **Who is responsible:** Driver responsible for 0-16 year olds, passengers over 16 responsible for themselves. **Enforcement:** Secondary, you *cannot* be stopped for not wearing a safety belt. **Fine:** $10 maximum†‡. **Exemptions:** Written medical, USPS carriers.
Montana	**Law applies to:** All occupants. **Who is responsible:** Driver responsible for all. **Enforcement:** Secondary, you *cannot* be stopped for not wearing a safety belt. **Fine:** $20. **Exemptions:** Written medical.
Nevada	**Law applies to:** All occupants. **Who is responsible:** Driver responsible for 0-18 year olds, passengers over 18 responsible for themselves. **Enforcement:** Secondary, you *cannot* be stopped for not wearing a safety belt. **Fine:** $25. **Exemptions:** Written medical, emergency personnel.
New Jersey	**Law applies to:** Front seat occupants. **Who is responsible:** Driver responsible for 0-18 year olds, passengers over 18 responsible for themselves. **Enforcement:** Secondary, you *cannot* be stopped for not wearing a safety belt. **Fine:** $20 maximum†, no points. **Exemptions:** Written medical, letter carriers.
New Mexico	**Law applies to:** Front seat occupants and rear seat occupants under 11 years old in passenger cars. **Who is responsible:** Front seat occupants responsible for themselves. **Enforcement:** Primary, you *can* be stopped for not wearing a safety belt. **Fine:** $25 - $50. **Exemptions:** Written medical, letter carriers.
New York*	**Law applies to:** Front seat occupants and rear seat occupants under 10 years old. **Who is responsible:** Driver responsible for 0-16 year olds, passengers over 16 responsible for themselves. **Enforcement:** Primary, you *can* be stopped for not wearing a safety belt. **Fine:** $50†. **Exemptions:** Written medical.

State	Safety Belt Law:
North Carolina	**Law applies to:** Front seat occupants. **Who is responsible:** Driver responsible for 0-15 year olds, passengers over 15 responsible for themselves. **Enforcement:** Primary, you *can* be stopped for not wearing a safety belt. **Fine:** $25 maximum. **Exemptions:** Written medical, certain delivery vehicles.
Ohio	**Law applies to:** Front seat occupants. **Who is responsible:** Driver and passenger can both be cited. **Enforcement:** Secondary, you *cannot* be stopped for not wearing a safety belt. **Fine:** $20 for driver, $10 on driver for each unbelted occupant, $30 maximum; $10 for occupant. **Exemptions:** Written medical, certain delivery vehicles.
Oklahoma	**Law applies to:** Front seat occupants. **Who is responsible:** Not specified, stipulates "front seat occupants must use belts." **Enforcement:** Primary, you *can* be stopped for not wearing a safety belt. **Fine:** $10 fine, $15 court costs. **Exemptions:** Written medical, trucks, RVs and vans.
Tennessee	**Law applies to:** All occupants. **Who is responsible:** Driver responsible for 4-16 year olds, passengers over 16 responsible for themselves. **Enforcement:** Primary you *can* be stopped for not wearing a safety belt. **Fine:** $25 per violation, with maximum of $50. No points. **Exemptions:** Written medical, certain delivery vehicles.
Texas	**Law applies to:** Front seat occupants in passenger cars and trucks over 1500 lbs. **Who is responsible:** Driver responsible for 0-15 year olds, passengers over 15 responsible for themselves. **Enforcement:** Primary, you *can* be stopped for not wearing a safety belt. **Fine:** $25 - $50. **Exemptions:** Written medical, USPS carriers.
Utah	**Law applies to:** Front seat occupants. **Who is responsible:** Driver responsible for 4-18 year olds, passengers over 18 responsible for themselves. **Enforcement:** Secondary, you *cannot* be stopped for not wearing a safety belt. **Fine:** $10. **Exemptions:** Written medical, letter carriers.
Virginia	**Law applies to:** Front seat occupants. **Who is responsible:** Driver responsible for 0-16 year olds, passengers over 16 responsible for themselves. **Enforcement:** Secondary, you *cannot* be stopped for not wearing a safety belt. **Fine:** $25. **Exemptions:** Written medical, postal carriers, law enforcement vehicles.
Washington	**Law applies to:** All occupants. **Who is responsible:** Driver responsible for 0-16 year olds, passengers over 16 responsible for themselves. **Enforcement:** Secondary, you *cannot* be stopped for not wearing a safety belt. **Fine:** Traffic infraction. Information not available to insurance company. **Exemptions:** Written medical.

†Driver responsible for compliance can be held liable.

‡Non-use may reduce insurance payments after an accident.

*Efforts under way to repeal the law.

How many times have you gone out of your way to prevent your children from being injured, taken special care to keep household poisons out of their reach, or watched carefully while they swam? If you are like most parents, you have probably done these things quite often. Yet, despite our concern about our children's welfare in these situations, most parents plunk their children in the back of a station wagon or let them roam around in a moving car. Ironically, of all hazards, it is the automobile that poses the greatest threat to your children's welfare.

After the first weeks of an infant's life, car accidents are the single leading cause of death and serious injury for children. Yet, nearly 80 percent of the children who died in cars could have been saved by the use of child safety seats or safety belts.

Being a safe driver yourself is no excuse not to have everyone buckled up. Quite often crashes or sudden swerves are caused by the recklessness of others. You simply can't protect children by holding them on your lap. Even in low-speed crashes or swerving, a child can be hurled against the inside of the car with a violent impact. At 30 mph, a crash or sudden braking can wrench your child from your arms with a tremendous force. Your child will continue to fly forward at the speed the car was traveling until he or she hits something. At this speed, even a tiny 10-pound infant would be ripped from your arms with a force of nearly 300 pounds.

To demonstrate the actual forces present even in low-speed craches, researchers at the University of Michigan set up a study using adult volunteers. Both male and female adults were given 17-pound dummies to represent the average six-month-old baby. Sitting in a seat, with safety belts on, each adult held one of the "babies" in tests simulating 15 and 30 mph crashes. Even knowing when the impact would occur and holding on with all their strength, none of the volunteers was able to keep the "baby" from being torn from his or her arms.

If you aren't wearing a safety belt, your own body will be an additional hazard to a child in your lap. You will be thrown forward with enough force to crush your child against the dashboard or the back of the front seat.

The best and only way to protect your child in an automobile is by using a safety seat. If no seat is available, buckle the child in the back seat with a conventional seat belt.

By getting into the habit of always using a child safety seat, you will be on the way to establishing the habit of regular safety belt use when your children get older. As a lifelong wearer of safety belts, your child will be reducing his or her chances of being killed or seriously injured in an accident by 50 percent.

National Passenger Safety Association

Some of the information on the following pages was compiled with the assistance of the National Passenger Safety Association. NPSA is a nonprofit organization of parents and professionals dedicated to ensuring safe transportation in automobiles.

For more information on membership, contact: National Passenger Safety Association, P.O. Box 65616, Washington, DC 20035-5616.

Seat Types

There are three major types of child safety seats: infant, convertible, and toddler.

Infant seats can be used from birth until your baby is able to sit up, usually at 9 to 12 months, or at a weight of 20 pounds. This seat can only be installed facing the rear of the car, keeping the baby in a semi-reclining position. In an accident, the crash forces are spread as gently as possible over the baby's back. A harness keeps the baby in the seat, which is anchored to the car by the car's safety belt. Look for seats with more than one harness position. They will fit the baby better as he or she grows.

Infant Seat

One of the benefits of purchasing an infant seat, as opposed to a convertible seat that can be used for infants and toddlers, is that you can easily remove and install the seat with the baby in place. Another benefit is that most infant car seats can be used as indoor baby seats. CAUTION: *Some indoor baby seats look remarkably similar to infant safety seats. These are not crashworthy and should never be used as car safety seats.*

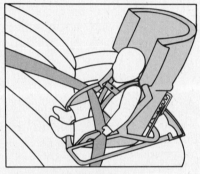

Five-Point Harness

Convertible seats can be used from birth until the child reaches 40 pounds. When used for an infant, the seat faces rearward in a reclining position, but once the baby is able to sit up, the frame can be adjusted upright and the seat turned to face forward. The safety harness can also be moved from the lower to the upper slots as the child gets taller.

Buying a convertible seat can save you the expense of buying both an infant and toddler seat. The easiest seats to use are those with a harness/partial shield. When using one of these seats it is extremely important that the straps fit snugly over the child's shoulders. There should only be enough room between the strap and shoulder to slip two fingers. One of the best ways to insure that the shoulder straps are adjusted correctly is to buy a retractable harness model. Like a car's safety belt, these automatically adjust to fit snugly on your child.

Convertible seats come in four basic types:

The five-point harness consists of two shoulder and lap straps converging at a buckle connected to a crotch strap. These straps are adjustable, allowing for growth and the child's comfort. The best models have adjustable crotch straps as well so you can pull the lap straps down across the child's thighs.

The harness/partial shield, which has a small pad joining the shoulder belts and requires

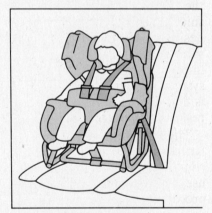

Harness/Partial Shield

only one buckle to secure your child, is generally more convenient than the five-point harness. In fact, many parents find this to be the simplest and easiest-to-use type of convertible seat.

The three-point harness/safety shield is another convenient model to use, since the safety harness is attached to the safety shield. As the shield

Shell Seat

comes down in front of the child, the harness comes over the child's shoulders. The shield in this type of seat is designed to provide some safety protection and is an important part of the restraint system. An additional feature is that the child has a place to rest his or her arms or a toy.

The five-point harness/armrest is a combination of designs, which uses the five-point harness to protect the child in the event of an accident. The armrest is designed for the child's convenience and is not a part of the safety restraint system. Use of the armrest without the five-point harness will not protect your child.

Toddler seats can be used for children between 20 and 60 pounds, depending on the type of seat purchased. There are three types of toddler seats: shell, shield, and harness.

The shell seat is similar to a convertible seat but does not recline. It should be used only when your child can sit up without support. The child is placed in a five-point harness within the safety seat. The seat is anchored by the car's safety belt. Some shell seats require a tether strap, which must be securely fastened to the car.

C Shield

The shield-type booster seat is used when your child is too big for a convertible or shell safety seat but too small to use safety belts. The shield has energy-absorbing padding inside a protective shield. Typically, the car's safety belt fastens in front

Harness-Type Seat

of the shield, anchoring it to the car. This type of seat is not recommended for children under 30 pounds. Because the shield does not provide much protection in a side collision, it should be used only in the center of your car's seat.

Harness-type seats are another type of booster seat. With the harness-type booster seat, you must use either the lap and shoulder belt or the harness that comes with the seat. The harness must be tethered (anchored) to the car. Never use a harness-type booster seat without upper chest protection.

Name of Seat	Price	Description
Infant Safety Seats		
Century 570, 580	$25/60	3 Pt. - 2 Position Harness/Pushbutton Release Buckle
Century Infant Love Seat	$30/40	3 Pt. - 2 Position Harness
Cosco First Ride	$35/45	3 Pt. Harness/Pushbutton Release Buckle
Cosco TLC	$24/40	3 Pt. - 2 Position Harness/Pushbutton Release Buckle
Evenflo Dyn-O-Mite	$28	3 Pt. Harness
Evenflo Infant Car Seat	$32	3 Pt. Harness
Ford Infant Carrier	$40	3 Pt. Harness
Kolcraft Rock 'N' Ride	$35/45	3 Pt. Harness
Strolee Rockit Seat 640	$30/50	3 Pt. - 1 Position Harness
Convertible Safety Seats		
Century 100	$40/50	5 Pt. - 2 Position Harness/Pushbutton Release Buckle/Armrest
Century 200	$50/65	3 Pt. - 2 Position Harness/Pushbutton Release Buckle/Partial Shield/Armrest
Century 300	$60/85	5 Pt. - 2 Position Harness/Pushbutton Release Buckle/Full Shield/Armrest
Century 400 XL	$70/100	3 Pt. - 2 Position Quick Lock Harness/Adjustable Full Shield/Armrest
Century 1000 S.T.E.	$60/80	5 Pt. - 3 Position Harness/Recessed Pushbutton Release Buckle/Armrest
Century 2000, 3000 S.T.E.	$70/120	3 Pt. - 3 Position Harness/Recessed Pushbutton Release/Adjustable Partial Shield/Armrest
Cosco Auto Trac	$80/90	2 Position/Automatic Adjustable Harness/Shield
Cosco Commuter	$70/100	3 Pt. - 2 Position Harness/Adjustable Shield
Cosco Commuter 5-Pt.	$55	5 Pt. - 2 Position Harness/Pushbutton Release Buckle/Adjustable Shield
Cosco Safe & Easy	$46	5 Pt. - 2 Position Harness/Pushbutton Release Buckle
Cosco Safe & Snug	$55	3 Pt. - 2 Position Harness/Adjustable Shield
Evenflo Bobby Mac Deluxe II	$50	3 Pt. Harness with Full Shield
Evenflo Convertible	$40	5 Pt. Harness
Evenflo Seven-Year	$100	3 Pt. - 2 Position Harness/Full Shield/Birth to 60 pounds
Evenflo One-Step	$50	3 Pt. Harness/Fully Adjustable Shield
Fisher-Price	$75/80	Harness/Body Pad/Shoulder Straps Connect to Partial Shield

Name of Seat	Price	Description
Gerry Guardian	$80	3 Pt. Harness/Full Shield/Both Retractable with Armrest
Kolcraft Hi Rider XL "7"	$60	3 Pt. Harness/Fully Adjustable Shield/Armrest
Kolcraft Ultra Ride	$90	5 Pt. Harness/Armrest
Nissan Infant/Child Seat	$95	3 Pt. Integral Double Shoulder Harness/Padded Breast Plate
Pride-Ride 825 & 827	$50	5 Pt. Harness
Pride-Ride 830 & 831	$85	5 Pt. Harness/Armrest
Pride-Ride 832	$95	5 Pt. Harness/Armrest
Pride-Ride 835 & 837	$70	5 Pt. Harness/Armrest
Strolee GT 2000	$60/80	5 Pt. Harness
Strolee GT 3000	$70/90	3 Pt. Harness/Retractable Shield
Strolee Wee Care 609, 614	$35/69	5 Pt. Harness
Strolee Wee Care 610, 618, 620	$39/85	5 Pt. Harness/Removable Armrest
Strolee Wee Care 615	$55/75	3 Pt. Harness/Retractable Shield
Volvo Child Seat	$100/150	5 Pt. Harness/Armrest/Toddler Rear Facing in Volvo
Booster Seats		
Century Commander Booster	$20/30	6 Position Adjustable Full Pivoting Growth Shield
Cosco Explorer 1	$26/30	Adjustable Side Shield/Reversible Height Base
Evenflo Booster	$41	2 Position Full Shield
Evenflo Wings	$25	Infinite Adjustable Full Shield
Ford Tot Guard	$65	Fully Adjustable Shield
Gerry Voyager	$40	2 Position Full Shield/Armrest
Kolcraft Flip "N" Go II	$20	Adjustable Partial Shield
Kolcraft Quick-Step Tot-Rider	$40	Partial T-Shield/Armrest
Pride-Trimble Click-N-Go 890,891,892	$23/30	3 Position Shield
Strolee Quick Click 605 Booster	$25/45	Fully Adjustable Shield
Special Needs		
Evenflo Britax	$385	For The Disabled Child Up to 80 pounds or 60 inches
Evenflo Swinger Infant Car Bed	$200	For The Infant Who Requires A Prone Position/Up to 26 inches or 18.7 pounds
E-Z-On Vest	$49	For The Person Up To 164 pounds/Model 101-TCX5 Up to 50 pounds
Tumbleforms Carrie Seating System	$595	For The Disabled Child 38 to 40 inches or 30-60 pounds/Lapbelt Secures Seat Not Child

Based on data collected by the American Academy of Pediatrics

Remember When Buying a Child Safety Seat

Shop around; the same car seat may sell at a wide range of prices in local stores. Put a car safety seat on your baby shower list—it is an excellent gift of love.

When buying, renting, or borrowing a used child safety seat, make certain it has not restrained a child in an accident. If it has, its structure may be weakened and it should no longer be used. If your own seat has restrained your child in a serious accident, replace it immediately.

Because it is difficult for many consumers to judge a safety seat adequately, the federal government conducted a small study of parents' reactions to eight different models. In the study, parents were asked to select and use a seat from among eight popular models. Only three parents kept the seats they originally picked. This stresses the importance of understanding how a seat works, how it fits in your car, and how comfortable it will be for your child before you buy. If the seat is difficult to use, your child might not get the protection he or she needs.

Three out of four child safety seats are being used incorrectly. According to a recent study conducted for the Physicians for Automotive Safety, the incorrect use of child safety seats has reached epidemic proportions. The problems fall into two categories: Incorrect installation of the seat, and incorrect use of the seat's restraining system to secure the child. The study revealed that 84 percent of those seats requiring a top-tether strap had the strap incorrectly installed. Overall, 75 percent of the seats in the national survey were incorrectly installed. In addition to improper top-tether attachment, the vast majority of seats had the car's safety belt improperly routed through the seat frame.

The incorrect installation of a child safety seat can deny the child the lifesaving protection offered by the seat and may even contribute to further injury. It is very important to read the installation instructions carefully.

Considering these guidelines, and the points below, most consumers have found that seats with a three-point retractable harness and a body or safety shield, such as the Gerry Guardian, Nissan or Fisher Price seats, are the easiest to use.

Buying Tips

1. Make sure the seat you buy can be properly installed in your car. Some car seats cannot be properly buckled into certain cars. Also, make sure the ceiling of the car is high enough to completely raise the armrest or safety shield.
2. Buy a seat that is installed using only the car's safety belts and does not need a separate tether (anchor) strap.
3. Only buy or rent seats made after January 1, 1981. These seats must meet a tough federal motor vehicle safety standard, which includes passing a simulated crash test. You will find the date of manufacture on a label on the car seat.
4. Look for an FAA-approved seat if you want to use it on an airplane.
5. Determine how many straps need to be fastened to use the seat. The easy-to-use seats require only one.
6. Make sure the seat is wide enough for growth and bulky winter clothes.
7. Make sure your child will be comfortable. Can he or she move his or her arms freely, sleep in the seat, and, if older, see out the window and over the armrest/shield?
8. Will the armrest/shield block the driver's rear view when it's upright?
9. If you have more than one car, is the seat light and easy to install?
10. *Always* use a locking clip in the front seat of imported cars.

Tips on Using the Seat and Buckling Up

Car seats for premature infants: Many infant car seats are unsafe for premature babies, but some can be used with a little coaxing, the *Journal of Pediatrics* reports.

More and more babies are leaving the hospital weighing less than five pounds, write Dr. Marilyn Bull and Karen Bruner Stroup, who placed premature infants in a dozen of the seats.

The crucial dimension, they report, is the distance from the seat back to the crotch strap. If that distance is greater than 14 centimeters, or 5½ inches, a small baby can tend to slouch forward, and a blanket must be used between the baby and the strap.

Even seats with the right back-to-crotch measure need blanket rolls along the sides to support the head. The report says larger infants can also benefit from supporting blankets.

Seats with lap pads or shields were "uniformly unacceptable" because the shields hit the baby in the face or neck.

The study used actual infants because no dummies of that size are currently made, so the crash-worthiness of the seats for premature infants is unknown.

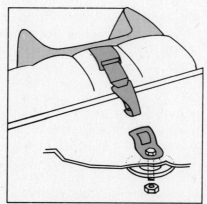

Tether straps: Some seats require the installation of a tether strap when used in the toddler position. This strap gives additional protection in a crash, especially in a side collision. If the seat is used in the car's front seat, the strap must be attached to the rear safety belt. In the rear seat, it must be attached to the window shelf or luggage area.

The tether strap is the nemesis of child safety seat users. Unfortunately, because most consumers find it very difficult to anchor this strap properly, the seats requiring a strap are rarely installed properly.

When correctly used, a seat with a tether strap provides extra protection. If you will not use the top strap every time, you shouldn't buy a seat that requires one. There are many seats that do not need an anchor strap.

The diagram shows the proper anchorage of a tether seat hook. The anchorage point should always be metal. Check with your car dealer if you are not sure of the proper anchorage point. *Avoid buying a seat that requires a top tether strap.*

Safety belts for kids: Normally, children under 40 pounds should always be in a child safety seat. If no seat is available, Physicians for Automotive Safety strongly recommends that a safety belt be used as long as the child is able to sit up unsupported.

When your child outgrows the safety seat, he or she should always use the car's safety belt. The belt should be snug and as low on the hips as possible. If the shoulder belt crosses the face or neck, place it behind the child's back after the buckle is fastened. Never use pillows or cushions to boost your child. In an accident, they may allow a child to slide under the lap belt or allow a child's head to strike the car's interior.

Never put a belt around you and a child in your lap. In an accident or sudden stop, both your weight and the child's would be forced into the belt, with the child absorbing a much greater share of the crash force. Most likely, the pressure would push the belt deeply into the child's body, causing severe injury or death.

Strapping two children into one belt also can be very dangerous. This makes the proper fit impossible.

Buckled up = better behavior:
In studies done at the University of Kansas Medical School, researchers concluded that "buckled up" equals better behavior. When not buckled up, children squirmed around, stood up, complained, fought, and pulled at the steering wheel. When buckled into car safety seats, however, they displayed 95 percent fewer incidents of bad behavior.

Children behave better when buckled up because they feel secure. In sudden stops and swerves, they are held snugly and comfortably in place. In addition, being in a seat can be more fun because most car safety seats are high enough to allow the child to see out of the window. Finally, children are less likely to feel carsick and more likely to fall asleep in a car seat.

Safety seats on aircraft: With the passage of child safety seat laws, many parents have become concerned about protecting children in aircraft. Safety seats offer children the same protection during takeoff, landing, and turbulence that safety belts offer adults. For a safety seat to be used on an aircraft, it must be approved by the Federal Aviation Administration. Call the FAA Public Inquiry Center at 202-267-3484 for a list of approved seats. (Open 8 a.m.-4 p.m. EST, 5 days a week.)

Used and loaner seats: If friends or family pass on a used safety seat to you, *be sure the seat was manufactured after January 1, 1981*, to ensure the best protection for your child. For information on the safety of older seats, contact Physicians for Automotive Safety, P.O. Box 430, Armonk, NY 10504. Let them know the make and model seat you have, and supply a stamped, self-addressed envelope for their response.

It may be possible to obtain a child safety seat through a "loaner" program in your community. This is a low-cost way of obtaining the latest in safety seats as well as proper instructions on their use. To find a loaner program in your area, write to the National Highway Traffic Safety Adminstration. Their address is in "The Complaint Chapter" under Federal Agencies.

Buckled up = fewer accidents:
A recent study at the University of North Carolina offered proof that hundreds of crashes each year are caused when unrestrained children distract the driver. Think of how disconcerting it is when your child falls off the seat, hangs out the window, pulls your hair, or tries to open the door.

With your children in safety seats, or buckled up when they get older, you can concentrate on your driving without worrying about their getting hurt. Everyone will be much calmer, including your children, when you arrive at your destination.

A final note for pregnant women: The American College of Obstetricians and Gynecologists strongly urges pregnant women always to wear a safety belt, including on the ride to the hospital to deliver the baby. In a car crash, the most serious risk to an unborn baby is that the mother will be injured. *Obstetricians recommend that the lap and shoulder belts be used with the lap belt as low as possible on the hips, under the baby.*

When packing your things for the hospital, make sure you include an infant car safety seat to bring your baby home. As the American Academy of Pediatrics says, "Make the first ride a safe ride!"

Ten Tips for Using Your Car Safety Seat

1. The safest place for your child's car seat is in the center position of the back seat.

2. Periodically check the seat's safety harness and the car seat belt of your automobile for a tight, secure fit.

3. Do not give your child lollipops or ice cream on a stick while riding. A bump or swerve could jam the stick into his or her throat.

4. Set a good example by buckling your seat belt every time you get in the car. Be sure all doors are locked, and teach children not to play with door handles or locks.

5. If someone else is driving, ride in the back seat with your baby. The back seat is safer.

6. Buy or make a fabric cover to improve the comfort of a vinyl seat. When the car is in the sun, cover the seat with a light-colored blanket to keep the metal parts from getting too hot.

7. In the winter, try to warm up the car and the safety seat before taking your baby out. Dress a baby in a legged suit. Drape an extra blanket over the seat after baby is buckled in. It can be removed if the car gets too warm.

8. Don't leave sharp or heavy objects loose in the car. Put groceries in the trunk. Anything loose can be deadly in a crash.

9. Make the car seat your child's "own special place," so he or she will enjoy being in it. Pick out some special toys or books that can be used only in the car seat to make using the seat a fun experience.

10. On long trips stop frequently (about every two hours) to give your child a little exercise. This extra time is a small price to pay for the additional protection a car seat offers your precious cargo.

Caution: Automatic Belts ≠ Child Safety Seats

Child safety seats should *never* be used in the front seat of cars equipped with two-point automatic safety belts. Next year, cars with these type of automatic belts must be equipped with a special hole to allow the easy installation of a lap belt. Until then, *never* use a child safety seat with automatic safety belts unless the car has a separate lap belt.

Child Safety Seat Laws—State by State

Every state now requires children to be in child safety seats or buckled up when riding in automobiles. The following table provides an overview of the requirements in your state.

You will note that most states use the child's age to define the law. For example, 0-3 years on the table includes birth through three years old. In most states (32) the laws are not limited to children riding with their parents. They require that any driver with child passengers ensure that those children are buckled up.

State	Child Restraint Law:
Alabama	**Law applies to:** All drivers. **Children covered:** 0-2 years. **Vehicles covered:** Vehicles registered in state except trucks or buses over one ton. **Fine:** $10. **Comments:** Violation does not affect insurance rates.
Alaska	**Law applies to:** All drivers. **Children covered:** 0-5 years. **Vehicles covered:** All vehicles except for school buses & emergency vehicles. **Fine:** Two points and up to $300.† **Comments:** Safety belts OK for 4 & 5 year-olds.
Arizona	**Law applies to:** Resident parent/guardian. **Children covered:** 0-4 years or under 40 lbs. **Vehicles covered:** Non-commercial vehicles registered by parent in state. **Fine:** $50.† **Comments:** Fine may be waived with proof of purchase.
Arkansas	**Law applies to:** Driver who regularly transports children. **Children covered:** 0-4 years. **Vehicles covered:** All vehicles, including pickups & vans. **Fine:** $10-$25.† **Comments:** Safety belt OK for 3 & 4 year-olds.
California	**Law applies to:** Resident parent/guardian. **Children covered:** 0-3 years or under 40 lbs. **Vehicles covered:** Vehicles under 6000 lbs. registered in state. **Fine:** $50-200.† **Comments:** If parent is not driving, safety belt may be substituted. Driver subject to fine if parent not in car.
Colorado	**Law applies to:** Resident driver. **Children covered:** 0-3 years and under 40 lbs. **Vehicles covered:** All vehicles driven by state residents. **Fine:** $25.†
Connecticut	**Law applies to:** All drivers. **Children covered:** 0-3 years. **Vehicles covered:** All passenger vehicles operating in state. **Fine:** $25-$100.† **Comments:** RVs and trucks over one ton exempted. Safety belt OK for 1-3 year-olds in back seat.
Delaware	**Law applies to:** Parent/guardian. **Children covered:** 0-3 years. **Vehicles covered:** Vehicles owned & operated by parent/guardian. **Fine:** $25.† **Comments:** State-wide loaner program available.

†Fine waivable on first offense or proof of safety seat ownership.

State	Child Restraint Law:
District of Columbia	**Law applies to:** Resident drivers or persons driving vehicles registered in D.C. **Children covered:** 0-5 years. **Vehicles covered:** Vehicles registered in D.C. **Fine:** $25.† **Comments:** Safety belt OK for 3-5 year-olds. Exemption if number in family exceeds number of seating positions.
Florida	**Law applies to:** All drivers. **Children covered:** 0-5 years. **Vehicles covered:** Passenger cars, vans or pickups registered in state. **Fine:** $15.† **Comments:** Safety belt OK for 4 year-olds.
Georgia	**Law applies to:** Resident driver who regularly transports children. **Children covered:** 0-3 years. **Vehicles covered:** Passenger cars, vans or pickups registered in state. **Fine:** $25.† **Comments:** Safety belt OK for 3 year-olds. Exemption for attending to personal needs of child.
Hawaii	**Law applies to:** All drivers. **Children covered:** 0-3 years. **Vehicles covered:** All vehicles. **Fine:** $100 maximum. **Comments:** Safety belt OK for 3 year-olds. $25 income tax credit for purchase of seat.
Idaho	**Law applies to:** Resident parent/guardian. **Children covered:** 0-3 years or under 40 lbs. **Vehicles covered:** All non-commercial vehicles. **Fine:** $100 maximum. **Comments:** Exemption if more passengers than belts and for attending to personal needs of child.
Illinois	**Law applies to:** Resident parent/guardian. **Children covered:** 0-5 years. **Vehicles covered:** All vehicles owned and operated by parent/guardian. **Fine:** $25-$50† first offense, $50 thereafter. **Comments:** Safety belt OK for 4 & 5 year-olds.
Indiana	**Law applies to:** All drivers. **Children covered:** 0-4 years. **Vehicles covered:** All vehicles registered in state except taxis & rental vehicles. **Fine:** $50-$500.† **Comments:** Safety belt OK for 3 & 4 years olds.
Iowa	**Law applies to:** All drivers. **Children covered:** 0-5 years. **Vehicles covered:** All vehicles weighing less than 10,000 lbs. **Fine:** $10.† **Comments:** Safety belt OK for 3-5 year-olds. Emergency vehicles exempt.
Kansas	**Law applies to:** Resident parent/guardian. **Children covered:** 0-3 years in front seat. **Vehicles covered:** All vehicles registered in state. **Fine:** $10.†
Kentucky	**Law applies to:** Resident parent/guardian. **Children covered:** Under 40″ tall. **Vehicles covered:** Vehicle owned and operated by parent. **Fine:** None.
Louisiana	**Law applies to:** Resident driver. **Children covered:** 0-4 years. **Vehicles covered:** All vehicles. **Fine:** $25-$50.† **Comments:** Tax credit for full purchase price. Safety belt OK for 3-4 year-olds in back seat. If more children than belts, unrestrained children to be in back seat.

†Fine waivable on first offense or proof of safety seat ownership.

State	Child Restraint Law:
Maine	**Law applies to:** Resident parent/guardian. **Children covered:** 0-11 years. **Vehicles covered:** All vehicles. **Fine:** $25 first offense, $50 thereafter. **Comments:** If driven by nonparent, safety belt OK for 1-3 year-olds.
Maryland	**Law applies to:** All drivers. **Children covered:** 0-4 years. **Vehicles covered:** Passenger or multi-purpose vehicles registered in state. **Fine:** $25.† **Comments:** Safety belt OK for 3-4 year-olds.
Massachusetts	**Law applies to:** All drivers. **Children covered:** 0-11 years. **Vehicles covered:** All vehicles. **Fine:** $25.† **Comments:** Safety belts OK for 0-11 year-olds. Exemption if all seating positions are filled or occupant is physically unable to use restraints.
Michigan	**Law applies to:** Resident driver. **Children covered:** 0-4 years. **Vehicles covered:** All vehicles. **Fine:** $10.† **Comments:** Safety belt OK for 1-4 year-olds if in back seat. Exemption while baby is being nursed.
Minnesota	**Law applies to:** All drivers. **Children covered:** 0-3 years. **Vehicles covered:** All vehicles. **Fine:** $25.
Mississippi	**Law applies to:** Resident parent/guardian. **Children covered:** 0-1 years. **Vehicles covered:** All vehicles registered in state. **Fine:** $10 Maximum†
Missouri	**Law applies to:** Resident driver. **Children covered:** 0-3 years. **Vehicles covered:** All vehicles registered in state. **Fine:** $25.† **Comments:** Safety belt may be substituted if in rear seat.
Montana	**Law applies to:** Resident parent/guardian. **Children covered:** 0-3 years or under 40 lbs. **Vehicles covered:** All vehicles owned/operated by parent. **Fine:** $10-$25.† **Comments:** Safety belt OK for 2 & 3 year-olds.
Nebraska	**Law applies to:** Resident driver. **Children covered:** 0-3 years. **Vehicles covered:** All vehicels since 1963, except taxis. **Fine:** $25.† **Comments:** Exemption for medical waiver from doctor. Safety belt OK for 1-3 year-olds.
Nevada	**Law applies to:** All drivers. **Children covered:** 0-4 years. **Vehicles covered:** All vehicles registered in state, except taxis & rental cars. **Fine:** $35-$100.† **Comments:** If more children than seating positions, preference must be given to children under 3 years old.
New Hampshire	**Law applies to:** All drivers. **Children covered:** 0-4 years. **Vehicles covered:** All vehicles, except those for hire. **Fine:** $30 maximum.† **Comments:** Safety belt is OK for 0-4 year-olds. Exception for children with physical problems.
New Jersey	**Law applies to:** All drivers. **Children covered:** 0-4 years. **Vehicles covered:** All vehicles. **Fine:** $10-$25.† **Comments:** Safety belt OK for children 18 months to 4 years old in rear seat.

†Fine waivable on first offense or proof of safety seat ownership.

State	Child Restraint Law:
New Mexico	**Law applies to:** All drivers. **Children covered:** 0-10 years. **Vehicles covered:** All vehicles registered in state. **Fine:** $50.† **Comments:** Safety belt OK for 1-4 year-olds in rear seat. Exception if all seating positions equipped with belts are occupied.
New York	**Law applies to:** All drivers. **Children covered:** 0-9 years. **Vehicles covered:** All vehicles registered in state. **Fine:** $25.† **Comments:** Safety belts mandatory for 4-9 year-olds.
North Carolina	**Law applies to:** All drivers. **Children covered:** 0-5 years. **Vehicles covered:** State registered vehicles owned/operated by parent. **Fine:** $25. **Comments:** Safety belts OK for 3-5 year-olds. Exemption for attending to personal needs of child or if all other seating positions are filled.
North Dakota	**Law applies to:** All drivers. **Children covered:** 0-5 years. **Vehicles covered:** All passenger vehicles. **Fine:** $20 maximum.† **Comments:** Safety belt OK for children over 2 years old.
Ohio	**Law applies to:** All drivers. **Children covered:** 0-3 years or under 40 lbs. **Vehicles covered:** All vehicles registerd in state except taxis. **Fine:** $10.† **Comments:** Safety belt OK for children over 1 year old only when driven by nonparent.
Oklahoma	**Law applies to:** Resident drivers. **Children covered:** 0-4 years. **Vehicles covered:** All vehicles. **Fine:** $50. **Comments:** If in rear seat, safety belt can be substituted for all children. If in front seat, safety belt can be substituted for 4 year-olds only.
Oregon	**Law applies to:** Resident drivers or residents of states with similar laws. **Children covered:** 0-15 years. **Vehicles covered:** All vehicles under 8,000 lbs. **Fine:** $50 maximum.† **Comments:** Safety belt OK for children over 1 year old. Exemption if all seating positions are occupied or for medical reasons and emergencies.
Pennsylvania	**Law applies to:** Parent/guardian. **Children covered:** 0-3 years. **Vehicles covered:** All vehicles registered in state. **Fine:** $25 maximum.† **Comments:** Safety belt OK in rear seat for children over 1 year old. Exemption for physical or medical reasons.
Rhode Island	**Law applies to:** All drivers. **Children covered:** 0-12 years. **Vehicles covered:** All vehicles. **Fine:** $10.†
South Carolina	**Law applies to:** All drivers. **Children covered:** 0-3 years. **Vehicles covered:** All vehicles registered in state. **Fine:** $25.† **Comments:** Safety belt OK in rear seat for children over 1 year old. Exemption if child is being fed or has medical problems.
South Dakota	**Law applies to:** All drivers. **Children covered:** 0-4 years. **Vehicles covered:** All vehicles. **Fine:** $20. **Comments:** Safety belt OK for children over 2 years old. Exemption for attending to personal needs of child or if all seating positions are occupied.

†Fine waivable on first offense or proof of safety seat ownership.

State	Child Restraint Law:
Tennessee	**Law applies to:** All drivers. **Children covered:** 0-3 years. **Vehicles covered:** All vehicles registered in state except RVs & one ton trucks. **Fine:** $2-$10. **Comments:** Exception while attending to needs of child.
Texas	**Law applies to:** Resident driver. **Children covered:** 0-3 years. **Vehicles covered:** All vehicles registerd in state, except those for hire. **Fine:** $25-$50.† **Comments:** Seat belt OK for children over 2 years old. Exception if all seating position are occupied.
Utah	**Law applies to:** Resident parent/guardian. **Children covered:** 0-4 years. **Vehicles covered:** All vehicles. **Fine:** $20.† **Comments:** Safety belt OK for children over 2 years old. Exemption if all seating positions are occupied.
Vermont	**Law applies to:** All drivers. **Children covered:** 0-4 years. **Vehicles covered:** All vehicles registered in state. **Fine:** $25.† **Comments:** Safety belt OK for children over 1 year old in rear seat. Exemption if number of children exceeds number of belts.
Virginia	**Law applies to:** All drivers. **Children covered:** 0-3 years. **Vehicles covered:** All vehicles registered in state. **Fine:** $25.† **Comments:** Safety belt OK for children over 3 years old or over 40 lbs. Exemption for medical reasons. Driver must carry physician statement.
Washington	**Law applies to:** Resident parent/guardian. **Children covered:** 0-4 years. **Vehicles covered:** All vehicles registered in state & owned & operated by parent/guardian. **Fine:** $30.† **Comments:** Safety belt OK for children over 1 year old.
West Virginia	**Law applies to:** All drivers. **Children covered:** 0-8 years. **Vehicles covered:** All vehicles. **Fine:** $10-$20.† **Comments:** Safety belt OK for children over 3 years old.
Wisconsin	**Law applies to:** Resident driver. **Children covered:** 0-3 years. **Vehicles covered:** All vehicles except taxis. **Fine:** $10-$200.† **Comments:** Safety belt OK for children over 2 years old. Fine increases for younger children and second offense.
Wyoming	**Law applies to:** All drivers. **Children covered:** 0-2 years old or under 40 lbs. **Vehicles covered:** All cars excluding small cars, pickups and vans. **Fine:** $25.

†Fine waivable on first offense or proof of safety seat ownership.

The **FUEL ECONOMY** Chapter

Even with today's lower gasoline prices, fuel efficiency is still an important consideration for most new car buyers. The EPA has come up with a new rating system that more closely approximates our expected mileage and most buyers have learned to use the EPA ratings to *compare* rather than *predict* fuel costs. But choosing a car on the basis of fuel efficiency is not always easy. Even among cars of the same size, fuel efficiency varies greatly. One compact car might get 36 miles per gallon (mpg) while another gets only 22 mpg. If you drive 15,000 miles a year and you pay $1.00 per gallon for fuel, the 36 mpg car will save you $265 a year over the "gas guzzler."

Estimating your fuel costs: The table on this page is a guide for estimating annual fuel costs. To use it, find a car's estimated mpg from the figures at the end of this chapter. Now find the mileage figure on the table below. Read across until you reach the column under the amount you typically pay for gas. This will be an estimate of what you can expect to pay for gas during an average year of driving. By calculating this for the different cars you are considering, you can easily see what differences in gas mileage will mean to your pocketbook. Don't forget to multiply this difference times the number of years you expect to keep the car.

A note about the EPA gas mileage estimates: Many of us do not believe the EPA figures because we often do not get the same mileage suggested by the EPA. This is because actual mileage depends on many factors which the EPA cannot possibly include in their tests: where you live, how you drive, and the exact condition of your car. The best way to use the EPA mileage estimates is on a relative basis. That is, if one car is rated at 20 mpg and another at 25, the 25 mpg car will nearly always perform better than the 20 mpg car.

Annual Cost of Fuel
(Based on 15,000 miles per year)

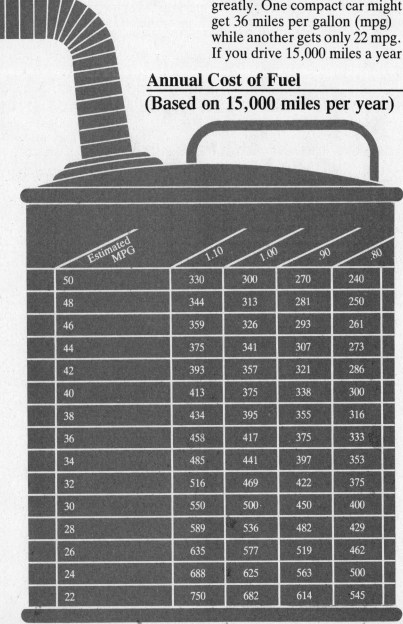

Estimated MPG	1.10	1.00	.90	.80
50	330	300	270	240
48	344	313	281	250
46	359	326	293	261
44	375	341	307	273
42	393	357	321	286
40	413	375	338	300
38	434	395	355	316
36	458	417	375	333
34	485	441	397	353
32	516	469	422	375
30	550	500	450	400
28	589	536	482	429
26	635	577	519	462
24	688	625	563	500
22	750	682	614	545

Factors Affecting Fuel Economy

Fuel economy is affected by a number of factors which you can consider before you buy. For example:

Transmission: Manual transmissions are generally more fuel efficent than automatic transmissions. In fact, a four-speed manual transmission can add up to 6.5 miles per gallon over a three-speed automatic. However, incorrect use of a manual transmission can waste gas, so choose a transmission that matches your needs and experience. Many transmissions now feature an overdrive gear. The overdrive feature can improve a vehicle's fuel economy by as much as 9 percent for an automatic and 3 percent for a manual transmission.

Axle Ratio: The relationship between the revolutions of the drive shaft (or transaxle) and the revolutions of the wheel is called the "axle ratio." Generally, a low ratio, such as 2.69, means less engine wear and better fuel economy than a higher ratio, such as 3.47. A lower axle ratio will result in slower acceleration, but will pay off in increased fuel economy in highway driving. In general, a 10 percent decrease in the axle ratio can improve fuel economy by 4 pecent. Ask the salesperson for an axle ratio of the car you are considering.

Engine: As you would expect, the size of your car's engine greatly affects your fuel economy. The smaller the engine, the better the fuel economy. A 10 percent increase in the size of an engine can increase fuel consumption by 6 percent. Diesel engines can provide as much as a 25 percent increase in fuel economy over the same size gasoline engine. However, diesel engines may be more expensive to maintain and emit more particulate pollution.

Tires: Radial tires can improve your mileage from 3 to 7 percent over conventional bias-ply tires. They also last longer and usually improve the way your car handles. For maximum fuel efficiency, tires should be inflated to the top of the pressure range stamped on the sidewall. Check tire pressure when the tires are cold—before you've driven a long distance. (See "The Tire Chapter" for a listing of the fuel efficiency and durability of various brands of tires.)

Cruise Control: Cruise control can save fuel because driving at a constant speed uses less fuel than changing speeds frequently.

Air Conditioning: Air conditioners add weight and require a car to have more horsepower to operate. They can cost you up to 3 miles per gallon in city driving. At highway speeds, however, using your air conditioner has about the same effect on fuel economy as the air resistance created by opening the windows. Installing an air conditioner cutoff switch that automatically disconnects the air conditioner during rapid accelerations can improve your gas mileage by about 4 percent.

Trim Package: Upgrading a car's trim, installing soundproofing, and adding undercoating can increase the weight of a typical car by 150 pounds. For each 10 percent increase in weight, fuel economy drops about 4 percent.

Power Options: Such features as power steering, brakes, seats, windows, and roofs can reduce your mileage by adding additional weight. Power steering alone can account for a 1 percent drop in fuel economy.

Here are a few things to know about fuel economy:

- Try to avoid short trips. They are expensive because they usually involve a "cold" vehicle. For the first mile or two a cold vehicle gets just 30 to 40 percent of the mileage it gets when fully warm.

- Your vehicle's normal gas mileage may be altered by such things as changes in vehicle load, traffic density, weather and road conditions, driving techniques, and vehicle condition.

- If you have a 2 to 3 mpg drop over several fill-ups that is not due to a change of driving pattern or vehicle load, first check tire pressure, then consider a tune-up.

Once you make your purchase, you may want to check the fuel economy your car is getting. Here's what to do:

Step One

The next time you fill your tank, note the mileage on the odometer.

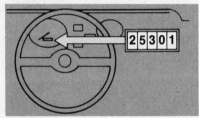

Step Two

When your tank is nearly empty, fill it up completely and write down the mileage and the number of gallons you buy.

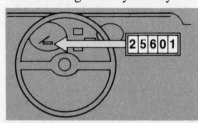

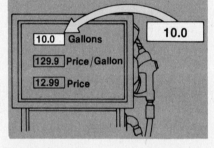

Step Three

Subtract the first odometer reading from the second and divide your answer by the number of gallons of gas you bought. This is your miles per gallon.

Current Mileage	25,601
Previous Mileage	− 25,301
	300

$$300 \div 10 = \textbf{30 MPG}$$

You will get the best estimate of your car's gas mileage by keeping a record over several tankfuls. There may be a small difference each time because of changes in weather, where you drive, the car's condition, and whether your driving was primarily city or highway.

Turbocharging

Beginning with the Europeans and now offered on most domestic cars, a turbocharger is basically an air pump that forces more air into the engine for combustion. Most turbochargers consist of an air compressor driven by a small turbine wheel powered by the engine's exhaust. Taking advantage of energy otherwise lost, the turbine forces the air/fuel mixture into the cylinders, improving the efficiency of the engine. Turbochargers often are used to increase the power and sometimes the fuel efficiency of small engines.

Engines equipped with turbochargers are certainly more expensive than standard engines. The extra power may not be necessary when you consider the extra expense and the fact that turbocharging adds to the complexity of the engine.

The octane rating of a gasoline is not a measure of power or quality. It is simply a measure of the gas's resistance to engine knock. Engine knock is the "pinging" sound you hear when the air/fuel mixture in your engine ignites prematurely during acceleration.

This gasoline octane rating appears on a yellow label on the fuel pump. Octane ratings vary with the different types of gas (premium or regular), in different parts of the country (higher altitudes require lower octane ratings), and even between brands (Texaco's gasolines may have a different rating than Exxon's).

Most new cars are designed to run on a posted octane rating of 87. This number is the average derived from testing each gasoline under two different conditions: Low- and high-speed use.

Determining the right octane rating for your car: By using a lower rate gasoline you can save money at the fuel pump. This simple procedure can help you select the right octane level for your car.

Step One: Have your engine tuned to exact factory specifications by a competent mechanic and make sure it is in good working condition.

Step Two: When the gas in your tank is very low, fill up with the gasoline you usually use. After you have driven 10 to 15 miles,

Octane Rating
87

come to a complete stop and accelerate rapidly. If your engine knocks (that pinging sound) during acceleration, you should switch to a higher octane rating. If there is no knocking sound, wait until your tank is very low and fill up with a lower rated gasoline. Then repeat the test. When you reach the level of octane that causes your engine to knock during the test, go back to the next highest rating.

NOTE: Your engine may knock when you are accelerating a heavily loaded car up a hill or sometimes when the humidity is low. This is normal and generally does not mean you need a higher-octane gas.

Detergent Gasoline

You have probably noticed that many of the oil companies are actively promoting detergent gasolines. The reason: The high repair bills associated with sophisticated fuel injection systems have been attributed to clogged fuel injectors caused by gasoline. Adding detergent agents to gasoline can reduce clogging and save consumers expensive repair bills.

This year, many auto manufacturers are strongly recommending the use of detergent gasolines with their fuel-injected cars. If you need a detergent gasoline, it pays to shop around. Some oil companies offer detergents only in their premium unleaded gasoline which often costs 15¢ a gallon more than regular. Other oil companies offer detergents in all grades of gasoline. By using a non-premium grade of detergent gasoline, you can save over $100 per year. Remember: Detergent gasolines are not necessary for cars with standard carburetors.

Hundreds of products on the market claim to improve your fuel economy. Not only do most of these products not work, but some may even damage your engine.

Sometimes the name or promotional material associated with these products implies they were endorsed by the federal government. In fact, *no government agency endorses any gas-saving products*. Many of the products, however, have been tested by the Environmental Protection Agency. Of nearly 100 products tested by the EPA, only six have been shown to actually improve your fuel economy. Even these, however, offer limited savings because of their cost and relatively small improvement in fuel efficiency.

PRODUCTS THAT MARGINALLY IMPROVE FUEL ECONOMY:

The products listed below have been tested by the EPA and may slightly improve your fuel economy without increasing harmful emissions.

Pass Master Vehicle Air Conditioner Cutoff and **P.A.S.S. Kit:** These products are virtually identical. During periods of rapid acceleration, they automatically turn off your air conditioner. This substantially reduces engine drain, allowing the engine to perform more efficiently. These products can improve fuel economy by 4 percent when the air conditioner is on.

IDALERT: This device sounds a buzzer after the car has been idling for a certain period of time. The sound of the buzzer indicates it would be more fuel-efficient to stop the engine and restart it when you are ready to go. The product was designed mainly for commercial use, where the potential for long periods of idling is high. It has not been widely accepted by consumers.

Autotherm: This item circulates the heat from the engine to the passenger compartment, keeping the car warm for up to two hours after the engine is turned off.

Autotherm saves fuel by allowing you to turn off your engine when sitting in a parked car in cold weather. This might be useful for police departments, whose officers will turn off their engines when they temporarily leave their cars, knowing that the passenger compartment will be warm when they return.

Kamei Spoilers: This device is a plastic air deflector that mounts under the front bumper. It improves fuel economy by reducing the aerodynamic drag. The EPA concluded that this device has the potential to improve the fuel economy of some vehicles. However, the 1 or 2 percent improvement in fuel economy is unlikely to offset the Kamei's cost during the life of the vehicle.

Morse Constant Speed Accessory Drive: This is a variable-ratio accessory drive to replace the fixed-ratio drive normally used to power the water pump and other accessories. Under heavy accessory use fuel economy improvements of up to 6 percent are possible. There is some question about whether this device will allow adequate engine cooling under all driving conditions. This product is currently not on the market.

If you are interested in more information on these products, write to the National Technical Information Service, Springfield, VA 22162.

Products That Don't Work

Purported gas-saving devices come in many forms. Listed below are the types of products on the market. Under each category are the names of devices actually tested or reviewed by EPA for which there was *no evidence of any improvement in fuel economy*.

AIR BLEED DEVICES

ADAKS Vacuum Breaker Air Bleed
Air-Jet Air Bleed
Aquablast Wyman Valve Air Bleed
Auto Miser
Ball-Matic Air Bleed
Berg Air Bleed
Brisko PVC
Cyclone - Z
Econo Needle Air Bleed
Econo-Jet Air Bleed Idle Screws
Fuel Max
Gas Saving Device
Grancor Air Computer
Hot Tip
Landrum Mini-Carb
Landrum Retrofit Air Bleed
Mini Turbocharger Air Bleed*
Monocar HC Control Air Bleed
Peterman Air Bleed*
Pollution Master Air Bleed
Ram-Jet
Turbo-Dyne G.R. Valve

DRIVING HABIT MODIFIERS

Fuel Conservation Device
Gastell

FUEL LINE DEVICES

Fuel Xpander
Gas Miser I
Greer Fuel Preheater
Jacona Fuel System
Malpassi Filter King
Moleculetor
Optimizer
PETRO-MIZER
POLARION-X
Russell Fuelmiser
Super-Mag Fuel Extender
Wickliff Polarizer

FUELS AND FUEL ADDITIVES

Bycosin*
EI-5 Fuel Additive*
Johnson Fuel Additive*
NRG #1 Fuel Additive
QEI 400 Fuel Additive*
Rolfite Upgrade Fuel Additive
Sta-Power Fuel Additive
Stargas Fuel Additive
SYNeRGy-1
Technol G Fuel Additive
ULX-15/ULX-15D
Vareb 10 Fuel Additive*
XRG #1 Fuel Additive

IGNITION DEVICES

Autosaver
Baur Condenser*
BIAP Electronic Ignition Unit
Fuel Economizer
Magna Flash Ignition Control System
Paser Magnum/Paser 500/Paser 500 HEI
Special Formula Ignition Advance Springs*

INTERNAL ENGINE MODIFICATIONS

ACDS Auto. Cylinder Deactivation System
Dresser Economizer*
MSU Cylinder Deactivation*

LIQUID INJECTION

Goodman Engine System, Model 1800*
Waag-Injection System*

MIXTURE ENHANCERS

Basko Enginecoat
Dresser Economizer
Electro-Dyne Superchoke*
Energy Gas Saver*

Environmental Fuel Saver*
Filtron Urethane Foam Filter*
Gas Saving and Emission Control Improvement Device
Glynn-50*
Hydro-Catalyst Pre-Combustion System
Lampkin Fuel Metering Device
Petromizer System
Sav-A-Mile
Smith Power and Deceleration Governor
Spritzer*
Turbo-Carb
Turbocarb

OILS AND OIL ADDITIVES

Analube Synthetic Lubricant
Tephguard*

VAPOR BLEED DEVICES

Atomized Vapor Injector
Econo-Mist Vacuum Vapor Injection System
Frantz Vapor Injection System*
Hydro-Vac
Mark II Vapor Injection System*
Platinum Gasaver
POWER FUeL
SCATPAC Vacuum Vapor Induction System
Turbo Vapor Injection System*
V-70 Vapor Injector

MISCELLANEOUS

BRAKE-EZ*
Dynamix
Fuel Maximiser
Gyroscopic Wheel Cover
Kat's Engine Heater
Lee Exhaust and Fuel Gasification EGR*
Mesco Moisture Extraction System
P.S.C.U. 01 Device
Treis Emulsifier

*For copies of the government reports on these products, you may write Mr. Merrill Korth, U.S. EPA, 2565 Plymouth Road, Ann Arbor, MI 48105.

For reports on the other products, contact the National Technical Information Service, Springfield, VA 22162. (703-487-4650)

Every year the Department of Energy publishes the results of the Environmental Protection Agency's (EPA) fuel economy tests in a comparative guide. Millions of these booklets have been distributed to consumers eager to purchase fuel-efficient automobiles. Because the success of the EPA program depends on consumers' ability to compare the fuel economy rat-

ings easily, the government has printed large numbers of the fuel economy guide. Recently, the government has decided to severely limit the availability of this information to the pubic. We have reprinted the EPA mileage figures for this year's cars.

The estimated mileage figure should be used to compare fuel efficiency among vehicles—not

to predict your exact mileage. Because EPA figures are based on laboratory tests, they often do not match your actual mileage. The mileage figures below and on the next few pages are the EPA city and highway figures. The city figures will be closest to the mileage you will actually receive.

1988 Fuel Economy Winners and Losers

"The Misers"	MPG City/Highway	Annual Fuel Cost†
Chevrolet Sprint Metro (TR: M5-ED:1.0L/3)	54/58	$268
Honda Civic CRX HF (TR: M5-ED:1.5L/4)	50/56	$288
Honda Civic CRX HF (TR: M5-ED:1.5L/4)	45/53	$312
Pontiac Firefly (TR: M5-ED:1.0L/3)	44/49	$326
Suzuki Forsa (TR: M5-ED:1.0L/3)	44/49	$326
Chevrolet Sprint (TR: M5-ED:1.0L/3)	44/49	$326
Ford Festiva (TR: M5-ED:1.3L/4)	39/43	$366
Daihatsu Charade (TR: M5-ED:1.0L/3)	38/42	$384
Ford Festiva (TR: M4-ED:1.3L/4)	38/40	$384
Pontiac Firefly (TR: A3-ED:1.0L/3)	38/40	$384
Suzuki Forsa (TR: A3-ED:1.0L/3)	38/40	$384
Chevrolet Sprint (TR: A3-ED:1.0L/3)	38/40	$384
"The Guzzlers"		
Lamborghini Countach (TR: M5-ED:5.2L/12)	6/10	$2156
Rolls-Royce Bentley 8/Mulsan/Cont. (TR: A3-ED:6.8L/8)	9/11	$1500
Rolls-Royce Corniche II/S.S./Spur (TR: A3-ED:6.8L/8)	9/11	$1500
Ferrari Testarossa (TR: M5-ED:4.9L/12)	10/15	$1364
BMW 5 and 6 Series (TR: M5-ED:3.5L/6)	10/19	$1327
Mercedes-Benz 560 SEC (TR: A4-ED:5.6L/8)	13/16	$1232
Mercedes-Benz 560 SEL (TR: A4-ED:5.6L/8)	13/16	$1232
Mercedes-Benz 560SL (TR: A4-ED:5.6L/8)	14/17	$1151
Mercedes-Benz 420SEL (TR: A4-ED:4.2L/8)	15/18	$1078
Jaguar XJ-S/XJ-SC (TR: A3-ED:5.3L/12)	13/17	$1071

Notes: Based on 1988 EPA figures. TR = Transmission   ED = Engine description.
†Based on driving 15,000 miles per year.

1988 EPA Figures

The following pages contain the EPA mileage ratings and the average annual fuel cost for most of the cars sold in the United States. We have arranged the car in alphabetical order. After the car name we have listed the engine size in liters and the transmission type. A = automatic, L = lockup and M = manual. A T following the car name indicates turbocharging and SW or Wag. indicates station wagon.

The table includes the EPA city (first) and highway (second) fuel economy ratings. The city numbers will most closely resemble your expected mileage for everyday driving. The third column presents the average annual fuel cost, which is based on driving 15,000 miles per year.

Passenger Cars

Car	City	Hwy	Cost	Car	City	Hwy	Cost
Acura Legend (2.7L/L4)	18	23	$750	Buick Skyhawk (2.0L/L3)	25	32	$536
Acura Legend (2.7L/M5)	19	24	$714	Buick Skyhawk (2.0L/L3)	26	32	$536
Alfa Romeo Milano (2.5L/A3)	18	22	$789	Bukc Skyhawk (2.0L/M5)	25	36	$518
Alfa Romeo Milano (2.5L/M5)	18	24	$750	Buick Skyhawk (2.0L/M5)	27	38	$484
Alfa Romeo Milano (3.0L/M5)	18	25	$750	Buick Skyhawk Wagon (2.0L/L3)	24	31	$578
Alfa Romeo Spider (2.0L/M5)	21	27	$626	Buick Skyhawk Wagon (2.0L/L3)	25	32	$536
Audi 80/90 (2.0L/A3)	23	27	$600	Bukck Skyhawk Wagon (2.0L/M5)	25	36	$518
Audi 80/90 (2.3L/M5)	20	25	$682	Buick Skyhawk Wagon (2.0L/M5)	27	38	$484
Audi 80/90 (2.0L/M5)	22	30	$600	Buick Skylark (3.0L/L3)	19	27	$682
Audi 80/90 Quattro (2.3L/M5)	18	24	$750	Buick Skylark (2.5L/L3)	23	31	$578
Audi 5000CS Quattro (2.2L/M5)	17	25	$750	Buick Skylark (2.3L/L3)	24	34	$536
Audi 5000CS Quattro Wagon (2.2L/M5)	17	25	$750	Buick Skylark (2.5L/M5)	23	33	$555
Audi 5000CS Turbo (2.2L/A3)	18	22	$750	Cadillac Allante (4.1L/L4)	16	24	$907
Audi 5000CS Turbo (2.2L/M5)	18	26	$714	Cadillac Brougham (5.0L/L4)	17	24	$750
Audi 5000S (2.3L/A3)	19	23	$750	Cadillac Cimarron (2.8L/L3)	20	27	$652
Audi 5000S (2.3L/M5)	20	25	$682	Cadillac Cimarron (2.8L/M5)	20	29	$652
Audi 5000S Quattro (2.3L/M5)	18	24	$750	Cadillac DeVille (4.5L/L4)	17	24	$789
Audi 5000S Wagon (2.3L/A3)	18	22	$750	Cadillac Eldorado (4.5L/L4)	17	24	$789
Audi 5000S Wagon (2.3L/M5)	18	24	$750	Cadillac Fleetwood (4.5L/L4)	17	24	$789
BMW 3-Series (2.3L/M5)	17	29	$862	Cadillac Seville (4.5L/L4)	17	24	$789
BMW 5-Series (2.7L/L4)	19	23	$714	Chevrolet Beretta (2.8L/L3)	20	26	$682
BMW 5-Series (3.4L/L4)	16	21	$834	Chevrolet Beretta (2.0L/L3)	24	31	$555
BMW 5-Series (2.7L/M5)	19	25	$714	Chevrolet Beretta (2.8L/M5)	19	29	$652
BMW 5-Series (3.4L/M5)	15	21	$882	Chevrolet Beretta (2.0L/M5)	25	35	$518
BMW 5-Series (3.5L/M5)	10	19	$1327	Chevrolet Camaro (2.8L/L4)	19	27	$682
BMW 6-Series (3.4L/L4)	14	18	$938	Chevrolet Camaro (5.0L/L4)	17	26	$750
BMW 6-Series (3.4L/M5)	15	20	$882	Chevrolet Camaro (5.0L/L4)	17	25	$907
BMW 6-Series (3.5L/M5)	10	19	$1327	Chevrolet Camaro (5.7L/L4)	16	25	$907
BMW 7-Series (3.4L/L4)	14	19	$938	Chevrolet Camaro (2.8L/M5)	17	27	$750
BMW 7-Series (3.4L/M5)	15	22	$882	Chevrolet Camaro (5.0L/M5)	16	25	$789
Buick Century (2.8L/L3)	20	27	$652	Chevrolet Camaro (5.0L/M5)	16	26	$862
Buick Century (2.5L/L3)	24	31	$578	Chevrolet Caprice (4.3L/L4)	19	27	$682
Buick Century (2.8L/L4)	21	29	$626	Chevrolet Caprice (5.0L/L4)	16	24	$789
Buick Century (3.8L/L4)	19	29	$682	Chevrolet Caprice Wagon (5.0L/L4)	17	24	$750
Buick Century Wagon (2.5L/L3)	22	29	$600	Chevrolet Cavalier (2.8L/L3)	20	27	$652
Buick Century Wagon (3.8L/L4)	19	29	$682	Chevrolet Cavalier (2.0L/L3)	25	32	$536
Buick Century Wagon (2.8L/L4)	20	29	$652	Chevrolet Cavalier (2.8L/M5)	20	29	$652
Buick Electra (3.8L/L4)	19	29	$682	Chevrolet Cavalier (2.0L/M5)	25	36	$518
Buick LeSabre (3.8L/L4)	19	29	$682	Chevrolet Cavalier Conv. (2.8L/L3)	20	27	$652
Buick LeSabre/Electra W. (5.0L/L4)	17	24	$750	Chevrolet Cavalier Conv. (2.8L/M5)	20	29	$652
Buick Reatta (3.8L/L4)	19	29	$682	Chevrolet Cavalier Wagon (2.8L/L3)	20	27	$652
Buick Regal (2.8L/L4)	20	29	$652	Chevrolet Cavalier Wagon (2.0L/L3)	25	32	$536
Buick Riviera (3.8L/L4)	19	29	$682	Chevrolet Cavalier Wagon (2.8L/M5)	20	29	$652

Chevrolet Cavalier Wagon (2.0L/M5)	25	36	$518	Dodge Colt (1.5L/M4)	34	38	$417
Chevrolet Celebrity (2.8L/L3)	20	27	$652	Dodge Colt (1.6L/M5)	25	31	$555
Chevrolet Celebrity (2.5L/L3)	24	31	$578	Dodge Colt (1.5L/M5)	32	37	$441
Chevrolet Celebrity (2.8L/L4)	21	29	$626	Dodge Colt Vista (2.0L/L3)	23	24	$652
Chevrolet Celebrity (2.8L/M5)	20	29	$652	Dodge Colt Vista 4WD (2.0L/M5)	21	27	$652
Chevrolet Celebrity Wagon (2.5L/L3)	24	31	$578	Dodge Colt Vista (2.0L/M5)	23	29	$600
Chevrolet Celebrity Wagon (2.8L/L4)	20	29	$652	Dodge Daytona (2.2L/A3)	20	25	$785
Chevrolet Celebrity Wagon (2.8L/M5)	19	28	$652	Dodge Daytona (2.5L/L3)	23	28	$600
Chevrolet Corsica (2.8L/L3)	20	26	$682	Dodge Daytona (2.2L/M5)	21	29	$719
Chevrolet Corsica (2.0L/L3)	24	31	$555	Dodge Daytona (2.5L/M5)	22	31	$600
Chevrolet Corsica (2.8L/M5)	19	29	$652	Dodge Diplomat (5.2L/L3)	17	23	$862
Chevrolet Corsica (2.8L/M5)	19	29	$652	Dodge Dynasty (3.0L/L3)	19	26	$714
Chevrolet Corsica (2.0L/M5)	25	35	$518	Dodge Dynasty (2.5L/L3)	23	28	$600
Chevrolet Corvette (5.7L/L4)	16	25	$907	Dodge Lancer (2.2L/A3)	20	25	$785
Chevrolet Corvette (5.7L/M4)	17	24	$907	Dodge Lancer (2.2L/L3)	23	28	$600
Chevrolet Corvette Conv. (5.7L/M4)	17	24	$907	Dodge Lancer (2.5L/L3)	23	28	$600
Chevrolet Corvette Conv. (5.7L/L4)	16	25	$907	Dodge Lancer (2.2L/M5)	21	29	$719
Chevrolet Monte Carlo (5.0L/L4)	17	24	$789	Dodge Lancer (2.5L/M5)	22	31	$600
Chevrolet Monte Carlo (4.3L/L4)	19	27	$682	Dodge Lancer (2.2L/M5)	25	34	$536
Chevrolet Nova (1.6L/L3)	27	31	$536	Dodge Omni (2.2L/L3)	25	30	$555
Chevrolet Nova (1.6L/L4)	24	28	$600	Dodge Omni (2.2L/M5)	25	34	$518
Chevrolet Nova (1.6L/M5)	25	29	$555	Dodge Shadow (2.2L/A3)	20	25	$785
Chevrolet Nova (1.6L/M5)	30	37	$454	Dodge Shadow (2.5L/L3)	23	28	$600
Chevrolet Spectrum (1.5L/A3)	31	33	$468	Dodge Shadow (2.2L/L3)	24	29	$578
Chevrolet Spectrum (1.5L/M5)	37	41	$384	Dodge Shadow (2.2L/M5)	21	29	$719
Chevrolet Spectrum Turbo (1.5L/M5)	28	36	$484	Dodge Shadow (2.5L/M5)	23	31	$578
Chevrolet Sprint (1.0L/A3)	38	40	$384	Dodge Shadow (2.2L/M5)	25	33	$536
Chevrolet Sprint (1.0L/M5)	44	49	$326	Dodge 600 (2.2L/A3)	20	25	$785
Chevrolet Sprint Metro (1.0L/M5)	54	58	$268	Dodge 600 (2.2L/L3)	23	28	$600
Chevrolet Sprint Turbo (1.0L/M5)	37	43	$384	Dodge 600 (2.5L/L3)	23	28	$600
Chrysler Conquest (2.6L/L4)	18	24	$862	Eagle Medallion (2.2L/A3)	20	26	$682
Chrysler Conquest (2.6L/M5)	18	22	$862	Eagle Medallion (2.2L/M5)	25	33	$536
Chrysler LeBaron (2.2L/A3)	20	25	$785	Eagle Medallion W. (2.2L/A3)	19	24	$714
Chrysler LeBaron (2.2L/L3)	23	28	$600	Eagle Medallion W. (2.2L/M5)	24	33	$536
Chrylser LeBaron (2.5L/L3)	23	28	$600	Eagle Premier (3.0L/L4)	18	27	$714
Chrysler LeBaron (2.2L/M5)	21	29	$719	Eagle Premier (2.5L/L4)	22	31	$600
Chrysler LeBaron (2.5L/M5)	22	31	$600	Eagle Premier (2.5L/M5)	24	32	$555
Chrysler LeBaron Conv. (2.2L/A3)	20	25	$785	Eagle Wagon 4WD (4.2L/A3)	16	19	$882
Chrysler LeBaron Conv. (2.5L/L3)	23	28	$600	Ferrari Testarossa (4.9L/M5)	10	15	$1364
Chrysler LeBaron Conv. (2.2L/M5)	21	29	$719	Ferrari Mondial/Cabriolet (3.2L/M5)	13	18	$1000
Chrysler LeBaron Conv. (2.5L/M5)	22	31	$600	Ferrari 328 GTS/GTB (3.2L/M5)	13	18	$1000
Chrysler LeBaron GTS (2.2L/A3)	20	25	$785	Ford Escort (1.9L/A3)	24	30	$555
Chrysler LeBaron GTS (2.5L/L3)	23	28	$600	Ford Escort (1.9L/M5)	26	34	$518
Chrysler LeBaron GTS (2.2L/L3)	23	28	$600	Ford Escort (1.9L/M5)	28	37	$484
Chrysler LeBaron GTS (2.2L/M5)	21	29	$719	Ford Escort (1.9L/M4)	33	42	$405
Chrysler LeBaron GTS (2.5L/M5)	22	31	$600	Ford Escort Wagon (1.9L/A3)	24	30	$555
Chrysler LeBaron GTS (2.2L/M5)	25	34	$536	Ford Escort Wagon (1.9L/M4)	33	42	$405
Chrys. NY/5th Ave. (3.0L/L3)	19	26	$714	Ford Escort Wagon (1.9L/M5)	28	37	$484
Chrysler New Yorker Turbo (2.2L/A3)	20	25	$785	Ford EXP (1.9L/A3)	24	30	$555
Chrys. Town & Country W. (2.2L/A3)	20	25	$785	Ford EXP (1.9L/M5)	26	34	$518
Chrys. Town & Country W. (2.5L/L3)	23	28	$600	Ford EXP (1.9L/M5)	28	37	$484
Daihatsu Charade (1.0L/M5)	38	42	$384	Ford Festiva (1.3L/M4)	38	40	$384
Dodge Aries (2.5L/L3)	23	27	$626	Ford Festiva (1.3L/M5)	39	43	$366
Dodge Aries (2.2L/L3)	25	30	$555	Ford Laser (1.6L/L4)	24	30	$578
Dodge Aries (2.2L/M5)	25	33	$536	Ford Laser (1.6L/M4)	26	30	$555
Dodge Aries Wagon (2.2L/L3)	23	28	$600	Ford LTD Crown Victoria (5.0L/L4)	17	24	$750
Dodge Aries Wagon (2.5L/L3)	23	28	$600	Ford LTD Crown Victoria W. (5.0L/L4)	17	24	$750
Dodge Aries Wagon (2.2L/M5)	25	33	$536	Ford Mustang (2.3L/L4)	21	27	$626
Dodge Colt (1.6L/L3)	24	26	$600	Ford Mustang (5.0L/L4)	18	27	$714
Dodge Colt (1.5L/L3)	30	32	$484	Ford Mustang (5.0L/M5)	16	24	$789

Ford Mustang (2.3L/M5)	25	30	$555	Mazda 929 (3.0L/M5)	18	24	$750
Ford Taurus (2.5L/A3)	21	26	$652	Mercedes-Benz 190D (2.5L/A4)	30	34	$445
Ford Taurus (3.0L/L4)	21	29	$626	Mercedes-Benz 190E (2.3L/A4)	21	24	$785
Ford Taurus (2.5L/M5)	23	32	$578	Mercedes-Benz 190E (2.3L/M5)	21	29	$719
Ford Taurus Wagon (3.0L/L4)	21	29	$626	Mercedes-Benz 190E (2.6L/A4)	20	23	$821
Ford Taurus Wagon (3.0L/L4)	19	26	$714	Mercedes-Benz 190E (2.6L/M5)	18	26	$821
Ford Tempo (2.3L/A3)	22	27	$626	Mercedes-Benz 260E (2.6L/A4)	20	24	$821
Ford Thunderbird (2.3L/L4)	17	23	$789	Mercedes-Benz 260E (2.6L/M5)	18	26	$862
Ford Thunderbird (5.0L/L4)	18	27	$714	Mercedes-Benz 300CE (3.0L/A4)	17	22	$907
Ford Thunderbird (2.3L/M5)	18	27	$714	Mercedes-Benz 300E (3.0L/A4)	17	22	$907
Ford Thunderbird (3.8L/L4)	21	27	$652	Mercedes-Benz 300E (3.0L/M5)	17	25	$862
Honda Accord (2.0L/L4)	23	29	$600	Mercedes-Benz 300SEL (3.0L/A4)	17	19	$959
Honda Accord (2.0L/L4)	24	30	$578	Mercedes-Benz 300TE (3.0L/A4)	17	20	$959
Honda Accord (2.0L/M5)	25	30	$555	Mercedes-Benz 420SEL (4.2L/A4)	15	18	$1078
Honda Accord (2.0L/M5)	27	34	$500	Mercedes-Benz 560SEC (5.6L/A4)	13	16	$1232
Honda Civic (1.5L/L4)	29	35	$484	Mercedes-Benz 560SEL (5.6L/A4)	13	16	$1232
Honda Civic (1.5L/M4)	35	38	$417	Mercedes-Benz 560SL (5.6L/A4)	14	17	$1151
Honda Civic (1.5L/M5)	33	37	$441	Mercury Cougar (5.0L/L4)	18	25	$750
Honda Civic CRX (1.5L/L4)	30	37	$454	Mercury Cougar (3.8L/L4)	21	27	$652
Honda Civic CRX (1.5L/M5)	34	39	$417	Mercury Grand Marquis (5.0L/L4)	17	24	$750
Honda Civic CRX (1.6L/M5)	29	36	$468	Mercury Grand Marquis W. (5.0L/L4)	17	24	$750
Honda Civic CRX HF (1.5L/M5)	50	56	$288	Mercury Merkur Scorpio (2.9L/L4)	17	23	$789
Honda Civic CRX HF (1.5L/M5)	45	53	$312	Mercury Merkur Scorpio (2.9L/M5)	17	23	$750
Honda Prelude (2.0L/L4)	20	26	$682	Mercury Merkur XR4Ti (2.3L/A3)	18	21	$789
Honda Prelude (2.0L/L4)	21	27	$652	Mercury Merkur XR4Ti (2.3L/M5)	20	25	$682
Honda Prelude (2.0L/M5)	23	27	$600	Mercury Sable (3.0L/L4)	21	29	$626
Hyundai Excel (1.5L/L3)	27	31	$518	Mercury Sable Wagon (3.0L/L4)	21	29	$626
Hyundai Excel (1.5L/M4)	27	33	$500	Mercury Sable Wagon (3.0L/L4)	19	26	$714
Hyundai Excel (1.5L/M5)	28	37	$484	Mercury Topaz (2.3L/A3)	22	27	$626
Isuzu Impulse (2.0L/L4)	20	26	$682	Mercury Tracer (1.6L/M5)	28	35	$484
Isuzu Impulse (2.3L/L4)	20	26	$682	Mercury Tracer (1.6L/A3)	25	29	$578
Isuzu Impulse (2.3L/M5)	20	26	$682	Mercury Tracer Wagon (1.6L/A3)	25	29	$578
Isuzu Impulse (2.0L/M5)	21	27	$652	Mitsubishi Cordia (2.0L/L3)	23	25	$626
Isuzu I-Mark (1.5L/A3)	31	33	$468	Mitsubishi Cordia (1.8L/M5)	22	28	$600
Isuzu I-Mark (1.5L/M5)	28	36	$484	Mitsubishi Cordia (2.0L/M5)	24	31	$578
Isuzu I-Mark (1.5L/M5)	37	41	$384	Mitsubishi Galant Sigma (3.0L/A4)	18	22	$750
Isuzu I-Mark (1.5L/M5)	33	39	$429	Mitsubishi Galant Sigma (3.0L/M5)	17	24	$750
Jaguar XJ-S (5.3L/A3)	13	17	$1071	Mitsubishi Mirage (1.6L/L3)	24	26	$600
Jaguar XJ-SC (5.3L/A3)	13	17	$1071	Mitsubishi Mirage (1.5L/L3)	29	32	$500
Jaguar XJ6 (3.6L/L4)	17	24	$750	Mitsubishi Mirage (1.5L/M5)	32	37	$441
Jaguar XJ6 (3.6L/L4)	18	25	$862	Mitsubishi Mirage (1.5L/M4)	34	38	$417
Lamborghini Countach (5.2L/M5)	6	10	$2156	Mitsubishi Mirage (1.6L/M5)	25	31	$555
Lincoln Mark VII (5.0L/L4)	17	24	$750	Mitsubishi Precis (1.5L/L3)	27	31	$518
Lincoln Town Car (5.0L/L4)	17	24	$750	Mitsubishi Precis (1.5L/M5)	28	37	$484
Maserati Q (2.2L/A3)	19	23	$821	Mitsubishi Precis (1.5L/M4)	27	33	$500
Mazda RX-7 (1.3L/L4)	17	23	$789	Mitsubishi Space Wagon (2.0L/L3)	23	24	$652
Mazda RX-7 (1.3L/M5)	17	23	$789	Mitsubishi Starion (2.6L/L4)	18	24	$862
Mazda RX-7 (1.3L/M5)	17	24	$750	Mitsubishi Starion (2.6L/M5)	18	22	$862
Mazda 323 (1.6L/L4)	24	30	$578	Mitsubishi Tredia (2.0L/L3)	23	25	$626
Mazda 323 (1.6L/M4)	26	30	$555	Mitsubishi Tredia (1.8L/M5)	22	28	$600
Mazda 323 (1.6L/M5)	21	24	$785	Mtisubishi Tredia (2.0L/M5)	24	31	$578
Mazda 323 (1.6L/M5)	22	27	$719	Nissan Maxima (3.0L/L4)	18	24	$750
Mazda 323 (1.6L/M5)	28	33	$500	Nissan Maxima (3.0L/M5)	18	26	$714
Mazda 323 Wagon (1.6L/A3)	24	28	$578	Nissan Maxima Wagon (3.0L/L4)	18	24	$750
Mazda 323 Wagon (1.6L/M5)	28	33	$500	Nissan Pulsar NX (1.6L/L3)	25	30	$555
Mazda 626/MX-6 (2.2L/L4)	19	25	$785	Nissan Pulsar NX (1.8L/L4)	21	28	$626
Mazda 626/MX-6 (2.2L/L4)	22	28	$626	Nissan Pulsar NX (1.8L/M5)	23	29	$600
Mazda 626/MX-6 (2.2L/M5)	21	28	$719	Nissan Pulsar NX (1.6L/M5)	26	34	$518
Mazda 626/MX-6 (2.2L/M5)	24	31	$578	Nissan Sentra (1.6L/L3)	26	29	$555
Mazda 929 (3.0L/L4)	19	23	$714	Nissan Sentra (1.6L/M4)	29	35	$468

Model	City	Hwy	Price		Model	City	Hwy	Price
Nissan Sentra (1.6L/M5)	29	36	$468		Plymouth Colt (1.6L/L3)	24	26	$600
Nissan Sentra Coupe (1.6L/L3)	26	29	$555		Plymouth Colt (1.5L/L3)	30	32	$484
Nissan Sentra Coupe (1.6L/M5)	29	36	$468		Plymouth Colt (1.5L/M4)	34	38	$417
Nissan Sentra Wagon (1.6L/L3)	26	28	$555		Plymouth Colt (1.6L/M5)	25	31	$555
Nissan Sentra Wagon (1.6L/M5)	28	35	$484		Plymouth Colt (1.5L/M5)	32	37	$441
Nissan Sentra Wagon 4WD (1.6L/M5)	25	29	$555		Plymouth Colt Vista (2.0L/L3)	23	24	$652
Nissan Stanza (2.0L/L4)	21	27	$652		Plymouth Colt Vista (2.0L/M5)	23	29	$600
Nissan Stanza (2.0L/M5)	22	28	$600		Plymouth Colt Vista 4WD (2.0L/M5)	21	27	$652
Nissan Stanza Wagon 2WD (2.0L/L4)	21	25	$652		Plymouth Gran Fury (5.2L/L3)	17	23	$862
Nissan Stanza Wagon 2WD (2.0L/M5)	22	27	$626		Plymouth Horizon (2.2L/L3)	25	30	$555
Nissan Stanza Wagon 4WD (2.0L/L4)	19	21	$750		Plymouth Horizon (2.2L/M5)	25	34	$518
Nissan Stanza Wagon 4WD (2.0L/M5)	20	23	$714		Plymouth Reliant (2.5L/L3)	23	27	$626
Nissan 200SX (3.0L/L4)	18	25	$714		Plymouth Reliant (2.2L/L3)	25	30	$555
Nissan 200SX (2.0L/L4)	22	28	$626		Plymouth Reliant (2.2L/M5)	25	33	$536
Nissan 200SX (3.0L/M5)	19	26	$714		Plymouth Reliant Wagon (2.5L/L3)	23	28	$600
Nissan 200SX (2.0L/M5)	23	28	$600		Plymouth Reliant Wagon (2.2L/L3)	23	28	$600
Nissan 300ZX (3.0L/L4)	17	24	$750		Plymouth Reliant Wagon (2.2L/M5)	25	34	$536
Nissan 300ZX (3.0L/L4)	18	26	$714		Plymouth Sundance (2.2L/A3)	20	25	$785
Nissan 300ZX (3.0L/M5)	17	25	$750		Plymouth Sundance (2.2L/L3)	23	28	$600
Nissan 300ZX 2+2 (3.0L/L4)	18	26	$714		Plymouth Sundance (2.5L/L3)	23	28	$600
Nissan 300ZX 2+2 (3.0L/M5)	17	25	$750		Plymouth Sundance (2.2L/M5)	21	29	$719
Oldsmobile Custom Cruiser (5.0L/L4)	17	24	$750		Plymouth Sundance (2.5L/M5)	23	31	$578
Oldsmobile Cutlass Calais (3.0L/L3)	19	27	$682		Plymouth Sundance (2.2L/M5)	25	33	$536
Oldsmobile Cutlass Calais (2.5L/L3)	23	31	$578		Pontiac Bonneville (3.8L/L4)	19	29	$682
Oldsmobile Cutlass Calais (2.3L/L3)	24	34	$536		Pontiac Fiero (2.8L/L3)	18	24	$750
Oldsmobile Cutlass Calais (2.5L/M5)	23	33	$555		Pontiac Fiero (2.5L/L3)	24	31	$578
Oldsmobile Cutlass Calais (2.3L/M5)	25	36	$518		Pontiac Fiero (2.8L/M5)	17	27	$714
Oldsmobile Cutlass Ciera (2.8L/L3)	20	27	$652		Pontiac Fiero (2.5L/M5)	24	35	$536
Oldsmobile Cutlass Ciera (2.5L/L3)	24	31	$578		Pontiac Firebird/Trans Am (5.7L/L4)	16	25	$907
Oldsmobile Cutlass Ciera (3.8L/L4)	19	29	$682		Pontiac Firebird/Trans Am (5.0L/L4)	16	24	$907
Oldsmobile Cutlass Ciera (2.8L/L4)	21	29	$626		Pontiac Firebird/Trans Am (5.0L/L4)	17	26	$750
Oldsmobile Cutlass Cruiser (2.5L/L3)	22	29	$600		Pontiac Firebird/Trans Am (2.8L/L4)	19	27	$682
Oldsmobile Cutlass Cruiser (3.8L/L4)	19	29	$682		Pontiac Firebird/Trans Am (5.0L/M5)	16	25	$789
Oldsmobile Cutlass Cruiser (2.8L/L4)	20	29	$652		Pontiac Firebird/Trans Am (5.0L/M5)	16	26	$862
Oldsmobile Cutlass Supreme (2.8L/L4)	20	29	$652		Pontiac Firebird/Trans Am (2.8L/M5)	17	27	$750
Oldsmobile Cutlass Supreme (2.8L/M5)	19	28	$652		Pontiac Firefly (1.0L/A3)	38	40	$384
Olds. Cutlass Supreme Classic (5.0L/L4)	18	25	$750		Pontiac Firefly (1.0L/M5)	44	49	$326
Oldsmobile Delta 88 (3.8L/L4)	19	29	$682		Pontiac Firefly Turbo (1.0L/M5)	37	43	$384
Oldsmobile Firenza (2.0L/L3)	25	32	$536		Pontiac Grand Am (2.0L/L3)	20	27	$750
Oldsmobile Firenza (2.0L/L3)	26	32	$536		Pontiac Grand Am (2.5L/L3)	23	31	$578
Oldsmobile Firenza (2.0L/M5)	25	36	$518		Pontiac Grand Am (2.3L/L3)	24	34	$536
Oldsmobile Firenza (2.0L/M5)	27	38	$484		Pontiac Grand Am (2.0L/M5)	20	30	$719
Oldsmobile Firenza Cruiser (2.0L/L3)	25	32	$536		Pontiac Grand Am (2.5L/M5)	23	33	$555
Oldsmobile Firenza Cruiser (2.0L/L3)	26	32	$536		Pontiac Grand Am (2.3L/M5)	25	36	$518
Oldsmobile Firenza Cruiser (2.0L/M5)	25	36	$518		Pontiac Grand Prix (2.8L/L4)	20	29	$652
Oldsmobile Firenza Cruiser (2.0L/M5)	27	38	$484		Pontiac Grand Prix (2.8L/M5)	19	28	$652
Oldsmobile Ninety-Eight (3.8L/L4)	19	29	$682		Pontiac Lemans (1.6L/L3)	27	32	$518
Oldsmobile Toronado (3.8L/L4)	19	29	$682		Pontiac Lemans (1.6L/M4)	30	39	$441
Peugeot 505 (2.8L/L4)	18	22	$862		Pontiac Lemans (1.6L/M5)	31	40	$429
Peugeot 505 (2.2L/L4)	18	22	$862		Pontiac Safari Wagon (5.0L/L4)	17	24	$750
Peugeot 505 (2.2L/L4)	19	22	$714		Pontiac Sunbird (2.0L/L3)	20	27	$750
Peugeot 505 (2.2L/M5)	18	23	$750		Pontiac Sunbird (2.0L/L3)	26	32	$536
Peugeot 505 (2.2L/M5)	18	24	$862		Pontiac Sunbird (2.0L/M5)	21	31	$719
Peugeot 505 (2.8L/M5)	18	22	$862		Pontiac Sunbird (2.0L/M5)	27	38	$484
Peugeot 505 Wagon (2.2L/L4)	18	22	$862		Pontiac Sunbird Conv. (2.0L/L3)	20	27	$750
Peugeot 505 Wagon (2.2L/L4)	19	22	$750		Pontiac Sunbird Conv. (2.0L/L3)	23	31	$578
Peugeot 505 Wagon (2.2L/M5)	18	22	$750		Pontiac Sunbird Conv. (2.0L/M5)	20	30	$719
Plymouth Caravelle (2.2L/A3)	20	25	$785		Pontiac Sunbird Conv. (2.0L/M5)	25	34	$536
Plymouth Caravelle (2.5L/L3)	23	28	$600		Pontiac Sunbird Wagon (2.0L/L3)	26	32	$536
Plymouth Caravelle (2.2L/L3)	23	28	$600		Pontiac Sunbird Wagon (2.0L/M5)	27	38	$484

Pontiac 6000 (2.8L/L3)	20	27	$652	Suzuki Forsa (1.0L/A3)	38	40	$384
Pontiac 6000 (2.5L/L3)	24	31	$578	Suzuki Forsa (1.0L/M5)	44	49	$326
Pontiac 6000 (2.8L/L4)	20	29	$652	Suzuki Forsa Turbo (1.0L/M5)	37	43	$384
Pontiac 6000 (2.8L/M5)	20	29	$652	Toyota Camry (2.0L/L4)	25	30	$555
Pontiac 6000 Wagon (2.5L/L3)	22	29	$600	Toyota Camry (2.0L/L4)	25	32	$536
Pontiac 6000 Wagon (2.8L/L4)	20	29	$652	Toyota Camry (2.0L/M5)	22	27	$626
Pontiac 6000 Wagon (2.8L/M5)	19	28	$652	Toyota Camry (2.0L/M5)	26	32	$536
Porsche 911 Carrera (3.2L/M5)	18	25	$821	Toyota Camry Wagon (2.0L/L4)	25	30	$555
Porsche 911 Turbo (3.3L/M4)	16	22	$959	Toyota Camry Wagon (2.0L/M5)	26	32	$536
Porsche 924 S (2.5L/A3)	20	23	$714	Toyota Celica (2.0L/L4)	22	28	$600
Porsche 924 S (2.5L/M5)	20	28	$652	Toyota Celica (2.0L/L4)	25	32	$536
Porsche 928 S4 (5.0L/A4)	16	21	$959	Toyota Celica (2.0L/M5)	19	26	$785
Porsche 928 S4 (5.0L/M5)	15	23	$959	Toyota Celica (2.0L/M5)	22	28	$600
Porsche 944 (2.5L/A3)	19	22	$750	Toyota Celica (2.0L/M5)	26	32	$536
Porsche 944 (2.5L/M5)	20	28	$652	Toyota Celica Conv. (2.0L/L4)	25	32	$536
Porsche 944 S (2.5L/M5)	19	26	$785	Toyota Celica Conv. (2.0L/M5)	26	32	$536
Porsche 944 Turbo (2.5L/M5)	19	27	$785	Toyota Corolla (1.6L/L3)	27	30	$536
Rolls-Royce Bentley Cont. (6.8L/A3)	9	11	$1500	Toyota Corolla (1.6L/L4)	27	34	$500
R-Royce Bentley 8/Mulsan (6.8L/A3)	9	11	$1500	Toyota Corolla (1.6L/M5)	25	29	$555
R-Royce Corniche II (6.8L/A3)	9	11	$1500	Toyota Corolla (1.6L/M5)	30	35	$468
R-Royce Silver Spirit/Spur (6.8L/A3)	9	11	$1500	Toyota Corolla FX (1.6L/L3)	27	31	$536
Saab 900 (2.0L/A3)	19	21	$750	Toyota Corolla FX (1.6L/L4)	23	29	$578
Saab 900 (2.0L/A3)	19	22	$750	Toyota Corolla FX (1.6L/M5)	25	29	$555
Saab 900 (2.0L/A3)	20	23	$714	Toyota Corolla FX (1.6L/M5)	30	37	$454
Saab 900 (2.0L/M5)	21	27	$652	Toyota Corolla Wagon (1.6L/L3)	27	30	$536
Saab 900 (2.0L/M5)	22	27	$626	Toyota Corolla Wagon (1.6L/M5)	30	35	$468
Saab 900 Conv. (2.0L/A3)	20	22	$714	Toyota Cressida (2.8L/L4)	18	24	$862
Saab 900 Conv. (2.0L/M5)	21	27	$652	Toyota MR2 (1.6L/L4)	22	27	$719
Saab 9000 (2.0L/L4)	17	24	$750	Toyota MR2 (1.6L/L4)	25	30	$555
Saab 9000 (2.0L/L4)	19	26	$682	Toyota MR2 (1.6L/M5)	26	31	$536
Saab 9000 (2.0L/M5)	20	28	$652	Toyota MR2 (1.6L/M5)	24	30	$664
Saab 9000 (2.0L/M5)	21	27	$652	Toyota Supra (3.0L/L4)	18	23	$862
Sterling (2.5L/L4)	18	23	$750	Toyota Supra (3.0L/M5)	18	23	$862
Sterling (2.5L/M5)	19	24	$714	Toyota Tercel (1.5L/L3)	28	33	$500
Subaru Hatchback (1.8L/L3)	23	25	$626	Toyota Tercel (1.5L/M4)	31	35	$468
Subaru Hatchback (1.8L/M5)	26	31	$536	Toyota Tercel (1.5L/M5)	31	37	$454
Subaru Hatchback 4WD (1.8L/M4)	25	29	$555	Toyota Tercel EZ (1.5L/M4)	35	41	$394
Subaru Justy (1.2L/M5)	37	39	$394	Toyota Tercel Wagon (1.5L/A3)	24	25	$626
Subaru Justy 4WD (1.2L/M5)	30	35	$468	Toyota Tercel Wagon (1.5L/M5)	26	30	$536
Subaru Sedan (1.8L/A3)	22	24	$652	Volkswagen Cabriolet (1.8L/A3)	22	24	$652
Subaru Sedan (1.8L/L3)	25	27	$578	Volkswagen Cabriolet (1.8L/M5)	24	27	$600
Subaru Sedan (1.8L/M5)	25	32	$536	Volkswagen Fox (1.8L/M4)	25	30	$555
Subaru Sedan 4WD (1.8L/A3)	23	24	$626	Volkswagen Fox Wagon (1.8L/M4)	25	30	$555
Subaru Sedan 4WD (1.8L/M5)	24	29	$578	Volkswagen Golf (1.8L/A3)	23	28	$600
Subaru 4WD Turbo (1.8L/L4)	21	27	$652	Volkswagen Golf (1.8L/M5)	25	33	$536
Subaru 4WD Turbo (1.8L/M5)	21	25	$652	Volkswagen GTI 16V (1.8L/M5)	22	29	$600
Subaru Wagon (1.8L/A3)	22	24	$682	Volkswagen Jetta (1.8L/A3)	23	28	$600
Subaru Wagon (1.8L/L3)	25	27	$600	Volkswagen Jetta (1.8L/M5)	25	34	$536
Subaru Wagon (1.8L/M5)	25	31	$536	Volkswagen Jetta GLI 16V (1.8L/M5)	22	29	$600
Subaru Wagon 4WD T (1.8L/L4)	21	27	$652	Volkswagen Quantum (2.2L/A3)	18	22	$750
Subaru Wagon 4WD (1.8L/A3)	23	23	$652	Volkswagen Quantum (2.2L/M5)	19	24	$714
Subaru Wagon 4WD (1.8L/M5)	24	29	$578	Volkswagen Quantum Syn. W (2.2L/M5)	17	21	$789
Subaru Wagon 4WD T (1.8L/M5)	21	25	$652	Volkswagen Quantum Wagon (2.2L/A3)	18	22	$750
Subaru XT (2.7L/L4)	20	28	$652	Volkswagen Quantum Wagon (2.2L/M5)	19	23	$714
Subaru XT (1.8L/L4)	24	31	$578	Volkswagen Scirocco 16V (1.8L/M5)	22	28	$600
Subaru XT (1.8L/M5)	25	32	$536	Volvo 240 DL/GL (2.3L/A4)	20	24	$682
Subaru XT-DL (1.8L/M5)	25	32	$536	Volvo 240 DL/GL (2.3L/M5)	22	27	$626
Subaru XT 4WD (2.7L/L4)	19	25	$714	Volvo 240 DL/GL Wagon (2.3L/A4)	20	24	$682
Subaru XT 4WD (2.7L/M5)	18	25	$714	Volvo 240 DL/GL Wagon (2.3L/M5)	22	28	$626
Subaru XT 4WD (1.8L/M5)	24	28	$578	Volvo 740/760 (2.8L/A4)	17	20	$834

Volvo 740/760 (2.3L/A4)	19	22	$750
Volvo 740/760 (2.3L/L4)	21	26	$652
Volvo 740/760 (2.3L/M4)	20	25	$682
Volvo 740/760 (2.3L/M5)	22	27	$626
Volvo 740/760 Wagon (2.3L/A4)	19	22	$750
Volvo 740/760 Wagon (2.3L/L4)	21	26	$652
Volvo 740/760 Wagon (2.3L/M4)	20	25	$682
Volvo 740/760 Wagon (2.3L/M5)	22	28	$626
Volvo 780 (2.8L/A4)	17	20	$834
Yugo GV (1.1L/M4)	28	31	$518
Yugo GV (1.3L/M5)	27	32	$518

Pickups, Minivans and 4x4s

Chevrolet Astro 2WD (4.3L/M5)	17	23	$789
Chevrolet Astro 2WD (4.3L/L4)	17	22	$789
Chevrolet C10 Pickup 2WD (5.0L/A3)	15	17	$938
Chevrolet C20 Pickup 2WD (5.0L/A3)	14	16	$1000
Chev. G10/20 Sptvan 2WD (5.0L/L4)	13	16	$1000
Chevrolet G10/20 Van 2WD (5.0L/A3)	15	17	$938
Chevrolet K10 Pickup 4WD (5.0L/A3)	13	14	$1154
Chevrolet R10 Suburban 2WD (5.7L/L4)	13	18	$1000
Chevrolet S10 Blazer 2WD (2.8L/L4)	17	24	$750
Chevrolet S10 Blazer 2WD (2.5L/L4)	20	25	$682
Chevrolet S10 Pickup 2WD (2.8L/L4)	17	25	$750
Chevrolet S10 Pickup 2WD (2.5L/L4)	21	28	$652
Chevrolet T10 Blazer 4WD (2.8L/L4)	16	22	$834
Chevrolet T10 Pickup 4WD (2.8L/L4)	17	24	$750
Chevrolet V10 Blazer 4WD (5.7L/L4)	13	17	$1071
Chevrolet V10 Suburban 4WD (5.7L/L4)	13	16	$1071
Dodge AD150 Rmchgr 2WD (5.2L/A3)	13	14	$1154
Dodge AW150 Rmchgr 4WD (5.9L/A3)	9	11	$1500
Dodge AW150 Rmchgr 4WD (5.2L/A3)	12	14	$1154
Dodge B150/B250 Van 2WD (5.2L/A3)	13	14	$1154
Dodge Cara/Ram Van 2WD (2.5L/A3)	20	23	$682
Dodge Dakota 2WD (3.9L/L3)	17	20	$834
Dodge Dakota 4WD (3.9L/L3)	15	19	$882
Dodge D100/150 P-up 2WD (5.2L/A3)	13	14	$1154
Dodge Power Ram50 4WD (2.6L/A4)	18	19	$834
Dodge Raider (2.6L/A4)	16	17	$882
Dodge Raider (2.6L/M5)	17	19	$834
Dodge Ram50 2WD (2.6L/A4)	20	22	$714
Dodge Ram50 2WD (2.0L/A4)	23	26	$626
Dodge W100/150 P-up 4WD (5.2L/A3)	13	14	$1154
Ford Aerostar Van (3.0L/L4)	17	23	$789
Ford Aerostar Van (3.0L/M5)	18	24	$750
Ford Bronco 4WD (5.8L/A3)	11	14	$1250
Ford Bronco 4WD (5.0L/A3)	12	13	$1154
Ford Bronco II 2WD (2.9L/L4)	17	22	$789
Ford Bronco II 2WD (2.9L/M5)	19	24	$714
Ford Bronco II 4WD (2.9L/L4)	17	21	$834
Ford Bronco II 4WD (2.9L/M5)	18	23	$750
Ford Courier (2.2L/L4)	20	25	$682
Ford Courier (2.2L/M5)	21	26	$652
Ford Courier 4WD (2.6L/M5)	17	21	$789
Ford E150 Club Wagon (5.8L/A3)	11	13	$1250
Ford E150 Club Wagon (4.9L/A3)	14	15	$1071
Ford F150 Pickup 2WD (5.8L/A3)	12	14	$1154
Ford F150 Pickup 2WD (5.0L/A3)	16	15	$1071
Ford Ranger Pickup 2WD (2.3L/L4)	22	27	$626
Ford Ranger Pickup 2WD (2.9L/M5)	19	24	$714
GMC C15 Pickup 2WD (6.2L/L4)	19	25	$678
GMC C15 Pickup 2WD (4.3L/M4)	17	22	$789
GMC G15/25 Rally 2WD (4.3L/M4)	15	18	$938
GMC G15/25 Vandura 2WD (4.3L/A3)	17	19	$834
GMC G15/25 Vandura 2WD (5.0L/L4)	15	20	$882
GMC K15 Pickup 4WD (4.3L/A3)	15	17	$938
GMC K25 Pickup 4WD (5.0L/L4)	13	17	$1000
GMC R15 Suburban 2WD (5.7L/L4)	13	18	$1000
GMC Safari 2WD (2.5L/L4)	20	25	$682
GMC S15 Jimmy 2WD (2.8L/M4)	18	23	$750
GMC S15 Pickup 2WD (2.5L/L4)	21	28	$652
GMC T15 Jimmy 4WD (2.8L/L4)	16	22	$834
GMC V15 Suburban 4WD (5.7L/M4)	12	14	$1250
Isuzu Trooper (2.6L/L4)	16	18	$882
Isuzu Trooper (2.6L/M5)	16	19	$882
Jeep Cherokee 2WD (2.5L/L4)	18	24	$750
Jeep Chero./Wag. 4WD (2.5L/L4)	18	23	$750
Jeep Comanche 2WD (2.5L/L4)	18	23	$750
Jeep Comanche 4WD (2.5L/L4)	18	23	$750
Jeep Grand Wagoneer 4WD (5.9L/A3)	11	13	$1250
Jeep Wrangler 4WD (4.2L/L4)	15	17	$938
Jeep J-10 STD Pickup 4WD (4.2L/M4)	16	19	$882
Land Rover LTD Range Rover (3.5L/L4)	14	14	$1232
Mazda B2200/B2600 (2.2L/L4)	20	25	$682
Mazda B2600 4X4 (2.6L/L3)	17	18	$834
Mitsubishi Montero (2.6L/A4)	16	17	$882
Mitsubishi Montero (2.6L/M5)	17	19	$834
Mitsubishi Truck 2WD (2.6L/A4)	20	22	$714
Mitsubishi Truck 4WD (2.6L/A4)	18	19	$834
Mitsubishi Wagon (2.4L/L4)	18	21	$789
Mitsubishi Van (2.4L/L4)	19	22	$750
Nissan Pathfinder 4WD (3.0L/L4)	15	17	$1000
Nissan Pathfinder 4WD (3.0L/M5)	14	18	$938
Nissan Cab Chassis 2WD (3.0L/L4)	12	12	$1250
Nissan Cab Chassis 2WD (3.0L/M5)	14	14	$1071
Nissan Truck 2WD (2.4L/M4)	21	24	$682
Nissan Truck 4WD (3.0L/L4)	15	17	$938
Nissan Van (2.4L/L4)	18	21	$789
Nissan Van (2.4L/M5)	18	22	$789
Plymouth Voyager 2WD (3.0L/L3)	18	23	$750
Plymouth Voyager 2WD (2.5L/M5)	21	28	$626
Suzuki Samurai (1.3L/M5)	28	29	$536
Toyota Truck 2WD (2.4L/A4)	22	23	$682
Toyota Truck 4WD (2.4L/L4)	18	21	$789
Toyota Van 2WD (2.2L/L4)	21	23	$682
Toyota Van 2WD (2.2L/M5)	22	23	$682
Toyota Van 4WD (2.2L/L4)	19	21	$750
Toyota 1-Ton Truck 2WD (2.4L/A4)	22	23	$682
Toyota 4-Runner 4WD (2.4L/L4)	17	19	$834
Toyota 4-Runner 4WD (2.4L/M5)	19	22	$750
Volkswagen Vanagon 2WD (2.1L/A3)	14	16	$1000
Volkswagen Vanagon 2WD (2.1L/M4)	16	18	$882
VW Vanagon Syncro 4WD (2.1L/C5)	15	15	$1000

The **MAINTENANCE** Chapter

Maintenance Costs

After buying a car, the cost of preventive maintenance and repairs will be a significant portion of your operating expenses. This chapter allows you to consider some of these costs before deciding which car to purchase.

Preventive maintenance is the periodic servicing specified by the manufacturer to keep your car running properly—for example, how often you should change the oil and oil filter. Every owner's manual contains a schedule of recommended servicing for at least the first 50,000 miles. The tables on the following pages estimate the cost of following the preventive maintenance schedule specified by the manufacturer for the first 50,000 miles. The tables also list the costs for nine repairs that typically occur during the first 100,000 miles. There is no precise way of predicting exactly when a repair will be needed. But if you keep a car for 75,000 to 100,000 miles, it is likely that you will experience most of these repairs at least once. The last column provides a general indication of how expensive these nine repairs are for one car compared to another. Repair cost is rated as "High" if the total for nine repairs is in the top third of all the cars rated and "Low" if the total is in the bottom third.

Most repair shops use "flat-rate manuals" to estimate repair costs. These manuals list the estimated time required for repairing many items. Each automobile manufacturer publishes its own manual and there are several independent manuals. For many repairs, the time varies from manual to manual. Certain repair shops use different manuals for different repairs. To determine a repair bill, a shop multiplies the time listed in its manual by its hourly labor rate, then adds the cost of parts.

The cost estimates are based on flat-rate manual repair times multiplied by a nationwide average labor rate of $35 per hour. All estimates include the cost of replaced parts and related adjustments.

Prices on the following tables may not predict the exact costs of these repairs. For example, the labor rate for your area may be more or less than the nationwide average. However, the prices will provide you with a relative comparison of maintenance costs for various automobiles.

A Hot Tip

A cold-running engine will dramatically reduce fuel efficiency. Most engines are designed to operate efficiently at 180 degrees. An engine running at 125 degrees can waste one out of every ten gallons of gas. Your engine temperature is controlled by a thermostat valve. This little device has a sensor that controls a valve letting in water from the radiator. A faulty thermostat can be a major cause of poor fuel economy. If you feel your car should be getting better fuel economy, have your thermostat checked. Thermostats are inexpensive and relatively easy to replace.

Maintenance Costs
Subcompact

Car	PM Costs to 50,000 miles	Water Pump	Alternator	Front Brake Pads	Starter	Carburetor (Fuel Injectors)	Fuel Pump	Struts (Front Shocks)	Lower Ball Joints	CVJ (Universal Joint)	Relative Maintenance Cost
Acura Integra	969	125	222	67	174	(155)	183	212	269	264	Med.
Chevy Nova	555	125	427	44	312	496	75	180	103	350	High
Chevy Spectrum	555	109	579	80	353	494	61	255	59	200	High
Chevy Sprint	555	181	559	89	360	512	75	255	161	275	High
Dodge Colt	540	100	428	79	294	560	80	286	231	231	High
Dodge Omni	540	107	203	83	185	360	188	160	179	240	Med.
Ford Escort	545	153	252	75	176	(320)	263	250	249	180	High
Ford Festiva	545	153	252	66	207	(495)	306	369	127	208	High
Honda Accord	680	94	248	65	182	520	136	198	254	354	High
Honda Civic	640	83	208	58	165	609	72	(173)	100	331	Med.
Honda CRX-Si	640	83	388	58	165	(248)	188	(173)	266	331	Med.
Honda Prelude	640	94	248	65	166	(231)	78	198	190	345	Med.
Hyundai Excel	895	127	299	50	239	541	74	194	66	149	Med.
Isuzu I-Mark	620	319	425	77	256	447	64	318	125	287	High
Mazda 323	660	132	177	61	183	(162)	250	184	119	202	Low
Mercury Tracer	545	153	252	66	156	(170)	295	250	110	230	Med.
Mitsubishi Cordia	867	156	386	81	215	936	81	327	203	125	High
Mitsubishi Mirage	867	153	420	71	216	756	81	296	205	265	High
Mitsubishi Precis	867	127	299	50	239	541	74	194	66	149	Med.
Mitsubishi Tredia	867	166	386	81	216	936	81	285	203	125	High
Nissan Pulsar	683	77	220	55	256	(266)	229	334	222	137	Med.
Nissan Sentra	683	62	364	71	180	505	48	335	255	227	High
Nissan Stanza	683	185	368	73	123	(153)	237	335	164	330	High
Plymouth Colt	540	100	428	79	294	560	80	286	231	231	High
Plymouth Horizon	540	107	203	83	185	360	188	160	179	240	Med.
Pontiac Lemans	555	135	140	70	701	(195)	140	190	290	260	High
Subaru DL/GL	698	135	500	75	570	535	93	390	310	210	High

Maintenance Costs
Subcompact

Car	PM Costs to 50,000 miles	Water Pump	Alternator	Front Brake Pads	Starter	Carburetor (Fuel Injectors)	Fuel Pump	Struts (Front Shocks)	Lower Ball Joints	CVJ (Universal Joint)	Relative Maintenance Cost
Subaru Justy	698	78	406	69	504	511	82	362	59	229	High
Toyota Corolla GTS	834	123	400	61	276	(243)	62	431	260	207	High
Toyota Corolla FX16	834	177	398	68	300	(245)	204	450	172	207	High
Toyota MR2	834	163	423	56	322	(243)	261	318	158	315	High
Toyota Tercel	834	115	386	61	293	328	58	311	173	286	High
Volkswagen Fox	825	222	419	108	361	(68)	184	(240)	97	155	Med.
Volkswagen Golf	825	222	231	61	128	(68)	113	(248)	62	196	Low
Volkswagen Jetta	825	222	408	98	278	(68)	171	(230)	62	177	Med.
Volkswagen Scirocco	825	215	423	81	278	(120)	83	141	68	430	Med.
Yugo GV	625	134	223	25	232	443	42	188	158	185	Med.
Average Maintenance/ Repair Cost	701	141	340	69	263	548 (203)	135	270 (213)	168	242	

Compacts

Car	PM Costs to 50,000 miles	Water Pump	Alternator	Front Brake Pads	Starter	Carburetor (Fuel Injectors)	Fuel Pump	Struts (Front Shocks)	Lower Ball Joints	CVJ (Universal Joint)	Relative Maintenance Cost
BMW 325i	1095	119	271	90	204	(123)	186	386	236	(75)	Med.
Buick Skyhawk	610	104	253	76	200	(250)	89	291	102	293	Med.
Buick Skylark	610	116	193	76	205	(185)	122	398	110	155	Med.
Cadillac Cimarron	610	104	253	76	200	(250)	89	291	102	293	Med.
Chevrolet Cavalier	610	104	253	76	200	(250)	89	291	102	293	Med.
Chev. Corsica/Beretta	555	104	253	76	200	(250)	89	291	102	293	Med.
Chrysler Conquest	595	98	284	68	373	(341)	309	359	90	(57)	High
Chrysler LeBaron	595	93	160	89	143	(68)	58	166	106	140	Low
Chrysler LeBaron GTS	595	93	171	75	165	(70)	58	155	109	140	Low
Dodge Aries	540	93	171	75	165	(70)	58	155	109	140	Low
Dodge Daytona	540	93	182	89	165	(70)	58	166	106	140	Low
Dodge Lancer	595	93	171	75	165	(70)	58	155	109	140	Low

Maintenance Costs
Compact

Car	PM Costs to 50,000 miles	Water Pump	Alternator	Front Brake Pads	Starter	Carburetor (Fuel Injectors)	Fuel Pump	Struts (Front Shocks)	Lower Ball Joints	CVJ (Universal Joint)	Relative Maintenance Cost
Dodge Shadow	540	100	164	79	143	(70)	61	173	147	233	Low
Ford Mustang	545	124	241	63	256	(191)	62	228	202	(46)	Low
Ford Tempo	545	137	249	69	153	(191)	121	205	239	215	Med.
Isuzu Impulse	620	98	328	67	293	(131)	217	(70)	110	180	Low
Mazda RX-7	660	198	178	57	151	(179)	253	281	180	(69)	Low
Mazda 626	660	124	174	104	105	(165)	253	268	101	192	Low
Mercury Topaz	545	137	249	69	153	(191)	121	205	239	215	Med.
Mitsubishi Starion	867	98	284	68	373	(341)	309	359	90	(57)	High
Nissan 200 SX	683	86	164	73	126	(136)	239	718	132	(43)	Med.
Oldsmobile Cut. Calais	610	116	193	76	205	(185)	122	398	110	155	Med.
Oldsmobile Firenza	610	104	253	76	200	(250)	89	291	102	293	Med.
Plymouth Reliant	540	93	171	75	165	(70)	58	155	109	140	Low
Plymouth Sundance	540	100	164	79	143	(70)	61	173	147	233	Low
Pontiac Sunbird	610	104	253	76	200	(250)	89	291	102	293	Med.
Pontiac Fiero	555	119	256	82	197	(215)	88	259	99	287	Med.
Pontiac Grand Am	610	116	193	76	205	185	122	398	110	155	Med.
Renault Medallion	595	115	192	86	189	(195)	120	202	195	(75)	Low
Toyota Camry	834	238	400	61	314	(150)	281	387	141	134	High
Toyota Celica	834	214	402	59	255	(147)	249	384	137	(59)	Med.
VW Quantum	825	100	411	130	280	(65)	150	308	160	171	Med.
Average Maintenance/ Repair Cost	651	117	241	79	207	185 (164)	137	283 (193)	133	205 (60)	

Intermediates

Car	PM Costs to 50,000 miles	Water Pump	Alternator	Front Brake Pads	Starter	Carburetor (Fuel Injectors)	Fuel Pump	Struts (Front Shocks)	Lower Ball Joints	CVJ (Universal Joint)	Relative Maintenance Cost
Acura Legend	969	112	237	73	185	(580)	313	(326)	121	228	High
Audi 5000S	1189	155	510	106	400	(300)	263	(320)	335	235	High
Buick Century	610	106	248	79	204	(226)	105	175	77	282	Low

Car	PM Costs to 50,000 miles	Water Pump	Alternator	Front Brake Pads	Starter	Carburetor (Fuel Injectors)	Fuel Pump	Struts (Front Shocks)	Lower Ball Joints	CVJ (Universal Joint)	Relative Maintenance Cost
Buick LeSabre	610	127	249	74	226	(218)	120	157	399	347	High
Buick Regal	610	127	249	74	226	(218)	120	157	399	347	High
Buick Riviera	668	118	227	78	260	(190)	176	118	311	241	Med.
Cadillac Eldorado	668	118	227	78	260	(190)	176	118	311	241	Med.
Cadillac Seville	668	152	240	80	215	(736)	115	171	257	239	High
Chevrolet Camaro	610	106	244	77	220	(351)	111	252	204	(66)	Med.
Chevrolet Celebrity	610	106	248	79	204	(226)	105	175	77	282	Low
Chevrolet Monte Carlo	668	117	247	86	227	(220)	105	(73)	129	(75)	Low
Chrysler New Yorker	595	83	171	83	145	(69)	57	114	102	202	Low
Dodge Dynasty	595	83	171	83	145	(69)	57	114	102	202	Low
Dodge 600	595	93	171	86	166	(70)	58	155	109	202	Low
Ford Taurus	585	130	270	81	170	(289)	138	255	216	239	Med.
Ford Thunderbird	620	147	252	79	202	(200)	213	151	270	(46)	Med.
Mercedes 190 E	1265	135	235	60	285	(125)	146	(370)	120	(185)	Med.
Mercury Cougar	620	147	252	79	202	(200)	213	151	270	(46)	Med.
Mercury Merkur	545	95	470	78	234	(428)	225	(276)	292	(140)	High
Mercury Sable	585	130	270	81	170	(289)	138	255	216	239	Med.
Mitsubishi Galant	867	156	412	95	219	(365)	74	152	70	190	Med.
Nissan Maxima GL	750	135	319	74	370	(118)	227	373	108	202	High
Nissan 300 ZX T	750	132	235	73	238	(671)	361	1215	99	207	High
Olds Cutlass Ciera	610	106	248	79	204	(226)	105	175	77	282	Low
Olds. Cut. Sup. Class.	610	111	259	86	238	774	57	(73)	129	(75)	High
Oldsmobile Delta 88	610	127	249	74	226	(218)	120	157	399	347	High
Oldsmobile Toronado	668	118	227	78	260	(190)	176	118	311	241	Med.
Peugeot 505 T	1125	216	280	50	477	(200)	245	385	250	393	High
Plymouth Caravelle	595	93	171	86	166	(70)	58	155	109	202	Low
Ply. Colt Vista Wag.	540	100	428	79	294	560	80	286	231	231	High

Maintenance Costs
Intermediate

Car	PM Costs to 50,000 miles	Water Pump	Alternator	Front Brake Pads	Starter	Carburetor (Fuel Injectors)	Fuel Pump	Struts (Front Shocks)	Lower Ball Joints	CVJ (Universal Joint)	Relative Maintenance Cost
Pontiac Bonneville	610	127	249	74	226	(218)	120	157	399	347	High
Pontiac Firebird	610	106	244	77	220	(351)	111	252	204	(66)	Med.
Pontiac Grand Prix	610	127	249	74	226	(218)	120	157	399	347	High
Pontiac 6000	610	106	248	79	204	(226)	105	175	77	282	Low
Saab 9000 Turbo	941	161	392	102	400	(463)	268	375	95	345	High
Sterling	1197	153	211	119	287	(452)	168	130	109	132	Med.
Toyota Cressida	834	138	395	56	325	(175)	239	167	165	(59)	Med.
Volvo DL	924	111	272	58	188	(382)	226	(170)	79	(25)	Low
Volvo 760	924	232	354	59	150	(425)	211	400	66	(31)	High
Average Maintenance/Repair Cost	725	127	273	79	238	667 (275)	154	229 (192)	197	277 (54)	

Large

Car	PM Costs to 50,000 miles	Water Pump	Alternator	Front Brake Pads	Starter	Carburetor (Fuel Injectors)	Fuel Pump	Struts (Front Shocks)	Lower Ball Joints	CVJ (Universal Joint)	Relative Maintenance Cost
Buick Electra	610	139	348	74	217	(270)	170	293	198	346	High
Cadillac Brougham	668	215	570	78	215	931	131	85	116	(52)	High
Cad. Fleetwood 60 Spec.	668	169	295	79	238	(200)	113	270	268	422	High
Chevrolet Caprice	668	131	248	77	232	(250)	66	(96)	120	(56)	Low
Chrysler 5th Ave	595	104	150	78	178	377	56	(58)	133	(66)	Low
Dodge Diplomat	595	104	150	78	178	377	56	(58)	133	(66)	Low
Ford LTD Crown Victoria	620	147	433	74	199	(380)	267	(106)	310	(46)	High
Lincoln Continental	620	147	433	74	199	(380)	267	220	385	250	High
Lincoln Mark VII	620	147	433	74	199	(380)	267	220	385	(46)	High
Lincoln Town Car	620	147	433	74	199	(380)	267	(106)	310	(46)	High
Mercury Grand Marquis	620	147	433	74	199	(380)	267	(106)	310	(46)	High
Oldsmobile 98	610	139	348	74	217	(270)	170	293	198	346	High
Plymouth Gran Fury	595	104	150	78	178	377	56	(58)	133	(66)	Low
Pontiac Safari	668	133	247	94	272	903	71	(78)	116	(49)	High
Average Maintenance/Repair cost	627	141	334	77	209	593 (321)	159	230 (83)	223	371 (53)	

Pickups, Minivans & 4x4s

Car	PM Costs to 50,000 miles	Water Pump	Alternator	Front Brake Pads	Starter	Carburetor (Fuel Injectors)	Fuel Pump	Struts (Front Shocks)	Lower Ball Joints	CVJ (Universal Joint)	Relative Maintenance Cost
AMC Jeep Cherokee 4X4	767	95	135	95	141	641	95	(76)	246	(51)	Med.
AMC Jeep Comanche	767	70	145	99	137	(308)	105	(60)	157	(49)	Low
AMC Jeep Wrangler	767	70	272	95	119	(308)	105	(74)	136	(54)	Low
Chevrolet Astro	690	92	164	78	216	(123)	93	(88)	156	(54)	Low
Chevrolet C-10 Pickup	690	114	244	82	263	(213)	75	(88)	150	(53)	Low
Chevy S-10 Blazer 4X4	690	89	147	81	229	(220)	106	(108)	118	(53)	Low
Chevrolet Suburban	690	110	251	78	240	(422)	127	100	106	(53)	Low
Dodge B 150 Van	605	98	87	87	177	280	57	(75)	130	(53)	Low
Dodge Caravan	605	94	162	97	145	372	59	205	173	201	Low
Dodge Dakota	605	94	93	75	176	354	54	(75)	124	(53)	Low
Dodge Raider	605	124	394	53	272	888	85	(74)	94	(44)	High
Ford Aerostar	540	138	249	92	220	(184)	221	87	130	(48)	Low
Ford Bronco II	540	128	252	92	227	(294)	213	81	234	(51)	Med.
Ford E-150 Club Wagon	540	115	253	63	203	(262)	209	82	84	(48)	Low
Ford F-150 Pickup	540	115	253	63	203	(262)	209	82	84	(48)	Low
Ford Ranger	540	140	250	93	221	(295)	208	84	93	(48)	Low
Isuzu Spacecab Pickup	665	104	344	69	415	444	94	(75)	128	(52)	Med.
Isuzu Trooper II 4X4	665	97	328	69	308	417	61	(54)	139	(52)	Low
Mazda B-2000 Pickup	660	124	136	77	115	445	81	(64)	66	(61)	Low
Mitsubishi Montero	895	124	394	53	272	888	85	(74)	94	(44)	High
Nissan Pickup	650	135	166	62	126	(594)	220	(56)	132	(48)	Low
Nissan Van	650	135	166	62	126	(110)	220	(56)	132	(48)	Low
Plymouth Voyager	605	94	162	97	145	372	59	205	173	201	Low
Suzuki Samari	615	165	325	80	250	340	50	85	220	(60)	Med.
Toyota Van Wagon	880	113	387	49	281	(187)	82	(200)	119	(56)	Low
Toyota 4-Runner 4X4	880	89	385	56	308	(166)	61	185	130	(72)	Low
Volkswagen Vanagon	885	241	401	106	292	88	241	191	208	128	Med.
Average Maintenance/ Repair Cost	675	115	242	78	216	461 (263)	121	125 (82)	139	177 (52)	

Service Contracts

Every year nearly 50 percent of new-car buyers purchase "service contracts." Ranging from $200 to $800 in price, a service contract is one of the most expensive options you can buy. In fact, dealers consider service contracts to be the second most important contribution to their profits (after financing). Should you buy one?

A service contract is different from a warranty because it pays for repairs or maintenance not covered by the warranty or that occur after the warranty runs out. It is purchased separately from the car. You should consider the following items before buying a service contract:

- How reputable is the company responsible for the contract? If the company offering the contract lacks funds or insurance and goes out of business, you will be out of luck. Chrysler, Ford, and General Motors offer their own service contracts and are responsible for about 60 percent of the service contracts sold. The rest are sold by independent companies. Check with your Better Business Bureau or local office of consumer affairs if you are not sure of the company's reputation.

- Exactly what does the contract cover and for how long? A service contract may cover all parts of the car or only major mechanical failures. In addition, there are many different time limits offered. These time limits will make a difference depending on whether you plan to do a lot of driving over a short period of time or plan to keep the car for a long time. For example, Ford offers three plans: 3-year/36,000 mile maximum coverage; 5-year/50,000 mile maximum coverage; and 5-year/50,000 mile powertrain coverage. Does the contract pay for preventive maintenance, towing, and rental car expenses? Be sure that these items are written into the contract. If they are not included, you can assume they are not covered.

- What does the service contract provide in addition to the coverage offered by the warranty? This year, many of the manufacturers are offering very good warranties. You may find that the service contract overlaps the "free" warranty. It is important to fully understand your free warranty and compare that with the terms of the service contract. You may find that the extra coverage is not a good value.

- How will the repair bills be paid? It is much better to have the service contract company pay your bills directly. Some contracts require you to pay the bill and they will reimburse you later.

- Where can the car be serviced? As long as you don't move and have regular access to the dealer who sold you the contract, this isn't a problem. But what if you have trouble while on the road? Are you free to take the car to any mechanic? What if you move?

- What other costs can be expected? Most service contracts will have a deductible expense. Compare the deductibles of the various plans offered. Also, some contracts will charge the deductible for each repair while others will charge the deductible per visit, regardless of the number of repairs made. Reimbursement for towing expenses may be limited and some contracts require a cancellation or transfer fee if you sell the car or want to end your contract.

Many automobile experts do not consider service contracts to be good investments. In most instances, defects in major components, such as the engine or transmission, should already be covered under a car's "warranty of merchantability."

The companies who sell the contracts are very sure that, on the average, your repairs are going to cost less than the price you pay for the contract. Otherwise, they wouldn't be in the business. One alternative to buying a service contract is to deposit the $400 to $500 average contract cost into a high interest-bearing savings account. If you have a major repair after your "free" warranty expires, chances are your reserve account will cover the cost. The greater likelihood, however, is that you will still have most of your nest egg, plus interest, for your next car purchase.

What's Not Covered Under a Service Contract

The following, taken directly from Ford's Extended Service Contract, shows what typically is not covered by a service contract.

1. Repairs covered by the manufacturer's New Vehicle Warranty.
2. Repairs caused by damage or unreasonable use (damage from road hazards, accident, fire or other casualty, misuse, negligence, racing, or failures caused by modifications or parts not authorized or supplied by Ford).
3. Damage from the environment (airborne fallout, chemicals, tree sap, salt, hail, windstorm, lightning, road hazards, etc.).
4. Repairs resulting from lack of required maintenance (failures caused by the owner neglecting to perform the required maintenance services set forth in the Owner's Guide for the vehicle). Costs of these routine maintenance services are not covered.
5. Maintenance service and wear item replacement. During the period covered by the Extended Service Contract, it may become necessary to repair or adjust items not specifically listed as covered under the Contract. Examples include:
- Replacement of spark plugs, wiper blades, emission control valves, brake/pad linings, manual clutch assembly, hoses, molded rubber or rubber-like items, or filters.
- Adjustment of carburetor, ignition, transmission bands, belts, or clutch system, and designated predelivery-type operations.
- Cleaning of fuel and cooling system; removal of sludge or carbon deposits.
- Adding of oil, coolant, refrigerants, fluids, or lubricants.
- Maintenance or replacement of other items not specifically covered under the Extended Service Contract.

Typically, these services and replacements are required because of normal wear and use and are the owner's responsibility. Costs for these services and parts are not covered by the Extended Service Contract.

6. Repairs to the vehicle if the odometer is altered, broken, or repaired/replaced so that the actual mileage cannot be determined.
7. To the extent allowed by law, LOSS OF USE OF VEHICLE (including other means of transportation except stated transportation reimbursement provision), LOSS OF TIME, INCONVENIENCE, COMMERCIAL LOSS, OR CONSEQUENTIAL DAMAGES.
8. Other
- Imported vehicles other than those named as eligible vehicles.
- Repairs caused by safety or other types of recalls.

Ten Tips for Dealing with a Mechanic

Call around. It doesn't make sense to choose a shop simply because it's nearby. Calling a few shops may turn up estimates cheaper by half.

But don't necessarily go for the lowest price. A good rule is to eliminate the highest and lowest estimates; the mechanic with the highest estimates is probably charging too much and the lowest may be cutting too many corners.

Check the shop's reputation. Call your local consumer affairs agency and the Better Business Bureau. But don't take their word as gospel: There are a lot of shops they've never heard of and others on which they don't have sufficient records. But if their reports on a shop aren't favorable, you can immediately disqualify it.

Develop a "sider." If you get to know a mechanic employed by a repair shop, don't be afraid to ask if he is available for work on the side—evenings or weekends. The labor will be cheaper.

Look for certification. Mechanics can be certified by the National Institute for Automotive Service Excellence, an industry-wide yardstick for competence. Certification is offered in eight areas of repair, and shops with certified mechanics are allowed to advertise this fact. But certification is not required by law; nor is it a guarantee that the job will be done properly. It's simply an assurance that the mechanic has some experience.

Take a look around. A well-kept shop is a sign of pride in workmanship. This has nothing to do with whether the waiting room is carpeted or air conditioned or offers free coffee, but rather whether the mechanics' work space is reasonably neat and well organized. A skilled and efficient mechanic would probably not be working in a messy shop.

Don't sign a blank check. Make sure that the service order you sign has relatively specific instructions, or at least a few words describing your car's symptoms. Signing a vague work order could make you liable to pay for work you didn't want. Be sure you are called for approval before the shop does work you have not ordered.

Show interest. Ask for an explanation of what's wrong with your car. You'll be surprised at how helpful a mechanic becomes just knowing that you're interested. Don't act like an expert. If you don't really understand what's wrong with your car, don't pretend that you do. It may only demonstrate your ignorance, setting you up to be taken by a dishonest mechanic. Express your satisfaction. If you're happy with the work, compliment the mechanic and ask for him (or her) the next time you come in. You'll get to know each other, and the mechanic will get to know your car.

Get a written estimate. This is a must for repairs of any size.

Things Your Mechanic Would Like to Tell You

- Read your owner's manual. Many repairs result from owners not following the manufacturer's maintenance schedule. Neglecting your car means big profits for repair shops.

- No mechanic does everything right all of the time. There are less-than-scrupulous mechanics, of course, but the complexities of the automobile are immense. The best mechanics aren't those who never make mistakes, but those who make sure that no customer is dissatisfied.

- Some repairs are preventive rather than corrective. It may be foolish to repair only what's broken. Fixing something in one part of the car often affects the workings elsewhere down the line. If the mechanic is trustworthy and suggests additional work, it may save you money in the long run.

- There is no correlation between price and quality of workmanship. This has been documented in study after study.

- Don't expect too much too quickly. It may be unfair to expect a mechanic to resolve in three hours what resulted from three years of abuse and neglect.

Keeping It Going

With the popularity of self-service gasoline stations, many of us are prone to overlook checking those items that can prevent serious problems down the road. The following service checks are ones you can make yourself. Spending 15 minutes a month may decrease the likelihood of a major problem later on.

Brakes: The most important safety item on the car is often the most ignored. A simple test will signal problems. If you have power brakes, you will need to have the engine on to do the test. Push the brake pedal down and hold it down. The pedal should stop firmly about halfway to the floor and stay there. If the stop is mushy or the pedal keeps moving slowly to the floor, you should have your brakes checked. Checking the brake fluid on most new cars is very easy. Your owner's manual tells you where the fluid reservoir is located. The reservoir indicates minimum and maximum fluid levels. If you add your own brake fluid, buy it in small cans and keep them very tightly sealed. Brake fluid absorbs moisture and excess moisture can damage your brake system. Have your brakes checked if you have to regularly replace the brake fluid.

Oil: A few years ago the phrase "fill it up and check the oil" was so common that it seemed like one word. Today, checking the oil often is the responsibility of the driver. To check your oil, first turn off the engine. Find the dipstick (look for a loop made of flat wire located on the side of the engine). If the engine has been running, be careful because the dipstick and surrounding engine parts will be hot. Grab the loop, pull out the dipstick, clean it off and reinsert it into the engine. Pull it out again and observe the oil level. You will note that "full" and "add" are marked at the end of the stick. If the level is between "add" and "full" you are OK. If it is below, you should add enough oil until it reaches the "full" line. To put in the oil, remove the cap at the top of the engine. You may have to add more than one quart. Regularly changing your oil is the single most important thing you can do to protect your engine. Many owner's manuals now contain instructions for changing the oil and filter. You should change the oil filter whenever you change the oil.

Transmission fluid: An automatic transmission is a very complicated item. As the repair prices on the previous pages indicate, it is also very expensive to replace. Checking your fluid level is easy and can prevent an expensive repair job. Like checking for your oil, you will first have to find the transmission fluid dipstick. Usually it is at the rear of the engine and looks like a smaller version of the oil dipstick. To get an accurate reading the engine should be warmed up and running. If the fluid is below the "add" line, pour in one pint at a time. Be sure you do not overfill the reservoir. While you are checking the fluid, note its color. It should be a bright, cherry red. If it is a darker, reddish brown, the fluid needs changing. If it is very dark, nearly black, and has a burnt smell (like varnish), your transmission may be damaged. You should take it to a specialist. Automatic transmission fluid is available at most department stores; check your owner's manual for the correct type for your car.

Power steering: The power steering fluid reservoir is usually behind the steering wheel and connected by a belt to the engine. To check, simply unscrew the cap and look in the reservoir. There will be markings inside; some cars have a little dipstick built into the cap.

Water: We've saved the easiest fluid for last. Most new cars have a plastic reservoir next to the radiator. This plastic bottle will have "full hot" and "full cold" marks on it. If the water is below the "full cold" mark, add water to bring it up to the "full cold" mark. (Antifreeze should be used if you want extra protection in cold weather.) *Note: If the car is hot, do not open the radiator cap. The pressure and heat that can be released could cause a severe burn.*

Belts: A loose belt in the engine

can be the cause of electrical problems, cooling problems, even air conditioning problems. You may have one or more belts connected to your engine. To check them, simply push down on the middle of each belt. It should feel tight. If you can push down more than half an inch, you should have the belts tightened.

Battery: If you have a battery with caps on the top, lift off the caps and check to see if the fluid comes up to the bottom of the filler neck. If it doesn't, add water (preferably distilled). If the temperature is freezing, add water only if you are planning to drive the car immediately. The newly added water can freeze and damage your battery. Maintenance-free batteries do not have refill caps and do not require additional fluid.

Look for corrosion around the battery connections. Corrosion can prevent electrical circuits from being completed, leading you to assume your perfectly good battery is "dead." If cables are corroded, remove and clean them with fine sandpaper or steel wool and baking soda. The inside of the connection and the battery posts should be shiny when you put the cables back on.

Tires: Improperly inflated tires are a major cause of premature tire failure. Check for proper inflation at least once a month. The most fuel-efficient inflation level is the maximum pressure listed on the side of the tire. Because many gas station pumps do not have gauges, and those that do are generally wrong, you should invest in your own tire gauge.

Spark plugs: Changing spark plugs is an easy, although not complete, form of a tune-up. For less than ten dollars you can change the plugs in most cars. Most new cars need resistor-type plugs. Your owner's manual tells you exactly what type of plugs your car needs. The only tool you need is a spark plug wrench, available at most department stores.

Many mechanics use the spark plug as a simple diagnostic tool. The normal color for the spark end of the plug is light tan or gray. If you find the spark end is black, contains any goo or appears to be damaged, it may indicate you need a complete tune-up or have some other problem.

Air filter: Probably the easiest maintenance item is changing your air filter. You usually can tell the filter needs changing simply by looking at it. If it appears dirty, change it. It is a simple task. If you are not sure how clear your filter is, try the following: When your engine has warmed up, put the car in park or neutral and, with the emergency brake on, let the car idle. Open the filter lid and remove the filter. If the engine begins to run faster, you need to change the filter.

Battery Safety

There are few motorists who have never had to "jump" start a car because of a "dead" battery. Surprisingly, that innocent-looking battery can be the cause of serious injuries.

Batteries produce hydrogen gas when they discharge or undergo heavy use (such as cranking the engine for a long period of time). A lit cigarette or a spark can cause this gas to explode. Whenever you are working with the battery, always remove the negative (or ground) cable first; it usually is marked with a "minus" sign. When you are done, reconnect it last. This will greatly reduce the chance of causing a spark that could ignite any hydrogen gas present.

For a safe "jump" start:
1. Connect each end of the red cable to the positive (+) terminal on each of the batteries.
2. Connect the end of the black cable to the negative (-) terminal of the *good* battery.
3. Connect the other end of the black cable to the engine block (or exposed metal away from the battery) of the car being started.
4. To avoid damage to the electrical parts of the car being started, make sure the engine is running at idle speed before disconnecting the cables.

Repair Protection by Credit Card

Paying auto repair bills by credit card can provide much needed recourse if you are having problems with an auto mechanic. The Federal Trade Commission provides the following example of a situation where paying by credit card could save the day:

Suppose you take your car to the mechanic because of a noise in the power steering. The shop does a rack-and-pinion overhaul. You pay $180 with your credit card and drive home. The next afternoon, the noise is back. Another mechanic looks at the car and finds that the real problem was fluid leaking from the power steering pump. That will cost another $125 to repair.

What happens if the first mechanic refuses to make good on his mistake? If you had paid the bill with cash, you would be out $180 and might have to file suit to recover your money. If you paid by check, it would probably be too late to stop payment. Payment with a credit card not only gives you extra time, but is also an effective tool for negotiating with the mechanic.

According to federal law, you have the right to withhold payment for sloppy or incorrect repairs. Of course, you may withhold no more than the amount of the repair in dispute.

In order to use this right, you must first try to work out the problem with the mechanic. Also, unless the credit card company owns the repair shop (this might be the case with gasoline credit cards used at gas stations), two other conditions must be met: The repair shop must be in your home state (or within 100 miles of your current address) and the cost of repairs must be over $50.

Until the problem is settled or resolved in court, the credit card company cannot charge you interest or penalties on the amount in dispute.

If you decide to take such action, send a letter to the credit card company with a copy to the repair shop, explaining the details of the problem and what you want as settlement. Send the letter by certified mail with a return receipt requested.

Sometimes the credit card company or repair shop will attempt to put a "bad mark" on your credit record. You may not be reported as delinquent if you have given the credit card company notice of your dispute. However, a creditor can report that you are disputing your bill and this can go in your record. The Fair Credit Reporting Act gives you the right to learn what information is in your file and challenge any information you feel is incorrect. You also have the right to have your side of the story added to your file.

Using a credit card will certainly not solve all your auto repair problems, but it can be a handy ally. For more information about your credit rights you can write to the Federal Trade Commission, Credit Practices Division, Washington, D.C. 20580.

Take a Tip from a Mechanic:

Before you pay for a repair, take the car for a test drive. The few extra minutes you spend checking out the repair could save you a trip back to the mechanic.

If you find the problem still exists, there will be no question that the repair wasn't properly completed. It is much more difficult to prove the repair wasn't properly made after you've left the repair shop.

The WARRANTY Chapter

Along with your new car comes a warranty—a promise from the manufacturer that your new car will perform as it should. Most of us never read the warranty—until it is too late. In fact, because warranties often are difficult to read and understand, most of us don't really know what our warranties offer. This chapter is designed to help you understand what to look for in a warranty when buying a new car.

Every new car comes with two types of warranties: one provided by the manufacturer and one implied by law. Warranties provided by the manufacturer can be either "full" or "limited." The best warranty you can get is a "full" warranty. Full warranties must meet the standards set by federal law under the Magnuson-Moss Warranty Act and must cover all aspects of the product's performance.

Any guarantee that is not a full warranty is called a "limited" warranty. If the warranty is limited, it must be clearly marked as such and you must be told exactly what the warranty covers. Most car manufacturers provide a limited warranty.

Warranties implied by law are defined by the Uniform Commercial Code (UCC). All states have passed a version of the UCC; Louisiana has not passed the portion of the UCC that gives warranty protection, however. The UCC provides an implied **warranty of merchantability** and a **warranty of fitness.** The "warranty of merchantability" means that your new car will be fit for the purpose for which it is used—in the case of a car, that means safe, efficient, and trouble-free transportation. The "warranty of fitness" gives you a promise that if the dealer tells you that a car can be used for a specific purpose, it will perform for that purpose.

Any claims made by the salesperson are considered warranties. These claims are called **express warranties,** and you should have them put in writing if you consider them to be important. If the car does not live up to any of the promises made to you in the showroom, you may have a case against the seller.

The manufacturer can limit the amount of time the limited warranty is in effect. And, in most states, the manufacturer can also limit the amount of time that the warranty implied by law is in effect.

EPA Mileage Label. Federal law requires that each new car have a label indicating the car's fuel mileage when it is tested according to government specifications. The label must also list the range of fuel mileage ratings of the other vehicles in that car's size class. In addition, every dealer is required to make available copies of the EPA *Gas Mileage Guide*. This free guide provides the mileage ratings for all new cars.

Car Label. By federal law, the manufacturer must label each new car indicating the make, identification number, name of the dealer, suggested base price, the prices of all of the options installed by the manufacturer, and the manufacturer's total suggested retail price. This information must be contained on a label affixed to the car's windshield—the label is commonly referred to as the "sticker." The law forbids removal or alteration of the sticker before delivery to the buyer.

Although the prices listed on new car stickers are only suggested prices and are not binding on dealers, they are useful when you comparison shop.

The Basic Warranty. Most manufacturers' warranties are similar. The differences are usually in the length of time or the amount of mileage covered, how the power train is warranted, and whether the car is warranted against rust.

Be careful not to confuse your warranty with a service contract. The service contract must be purchased separately; the warranty is yours at no extra cost when you buy the car. Here are some of the key items to look for:

What the Warranty Covers

The manufacturer warrants that the materials used to make the car and the way the car was made are free from defects, provided that the car is used in a normal fashion for 12 months or 12,000 miles, whichever comes first, from the date the car is delivered to the buyer.

While the warranty is in effect, the manufacturer will perform, at no charge to the owner, repairs which are necessary because of defects in materials or the way the car was manufactured.

What the Warranty Does Not Cover

The warranty does not cover parts that have to be replaced because of normal wear, such as filters, fuses, light bulbs, wiper blades, clutch linings, brake pads, or the addition of oil, fluids, coolants, and lubricants. Tires, batteries, and the emission control system are covered by separate warranties. A separate rust warranty also is provided.

The cost for required maintenance, such as that listed in the owner's manual, is not covered by the warranty. Failures resulting from misuse, negligence, changes you make in the car, accidents, or lack of required maintenance are not covered by the warranty.

Any implied warranties, including the warranties of merchantability and fitness for a particular purpose, are limited to 12 months or 12,000 miles. The manufacturer is not responsible for consequential damages, such as the loss of time or use of your car, or any expenses they might cause.

Some states do not allow the implied warranties to be limited to a specific amount of time or the consequential damages to be limited or excluded. If this is true in your state, these limitations do not apply to you. In addition to the rights granted to you in this warranty, you may have other rights granted to you under the laws of your state.

What You Must Do

You must operate and maintain your car according to the instructions in your owner's manual. You must keep a record of all maintenance performed on your car.

To Repair Your Car under the Warranty

Take your car to an authorized dealer or service center. The work will be done in a reasonable amount of time during normal business hours.

Rust Warranty

All American manufacturers and several foreign manufacturers warrant against rust, usually for 36 months. Many provide a 60-month warranty at no additional charge.

Some dealers offer extra rust protection at an additional cost. Before you purchase this option, you should compare the extra protection offered with the warranty already included in the price of the car; it may already include some protection against rust.

Emission System Warranty

The emission system is warranted by federal law. Any repairs required during the first five years or 50,000 miles will be paid for by the manufacturer if:
- an original engine part fails because of a defect in materials or workmanship; and
- the part failure causes your car to exceed federal emissions standards.

Using leaded fuel in a car designed for unleaded fuel will void your warranty and may result in the car not passing your state's inspection. Because an increasing number of states are requiring an emissions test before a car can pass inspection, you may have to pay to fix the system if you used the wrong type of fuel. Repairs to emission system are usually very expensive.

Other Warranties

Separate warranties are usually provided for tires and the battery. Options, such as a stereo system, should have their own warranties as well. Service should be provided through the dealer.

Getting Information from Uncle Sam

Sometimes, simple requests for information from the federal government go unheeded, or the agency will tell you the information "isn't public." The truth is, there is very little information that the government can keep secret. Thanks to the Freedom of Information Act, it is now easier to get certain information from the government. This act gives you access to information from virtually every federal agency. In order to get the information mentioned in "Secret Warranties," address your request to:

Executive Secretariat
National Highway Traffic Safety Administration
Washington, DC 20590.

On the front of the envelope, write "Freedom of Information Act Request." This should also appear at the top of your letter. In the letter, simply state your request. By law, the federal agency has 10 working days to respond.

Secret Warranties

While manufacturers deny the existence of "secret warranties," many consumers have found that certain repairs often are made at no charge long after the warranty period has expired. Rather than use the term "secret warranty," manufacturers often call these free repairs "policy adjustments" or "goodwill service." Whatever they are called, most consumers do not know about them.

If dealers report a number of complaints about a particular part and the manufacturer determines the problem is due to faulty design or assembly, the manufacturer may permit dealers to repair the problem "under warranty." In the past, this practice often was reserved for customers who made a big fuss. The availability of the free repair never was publicized.

Secret warranties are disclosed in service bulletins that the manufacturers send to dealers. These bulletins outline free repair or reimbursement programs as well as discuss other problems with possible causes and fixes.

Because of problems with secret warranties in the past, Ford and General Motors are now required to make many of their bulletins available to the public. To get this information from Ford, call their toll-free "defect line": 800-241-FORD. General Motors bulletins from 1985 on (which may cover earlier years) and indexes to the bulletins are available at GM dealers. You may also call (toll-free) 800-551-4123 to obtain a form to order them directly from GM. The indexes are free, but there is a charge for the bulletins.

Service bulletins are also on file at the National Highway Traffic Safety Administration. To obtain copies of the bulletins on file, send a letter to NHTSA's Technical Reference Library, Room 5108, NHTSA, Washington, DC, 20590. If you write to the government, it is best to ask for "service bulletins" rather than "secret warranties." If you have trouble getting a response, you may want to send a "Freedom of Information" request.

If you feel the problem you are having with your car after the warranty expires is a result of a premature failure, sometimes a friendly service manager (not the service writer) or the manufacturer's zone manager may be able to help out.

If the polite approach does not work, it may take a fuss to discover a secret warranty and have it applied to you. Finding a service bulletin on your problem can help you do that. You can also contact the Bureau of Consumer Protection of the Federal Trade Commission, and the Center for Auto Safety. (Their addresses can be found in "The Complaint Chapter.")

If you find that a secret warranty is in effect and repairs are being made at no charge after the warranty has expired, contact the Center and they will publish the information so others can benefit.

Consumer Advisory: Dealer Options and Your Warranty

Make sure that "dealer-added" options will not void your warranty. For example, some consumers who have purchased cruise control as an option to be installed by the dealer have found that their warranty is void when they take the car in for engine repairs. If you are in doubt, contact the manufacturer before you authorize the installation of dealer-supplied options. If the manufacturer says that adding the option will not void your warranty, get it in writing.

Comparing Warranties

Warranties are difficult to compare because they contain lots of fine print and confusing language. The following table will help you compare this year's new car warranties. Because the table does not contain all the details about each warranty, you should review the actual warranty to make sure you understand the fine points. Remember, you have the right to inspect a warranty before you buy—it's the law.

The table provides information on six basic areas covered by a typical warranty:

The *Basic Warranty* covers most parts of the car against manufacturer's defects. The tires, batteries, and items you may add to the car are covered under separate warranties. The table describes coverage in terms of months and miles; 24/24,000 means the warranty is good for 24 months or 24,000 miles, whichever comes first.

The *Powertrain Warranty* usually lasts longer than the basic warranty. Because each manufacturer's definition of the powertrain is different, it is important to find out exactly what your warranty will cover. Powertrain coverage should include any parts of the engine, transmission, and drive-train. The warranty on some luxury cars will often cover some additional systems such as steering, suspension, and electrical.

The *Corrosion Warranty* usually applies only to actual holes due to rust. Read this section carefully because most corrosion warranties *do not* apply to what the manufacturer may describe as "cosmetic" rust or bad paint.

The *Transferable* column indicates whether the warranty will transfer to the new owner if you sell your car during the coverage period.

The *Deductible* column indicates how much you will have to pay when you take the car in for warranty work. Most deductibles apply only to powertrain problems. The last column indicates whether the manufacturer has specifically included your right to *arbitration* in the warranty. This can be very useful in settling repair disputes. See "The Complaint Chapter" for a complete discussion of how arbitration works.

Warranties: The Best and The Worst

The *Warranty Rating Index* will help you compare the overall benefits of the 1988 warranties. The higher the index number, the better the warranty. The index number incorporates the important features of each warranty. In developing the index, we gave the most weight to the basic and powertrain components of the warranties. The corrosion warranty was weighted somewhat less and the transferability, deductible and arbitration features received the least weight. We also considered special features like extended coverage of steering, brake, and suspension systems. After evaluating all the features of the 1987 warranties—here are this year's best and worst.

The Best	The Worst
Company	**Company**
Cadillac Allante	Yugo
Lincoln/Merkur	Jeep
Porsche	Suzuki
Chrysler Fifth Avenue	Isuzu
Volvo	Honda

Manufacturer	Basic Warranty	Powertrain Warranty	Corrosion Warranty	Transferable	Deductibles	Arbitration	Index*
Acura	36/36,000	36/36,000	36/unlimited	yes	none	no	733
Audi	36/50,000	36/50,000	72/unlimited	yes	none	yes	1065
BMW	36/36,000	36/36,000	72/unlimited[1]	yes	none	no	867
Buick	12/12,000	72/60,000	72/100,000	yes[2]	$100[3]	no	851
Electra, Riv.	12/12,000[4]	72/60,000	72,100,000	yes[5]	$100	no	947
Cadillac	12/12,000[6]	72/60,000	72/100,000	yes[5]	$100	no	1023
Allante	12/12,000[7]	84/100,000	84/100,000	yes[8]	$25[9]	no	1341
Cimarron	12/12,000	72/60,000	72/100,000	yes[2]	$100[3]	no	851
Chevrolet	12/12,000	72/60,000	72/100,000	yes[2]	$100[3]	no	851
Chrysler	12/12,000	84/70,000	84/100,000	yes[2]	$100	yes	991
Fifth Ave.	12/12,000[6]	84/70,000	84/100,000	yes[2]	$100	yes	1163
New Yorker	60/50,000[10]	84/70,000	84/100,000	yes[2]	$100	yes	1185
Dodge	12/12,000	84/70,000	84/100,000	yes[2]	$100	yes	991
Eagle	12/12,000	84/70,000	84/100,000	no	$100[3]	yes	976
Ford	12/12,000	72/60,000	72/100,000	yes	$100[3]	yes	911
Honda	12/12,000	24/24,000	36/unlimited	yes	none	yes	559
Hyundai	12/12,500	36/36,000	36/unlimited	yes	none	no	583
Isuzu	12/12,000[7]	24/24,000	36/unlimited	yes	none	no	557
Jaguar	36/36,000	36/36,000	72/unlimited	yes	none	no	917
Jeep	12/12,000	36/36,000	36/36,000	no	$100[3]	yes	506
Lincoln	12/12,000[11]	72/60,000	72/100,000	yes[12]	$100[3]	yes	1237
Mazda	36/50,000	36/50,000	60/unlimited	yes	none	no	967
Mercedes	48/50,000	48/50,000	48/50,000	yes	none	no	957
Mercury	12/12,000	72/60,000	72/100,000	yes	$100[3]	yes	911
Merkur	12/12,000[11]	72/60,000	72/100,000	yes[12]	$100[3]	yes	1237
Mitsubishi	12/12,000(13)	36/50,000	60/unlimited	yes	none	no	767
Nissan	12/12,500[7]	36/36,000	60/unlimited	yes	none	yes	824

* Higher numbers indicate better warranties. See the preceeding page for a description of the index.

Manufacturer	Basic Warranty	Powertrain Warranty	Corrosion Warranty	Transferable	Deductibles	Arbitration	Index*
Oldsmobile	12/12,000	72/60,000	72/100,000	yes[2]	$100[3]	no	851
Toronado, 98	12/12,000[4]	72/60,000	72/100,000	yes[5]	$100	no	947
Peugeot	36/36,000	60/50,000	36/36,000	yes	none	no	837
Plymouth	12/12,000	84/70,000	84/100,000	yes[2]	$100	yes	991
Pontiac	12/12,000	72/60,000	72/100,000	yes[2]	$100[3]	no	851
Porsche	24/unlimited	24/unlimited	120/unlimited	yes	none	yes	1166
Renault	12/12,000	72/60,000	72/100,000	no	$100[3]	yes	886
Rolls-Royce	36/unlimited	36/unlimited	36/unlimited	yes	none	no	948
Saab	36/36,000	36/36,000	72/unlimited	yes	none	yes	967
Sterling	36/36,000	36/36,000	72/unlimited	yes	none	yes	967
Subaru	12/unlimited	36/36,000	36/36,000	yes	none	no	631
Suzuki	12/12,000	24/24,000	36/unlimited	yes	none	no	509
Toyota	36/36,000	36/36,000	60/unlimited	yes	none	no	869
Volkswagen	24/24,000	24/24,000	72/unlimited	yes	none	yes	799
Volvo	12/unlimited[7]	36/unlimited	96/unlimited[1]	yes	none	yes	1092
Yugo	12/12,000	12/12,000	none	yes	none	no	243

*Higher numbers indicate better warranties. See the preceeding page for a description of the index.

1. Once a year inspection required.

2. Second owner only can obtain first owner powertrain coverage for $100 transfer fee. Powertrain warranty ceases at 24/24,000 for subsequent owners.

3. Powertrain only.

4. Certain components covered by the basic warranty such as brake, steering and suspension systems, selected electrical components and others are covered for 36/36,000 with a $100 deductible and can be transferred to the second owner for a $100 fee.

5. Second owner only can obtain first owner major assembly/powertrain coverage for $100 transfer fee. Powertrain warranty ceases at 24/24,000 for subsequent owners.

6. Certain components covered by the basic warranty such as brake, steering and suspension systems, selected electrical components and others are covered for 60/50,000 for second owner with a $100 deductible and $100 transfer fee.

7. Certain components covered by the basic warranty such as brake, steering and suspension systems, selected electrical components and others may be covered for as long as the powertrain warranty.

8. Second owner only can obtain first owner major assembly/powertrain coverage. Powertrain warranty ceases at 36/36,000 for subsequent owners.

9. Original and second owners pay $25 major assembly/powertrain deductibles. Subsequent owners pay $100 deductible on powertrain coverage.

10. This non-transferable, no deductible warranty extends only to the original owner and includes basic, powertrain and corrosion coverage. The basic warranty for subsequent owners is 12/12,000.

11. Powertrain coverage extends to all major components of the car. Lincoln and Merkur's basic warranty also includes car rental payments of a maximum of $30/day for 5 days.

12. Second owner only can obtain first owner major assembly coverage for $25 transfer fee. Subsequent owners will generally receive the unexpired portion of a base 36/36,000 power train coverage.

13. 36/36,000 warranty on selected electrical components.

The **INSURANCE** Chapter

Insurance is an often-overlooked expense of owning a car. As you shop for a car, be aware that the car's design and accident history may affect your insurance rates. Some cars cost less to insure because experience has shown that they are damaged less or are less expensive to fix after a collision.

A car's design can affect both the chances and severity of an accident. Good maneuverability may help to avoid a collision in the first place. A car with a well-designed bumper may escape damage altogether in a low-speed crash. Some cars are easier to repair than others or may have less expensive parts. Cars with four doors tend to be damaged less than cars with two doors.

In addition, there is a car's record of injury loss. The tables toward the end of this chapter show differences in injury losses among various cars on the road. The information is based on the average amount that insurance companies pay claimants (per car, per year) for injuries.

Insurance companies use this and other information to determine whether or not to offer a discount on insurance premiums for a particular car, or whether to levy a surcharge.

The reason one car may get a discount on insurance while another a surcharge depends upon the design of the car and the way it is traditionally driven. Sports cars, for example, are usually surcharged due in part to the driving habits of the owners. Four-door sedans and station wagons often get discounts.

Not all companies offer discounts or surcharges and many cars receive neither. Some companies offer a discount or impose a surcharge on collision premiums only; others apply discounts and surcharges on both collision and comprehensive coverage. Discounts and surcharges usually range from 10 to 30 percent. Allstate offers discounts of up to 35 percent on certain cars. One company may offer a discount on a particular car while another may not.

Check with your insurance agent to find out whether your company has a rating program. The tables on the next two pages indicate which of the new cars may qualify for a discount on insurance.

Types of Coverage

More and more consumers are saving considerable amounts of money by shopping around for the best insurance buy. In order to be a good comparison shopper, you need to know a few things about automobile insurance. There are six basic types of coverage you can buy:

Bodily injury liability: This provides money to pay claims against you and the cost of your legal defense if your car injures or kills someone.

Property damage liability: This provides money to pay claims and defense costs if your car damages someone else's property.

Medical payments insurance: This pays for the medical expenses of the driver and passengers in your car resulting from an accident.

Uninsured motorists protection: This pays for injuries caused by an uninsured or a hit-and-run driver.

Collision insurance: This pays for the damage to your car after an accident.

Comprehensive physical damage insurance: This pays for damages when your car is stolen or damaged by fire, floods, or other perils.

Note: Certain states have "no-fault" insurance. This usually requires that you purchase personal insurance protection and there are some restrictions on liability lawsuits.

Insurance Costs

Subcompact

Car	Insurance Rate
Acura Integra	Surcharge
Chevrolet Nova	Regular
Chevrolet Spectrum	Regular
Chevrolet Sprint	Regular
Dodge/Plymouth Colt	Surcharge
Dodge Omni	Regular
Ford Escort	Regular
Ford Festiva	Surcharge
Honda Civic	Regular
Honda CRX-Si	Surcharge
Honda Prelude	Surcharge
Hyundai Excel	Regular
Isuzu I-Mark	Regular
Mazda 323	Surcharge
Mercury Tracer	Regular
Mitsub. Cordia/Tredia	Surcharge
Mitsubishi Mirage	Surcharge
Mitsubishi Precis	Surcharge
Nissan Pulsar/Sentra	Surcharge
Nissan Stanza	Regular
Plymouth Horizon	Regular
Pontiac LeMans	Regular
Subaru DL/GL	Surcharge
Subaru Justy	Surcharge
Toyota Corolla/FX16	Regular
Toyota MR-2	Surcharge
Toyota Tercel	Regular
Volkswagen Fox	Regular
VW Golf/Jetta	Surcharge
Volkswagen Scirroco	Surcharge
Yugo GV	Surcharge

Compact

Car	Insurance Rate
BMW 325i	Regular
Buick Skyhawk	Regular
Buick Skylark	Discount
Cadillac Cimarron	Discount
Chevrolet Cavalier	Regular
Chevrolet Beretta	Regular
Chevrolet Corsica	Discount
Chrysler Conquest	Surcharge
Chrysler LeBaron/GTS	Discount
Dodge Aries/Ply. Reliant	Discount
Dodge Daytona	Surcharge
Dodge Lancer	Discount
Ford Mustang	Surcharge
Ford Tempo/Merc. Topaz	Discount
Honda Accord	Regular
Isuzu Impulse	Surcharge
Mazda RX-7	Surcharge
Mazda 626	Regular
Mitsubishi Starion	Surcharge
Nissan 200 SX	Surcharge
Olds Cut. Calais	Regular
Oldsmobile Firenza	Regular
Ply. Sundance/Dodge Shadow	Regular
Pontiac Fiero	Surcharge
Pontiac Grand Am	Surcharge
Pontiac Sunbird	Regular
Renault Medallion	Discount
Toyota Camry	Discount
Toyota Celica	Surcharge
VW Quantum	Regular

Insurance Costs

Intermediate

Car	Insurance Rate
Acura Legend	Regular
Audi 5000S	Surcharge
Buick Cent./Buick LeSab.	Discount
Buick Regal/Riviera	Regular
Cad. Eldo./Seville	Regular
Chevy Camaro/Pont. Fbird	Surcharge
Chevrolet Celebrity	Discount
Chevrolet Monte Carlo	Surcharge
Chrysler New Yorker	Discount
Dodge Dynasty/Ply. Carav.	Regular
Dodge 600	Discount
Ford Taurus/Merc. Sable	Discount
Ford Tbird/Merc. Cougar	Surcharge
Mercedes 190 E	Regular
Mercury Merkur	Surcharge
Mitsubishi Galant	Discount
Nissan Maxima	Regular
Nissan 300 ZX T	Surcharge
Olds Cutlass Ciera	Discount
Olds Cut. Sup. Classic	Regular
Oldsmobile Delta 88	Discount
Oldsmobile Toronado	Regular
Peugeot 505 T	Regular
Plymouth Colt Vista Wag.	Discount
Pontiac Bonneville	Discount
Pontiac Grand Prix	Regular
Pontiac 6000	Discount
Saab 9000 T	Regular
Sterling	Regular
Toyota Cressida	Regular
Volvo DL/740	Discount

Large

Car	Insurance Rate
Buick Electra	Discount
Cadillac Brougham/Fltwd. 60	Discount
Chevrolet Caprice	Discount
Chrysler 5th Ave/Dodge Dip.	Discount
Ford LTD Crown Victoria	Discount
Lincoln Continental	Discount
Lincoln Mark VII/Town Car	Regular
Mercury Grand Marquis	Discount
Oldsmobile 98	Discount
Plymouth Gran Fury	Discount
Pontiac Safari Wagon	Discount
Chevrolet Astro/Subur.	Discount
Chevy C-10 P-up/S-10 Blzr.	Regular
Dodge B 150 Van	Discount
Dodge Caravan/Ply. Voy.	Discount
Dodge Dakota/Raider	Regular
Ford Aerostar	Discount
Ford Bronco II	Regular
Ford E-150 Club Wagon	Discount
Ford F-150 Pickup	Regular
Ford Ranger	Surcharge
Isuzu Spacecab/Trpr. II P-up	Regular
Jeep Chero./Comch./Wrg.	Regular
Mazda B-2000	Regular
Mitsubushi Montero	Regular
Nissan Pickup	Surcharge
Nissan Van	Discount
Suzuki Samurai	Regular
Toyota Van Wagon	Discount
Toyota 4-Runner 4x4	Surcharge
Volkswagen Vanagon	Discount

"No-Fault" Insurance

One of the major expenses of automobile accidents has been the cost of determining who is "at fault." Often, both parties were required to hire lawyers, court decisions took a long time, and the decisions were often inconsistent. This resulted in some victims receiving considerably less than others for the same losses.

As a result, many states have instituted "no-fault" automobile insurance systems. The concept is that each person's losses are covered by his or her insurance company, regardless of who is at fault. Lawsuits are permitted only under certain conditions. While the concept is the same from state to state, the details of the no-fault laws may vary. The variations include the amounts paid in similar situations, conditions governing the right to sue, and the inclusion or exclusion of property damage.

Because of these variations, it is important to understand the no-fault laws in your state. It will be easier to understand these laws if you understand the six basic types of insurance coverages. They are all applicable under no-fault laws.

While the concept of no-fault insurance is that your insurance company pays for your losses regardless of who is responsible, some states with no-fault insurance still permit lawsuits to determine who is at fault. The following list, which is divided into five categories, provides a general description of the no-fault laws in each state. The first category lists those states whose no-fault laws are closest to the true concept of "no-fault." The remaining categories list the states whose no-fault laws are less and less consistent with the no-fault concept. The final category includes those states which do not have no-fault laws.

In the table, the term "first-party" insurance refers to the insurance you buy to protect yourself and family; liability insurance refers to insurance covering losses to others resulting from your accident.

"No-Fault" States

1. First-party and liability insurance required—lawsuits restricted.

Colorado	Kansas	New Jersey
Connecticut	Kentucky	New York
Georgia	Massachusetts	North Dakota
Hawaii	Michigan	Utah
	Minnesota	

2. First-party required and liability optional—lawsuits restricted.

Florida	Puerto Rico

3. First-party and liability insurance required—lawsuits unrestricted.

Delaware	Oregon
Maryland	Pennsylvania

4. Liability required and first-party optional—lawsuits unrestricted.

District of Columbia	South Carolina	Texas

5. Insurance optional—lawsuits unrestricted.

Arkansas	South Dakota
New Hampshire	Virginia

States without "No-Fault"

Alabama	Maine	Rhode Island
Alaska	Mississippi	Tennessee
Arizona	Missouri	Vermont
California	Montana	Washington
Idaho	Nebraska	West Virginia
Illinois	Nevada	Wisconsin
Indiana	New Mexico	Wyoming
Iowa	North Carolina	Guam
Louisiana	Ohio	Virgin Islands
	Oklahoma	

Getting the Best Buy on Insurance

Depending on where you live, shopping around for auto insurance can save you money. Each state has a different law for determining how much companies can charge for automobile insurance. These insurance-pricing policies fall into three categories:

Noncompetitive: All insurance companies are required to charge the same price for the coverage offered. This rate is determined by an insurance commission or rating bureau.

Prior Approval: Prices must be approved by an insurance commission. Because prices are submitted to a central commission for approval, variations tend to be slight.

Competitive: In competitive states the insurance companies can charge whatever they think the market will bear. No state approval is necessary.

The following map indicates each state's insurance pricing system. If you live in a "noncompetitive" state, shopping around will *not* get you a better buy. In those states the location or reputation of the agent will be your most important consideration.

In a "prior approval" state, rates tend to vary slightly. Because pricing is less competitive, the service offered by one agent may override the savings offered by another.

In "competitive" states you will find wide price variations among the different companies. Shopping around can significantly reduce your insurance costs.

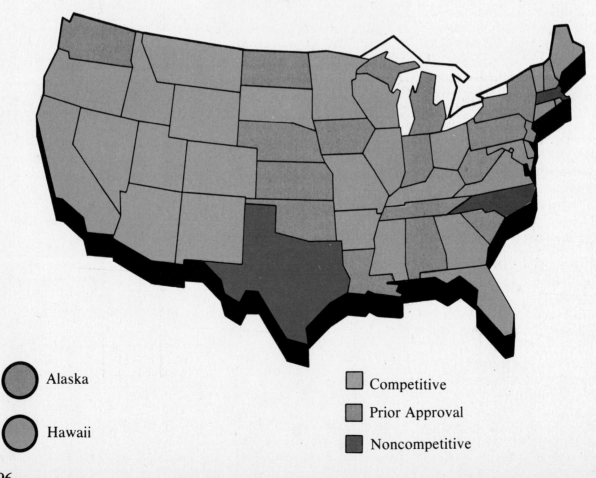

○ Alaska

○ Hawaii

▢ Competitive

▢ Prior Approval

▢ Noncompetitive

Reducing Insurance Costs

After you have shopped around and found the best deal by comparing the costs of different coverages, there are some other factors that will affect your final insurance bill. Among them are:

Your annual mileage: The more you drive, the more your vehicle will be "exposed" to a potential accident. The annual coverage for a car rarely used will be less than the coverage for a frequently used car.

Where you drive: If you regularly drive and park in the city you will most likely pay more than if you drive in rural areas.

Youthful drivers: Usually the highest premiums are paid by male drivers under the age of 25. Whether or not the under 25-year-old male is married will also affect his insurance rates. (Married males pay less.) As the driver gets older, the rates are lowered.

In addition to shopping around, taking advantage of premium discounts can reduce your insurance costs. Most insurance companies offer discounts from 5 to 30 percent on various parts of your insurance bill. The availability of discounts varies among companies and often depends on where you live. Many consumers do not benefit from these discounts simply because they don't ask.

To determine whether you are getting all the discounts to which you're entitled, ask your insurance company for a complete list of discounts it offers in your state. It is good to ask for this list when shopping around for insurance.

According to data compiled by the Insurance Information Institute, here are 20 ways to save money on personal auto premiums:

Driver Education. Many insurance companies offer a discount to young people who have successfully completed a state-approved driver education course. Typically, this can mean a $40 reduction in the cost of coverage.

Student Discounts. Many insurance companies offer discounts of up to 25 percent on insurance to full-time high school or college students who are in the upper 20 percent of the class, on the dean's list, or have a B or better average.

Deductibles. Opting for the largest reasonable deductible is the obvious first step in reducing premiums. Increasing your deductible to $500 from $200 could cut your collision premium about 20 percent. Raising the deductible to $1,000 from $200 could lower your premium about 45 percent. Discounts may vary by company.

Collision Coverage. The older the car the less the need for insuring for collision. Consider dropping collision insurance entirely on an older car, because regardless of how much coverage you carry, the insurance company will pay only up to the car's "book value." For example, if your car requires $1,000 in repairs but its "book value" is only $500, the insurance company is required to pay only $500.

Desirable Cars. Premiums are usually much higher for cars with high collision or bodily injury claims or that are the favorite target of thieves. Loss data on almost 200 makes and models is published in the Highway Loss Data Institute composite chart compiled by the Insurance Institute for Highway Safety, Publications Dept., Watergate 600, Suite 300, Washington, D.C. 20037.

Multi-Car Discount. Consumers insuring more than one car in the household with the same insurer can save up to 20 percent.

Insuring Driving Children. If children are away at school, they don't drive the family car very often, and it's usually cheaper to insure them on the parents' policy rather than separately.

Mature Driver Credit. Drivers ages 50 and older may qualify for up to a 10 percent discount, depending on the company.

Passive Restraints. Many companies offer discounts for automatic seat belts and air bags with a range of 10 percent to 30 percent.

Good Driver Discounts. Discounts vary but many companies offer them to drivers with an accident and violation-free record and to motorists driving fewer than a certain number of miles per year.

Car Pooling. Commuters sharing driving responsibilities may qualify for discounts or a lower price bracket.

Account Credit. Some companies offer discounts of up to 10 percent for insuring your home and auto with the same company.

First Accident Allowance. Some insurers offer a "first accident allowance," which guarantees that if a customer achieves five accident-free years, his rates won't go up after his first at-fault accident.

Anti-Theft Device Credits. Discounts of 5 to 15 percent are offered in some states for cars equipped with a hood lock and an alarm or a disabling device (active or passive) that prevents the car from being started.

Sole Female Driver. Some companies offer discounts of 10 percent for females, ages 30 to 64, who are the only driver in a household, citing favorable claims experience.

Non-Drinkers and Non-Smokers. A limited number of companies offer incentives to abstain.

Occupation Discounts. Some companies give discounts to certain professions whose members have proved to be less accident-prone.

Uninsured Motorist Coverage. In states where it isn't required, consumers with applicable health insurance may not want this coverage.

Optional Coverages. Consumers with substantial health insurance could decide not to take medical payments coverage.

Rental Cars. If you regularly rent cars, special coverage on your personal auto insurance can cover you while renting for far less than rental agencies offer.

The risk of your car being stolen is an important factor in the cost of your insurance. The market is flooded with expensive devices designed to prevent theft, yet nearly 80 percent of all stolen cars were unlocked and 40 percent actually had the keys in the ignition. Most of these thefts were by amateurs. While the most important thing you can do to protect your car is to keep it locked and remove the keys, this will not protect you from the pros. If you live or travel in an area susceptible to car thefts or have a high-priced car, there are some steps you can take to prevent theft.

Inexpensive Theft Prevention

- Replace door lock buttons with tapered tips. This will make it difficult to hook the lock with a wire hanger. (But it will also deter you from breaking into your own car!)
- Buy an alarm sticker (even though you don't have an alarm) and put it on one of your windows.
- Buy an electric etching tool (about $15) and write your driver's license number in the lower corners of the windows or on unpainted metal items where it can be seen. Many new car dealers offer this service for approximately $150. Their marking techniques will be more sophisticated and will be entered into a nationwide computer system available to law enforcement officials. Many police departments offer a similar service at no charge. They will provide a sticker and enter the number into their records.

The purpose of these identifying marks is to deter the professional thief who is planning to take the car apart and sell the various components. Because the parts can be traced, your car becomes much less attractive.

- Remove the distributor wire. This is a rather inconvenient but effective means of rendering your car inoperable. However, if you are parking in a particularly suspect place or leaving your car for a long time you may want to try this. On the top of the distributor, there is a short wire running to the coil. Removing the wire makes it impossible to start the car.

More Serious Measures

- Cutting off the fuel to the engine will keep someone from driving very far with your car. For around $125 you can have a fuel cutoff device installed which will enable you to open or close the gasoline line to the engine. One drawback is that the thief will be able to drive up to a few blocks before he or she runs out of gas. If your car is missing, check your neighborhood first!
- Another device to deter the pro is to install a second ignition switch. In order to start your car, you will have to activate a hidden switch. Time is the thief's worst enemy and the longer it takes to start your car, the more likely the thief is to give up.
- The most common anti-theft devices on the market are alarms. These can cost anywhere from $100 to $500 installed. Their complexity ranges from simply setting off your horn when someone opens your door to setting off elaborate sirens when someone merely bumps the car. Alarms require that the car have an exterior key-operated switch so that you can turn it off and on. Some people simply buy the switch, mount it on their car, and hope that its presence will intimidate the thief.

The Highway Loss Data Institute regularly compiles statistics on car thefts. In rating the cars, they consider the frequency of the theft and the loss resulting from the theft. The result is an index based on "relative average loss payments per insured vehicle year." The value of 100 represents the average of all cars for the model year. Values over 100 indicate that the car model has a higher history of being stolen or broken into.

Theft Index

Car	Theft Rate Index
Dodge Aries SW	4
Dodge Colt Vista SW	11
Plymouth Caravelle 4dr.	11
Toyota Tercel SW	13
Chevrolet Cavalier SW	14
Chevrolet Citation 4dr.	14
Ford LTD SW	14
Subaru DL/GL SW	14
Chevrolet Spectrum 2dr.	15
Mercury Topaz 4dr.	15
Plymouth Reliant 4dr.	15
Plymouth Reliant SW	15
Ford Escort SW	16
Honda Civic SW	16
Mercury Marquis 4dr.	16
Chevrolet Chevette 4dr.	17
Ford Tempo 4dr.	17
Plymouth Horizon 4dr.	17
Plymouth Voyager Van	17
Buick Century SW	18
Mazda GLC 2dr.	18
Mercury Topaz 2dr.	18
Chevrolet Nova 4dr.	19
Chevrolet Sprint 2dr.	19
Oldsmobile Cutlass Ciera SW	19
Toyota Tercel 2dr.	19
Chevrolet Celebrity SW	20
Dodge Aries 4dr.	20
Dodge Caravan Van	20
Dodge 600 4dr.	20
Ford LTD 4dr.	20
Ford Tempo 2dr.	20
Subaru DL/GL 4WD SW	20
Toyota Tercel 4WD SW	20
Dodge Omni 4dr.	21

Car	Theft Rate Index
Ford Escort 4dr.	21
Volvo 240 SW	21
Buick Skyhawk 4dr.	22
Buick Skylark 4dr.	22
Plymouth Gran Fury 4dr.	22
Dodge Aries 2dr.	23
Renault Alliance 4dr.	23
Ford Escort 2dr.	24
Honda Civic 2dr.	24
Mercury Lynx 2dr.	24
Nissan Maxima SW	24
Nissan Sentra SW	24
Pontiac 6000 SW	24
Chevrolet Cavalier 4dr.	25
Dodge Colt 4dr.	25
AMC Renault Encore 2dr.	26
Ford Crown Victoria SW	26
Plymouth Reliant 2dr.	26
Subaru Hatchback 2dr.	26
Chrysler LeBaron 4dr.	28
Mercury Grand Marquis SW	28
Plymouth Turismo 2dr.	28
Chevrolet Celebrity 4dr.	29
Plymouth Colt 2dr.	29
Chevrolet Celebrity 2dr.	30
Oldsmobile Firenza 4dr.	30
AMC Renault Alliance 2dr.	31
Dodge 600 2dr.	31
Pontiac Sunbird 2dr.	32
Toyota Tercel 4dr.	32
Chevrolet Cavalier 2dr.	33
Dodge Colt 2dr.	33
Dodge Diplomat 4dr.	33
Chrysler LeBaron GTS 4dr.	34
Oldsmobile Ninety-Eight 2dr.	35

Car	Theft Rate Index
Chevrolet Chevette 2dr.	36
Nissan Sentra 2dr.	36
Volvo 240 4dr.	36
Honda Civic 4dr.	37
Nissan Sentra 4dr.	37
Plymouth Colt 4dr.	37
Pontiac Sunbird 4dr.	37
Subaru DL/GL 4dr.	37
Ford Crown Victoria 4dr.	38
Toyota Corolla 4dr.	38
Chrysler LeBaron 2dr.	39
Chevrolet Astro Van	41
Nissan Stanza 4dr.	41
Buick Century 4dr.	42
Nissan Maxima 4dr.	42
American Eagle SW	43
Renault Encore 4dr.	43
Buick Skyhawk 2dr.	44
Chevrolet Spectrum 4dr.	44
Honda Accord 2dr.	44
Dodge Lancer 4dr.	46
Oldsmobile Cutlass Ciera 4dr.	46
Chevrolet Caprice SW	48
Chrysler LeBaron Conv. Spec.	48
Dodge Charger 2dr.	48
Mazda GLC 4dr.	49
Nissan Pulsar 2dr.	49
Oldsmobile Calais 2dr.	50
Oldsmobile Cutlass Ciera 2dr.	51
Mercury Cougar 2dr.	53
Chevrolet Impala 4dr.	54
Mercury Capri Spec.	57
Nissan 200SX 2dr.	58
Honda Civic CRX Spec.	59
Lincoln Town Car Spec.	59

Theft Index

Car	Theft Rate Index
Ford Thunderbird 2dr.	61
Buick Century 2dr.	62
Honda Accord 4dr.	62
Lincoln Continental Spec.	62
Pontiac Parisienne SW	62
Chrysler NY 5th Ave. 4dr.	63
Mitsubishi Mirage 2dr.	66
Olds Custom Cruiser SW	66
Mitsubishi Galant 4dr.	67
Chrysler New Yorker 4dr.	68
Ford EXP Spec.	68
Mazda 626 4dr.	68
Mitsubishi Tredia 4dr.	70
Oldsmobile Cutlass 4dr.	71
Pontiac Grand Am 2dr.	71
Toyota Camry 4dr.	72
Dodge Daytona 2dr.	73
Pontiac Parisienne 4dr.	74
Volkswagen Vanagon Van	74
Buick Electra 4dr.	77
Toyota Corolla 2dr.	80
Chevrolet Caprice 2dr.	81
Oldsmobile Ninety-Eight 4dr.	82
Cadillac Cimarron 4dr.	83
Honda Prelude 2dr.	84
Oldsmobile Delta 88 4dr.	85
Pontiac Bonneville 4dr.	88
Chrysler Laser 2dr.	90
Subaru GL 4WD 4dr.	95
Chevrolet Caprice 4dr.	96
Dodge 600 Conv. Spec.	96
Mazda 626 2dr.	98
Buick LeSabre 4dr.	99
Volkswagen Golf 4dr.	99

Car	Theft Rate Index
AVERAGE	100
Mitsubishi Cordia 2dr.	102
Pontiac 6000 4dr.	105
Toyota Van	106
Volkswagen Golf 2dr.	106
Volvo 740/760 Spec.	107
Ford Mustang Spec.	108
Buick Somerset 2dr.	115
Mercury Grand Marquis 2dr.	128
Buick LeSabre 2dr.	129
Isuzu Impulse 2dr.	130
Mercury Grand Marquis 4dr.	134
Ford Crown Victoria 2dr.	139
Oldsmobile Delta 88 2dr.	144
Cadillac DeVille 4D Spec.	148
Nissan 300ZX 2+2 Spec.	148
Jaguar XJ6 Spec.	152
Audi 4000 4dr.	154
Pontiac Fiero Spec.	154
Lincoln Mark VII Spec.	162
Toyota MR2 Spec.	162
Ford Mustang Conv. Spec.	167
Audi 5000 Spec.	168
Volkswagen Quantum 4dr.	202
Toyota Cressida 4dr.	211
Volkswagen Jetta 4dr.	215
Nissan 300ZX Spec.	217
Volkswagen Jetta 2dr.	218
BMW 318i/325e 4dr. Spec.	222
Cadillac DeVille 2d Spec.	223
Oldsmobile Cutlass 2dr.	227
Oldsmobile Toronado Spec.	231
Peugeot 505 4dr.	232
Pontiac Grand Prix 2dr.	234

Car	Theft Rate Index
Buick Regal 2dr.	237
Toyota Celica 2dr.	242
BMW 500 series Spec.	251
Volkswagen Scirocco 2dr.	267
BMW 318i/325e 2d Spec.	279
Mercedes 300D Spec.	280
Saab 900 4dr.	322
Chevrolet Monte Carlo 2dr.	323
Cadillac Brougham 4D Spec.	326
Porsche 944 Coupe Spec.	335
Volkswagen GTI 2dr.	345
Mazda RX-7 Spec.	379
Saab 900 2dr.	382
Buick Riviera Spec.	394
Toyota Celica Supra Spec.	397
Pontiac Firebird Spec.	417
Chevrolet Camaro Spec.	434
Cadillac Seville Spec.	488
Mercedes 190 D/E Spec.	547
Mercedes 300 SD/380 SE Spec.	573
Volkswagen Cabriolet Spec.	597
Cadillac Eldorado Spec.	673
Mercedes 500 SEL Spec.	707
Mercedes 380 SL Coupe Spec.	741
Chevrolet Corvette Spec.	795

In order to determine rates, insurance companies often use information like that collected by the Highway Loss Data Institute. The following tables present the history of occupant injury in many of this year's models. although the research is based on data if the design of the model studied is similar to this year's model. In fact, this is how the insurance companies determine the rates for the new cars.

The ratings, ranging from very good to very poor, are based on the frequency of all medical claims filed for cars under personal injury protection coverage. It will nearly always cost you more to insure cars rated "poor" than "good."

You will note that a car's accident history may not match its crash test performance. Such discrepancies arise because the accident history includes drive performance. A sports car, for example, may have good crash test results but a poor accident history because its owners tend to drive recklessly

Finally, because these ratings are based on accident *history*, and most people do not wear safety belts, buying a car with automatic crash protection will improve its occupant injury rating.

Occupant Injury History*

Subcompacts	2 Door	4 Door	Station Wagon
Chevrolet Nova		Average	
Chevrolet Spectrum	Very Poor	Very Poor	
Chevrolet Sprint	Very Poor		
Dodge Colt	Very Poor	Very Poor	
Dodge Omni		Average	
Ford Escort	Poor	Poor	Average
Honda Accord	Average	Average	
Honda Civic	Average		Average
Honda CRX-Si	Poor		
Honda Prelude	Average		
Hyundai Excel		Very Poor	
Mazda 323		Very Poor	
Mitsubishi Cordia	Very Poor		
Mitsubishi Mirage	Very Poor		
Mitsubishi Tredia		Very Poor	
Nissan Pulsar	Very Poor		
Nissan Sentra	Very Poor	Very Poor	Average
Nissan Stanza			Average
Plymouth Colt	Poor	Very Poor	
Plymouth Horizon		Average	
Subaru DL/GL		Very Poor	Average
Subaru Hatchback	Average		
Toyota Corolla	Very Poor	Average	
Toyota MR-2	Average		
Toyota Tercel	Average	Poor	Average
VW Cabriolet Conv.	Average		
Volkswagen Golf	Average	Average	
Volkswagen GTI	Average		
Volkswagen Jetta		Average	
Volkswagen Scirroco	Average		

Occupant Injury History*

Compacts	2 Door	4 Door	Station Wagon
Audi 4000		Average	
BMW 325 e/es	Average	Average	
Buick Skyhawk	Poor	Average	Average
Buick Regal	Average		
Cadillac Cimarron		Average	
Chevrolet Cavalier	Very Poor	Average	Average
Chrysler LeBaron	Average	Average	Good
Chrysler LeBaron GTS		Average	
Dodge Aries	Average	Average	Average
Dodge Daytona	Average		
Dodge Lancer		Average	
Dodge Shadow		Average	
Ford Mustang	Poor		
Ford Mustang Conv.	Average		
Ford Tempo	Poor	Average	
Isuzu Impulse	Poor		
Mazda RX-7	Average		
Mazda 626	Average	Average	
Mercury Topaz	Poor	Average	
Mitsubishi Starion	Average		
Nissan 200 SX	Poor		
Oldsmobile Calais	Average	Average	
Oldsmobile Firenza	Average	Average	Average
Plymouth Colt Vista Wagon			Average
Plymouth Reliant	Average	Average	Average
Pontiac Sunbird	Poor	Average	Average
Pontiac Fiero	Average		
Pontiac Grand Am	Average	Average	
Toyota Camry		Average	
Toyota Celica	Average		
VW Quantum			Good

Intermediates	2 Door	4 Door	Station Wagon
Audi 5000S		Average	
BMW 500 Series		Very Good	
BMW 733/735i		Very Good	
Buick Century	Average	Average	Good
Buick LeSabre		Good	
Buick Regal	Average		
Chevrolet Camaro	Poor		
Chevrolet Celebrity	Average	Average	Average
Chevrolet Corvette	Average		
Chevrolet Monte Carlo	Average		
Chrysler New Yorker		Average	
Dodge 600	Average	Average	
Dodge 600 Conv.	Average		
Ford Taurus		Good	
Ford Thunderbird	Average		
Mercury Cougar	Average		
Mitsubishi Galant		Average	
Nissan Maxima GL		Average	Average
Nissan 300 ZX T	Average		
Oldsmobile Cutlass Ciera	Average	Average	Good
Olds. Cut. Supreme Classic	Average	Good	
Oldsmobile Delta 88		Good	

Occupant Injury History *

Intermediates	2 Door	4 Door	Station Wagon
Peugeot 505 T		Good	
Plymouth Caravelle		Average	
Pontiac Bonneville		Average	
Pontiac Firebird	Average		
Pontiac Grand Prix	Average		
Pontiac 6000	Average	Average	Very Good
Porsche 944	Very Good		
Saab 900	Good	Very Good	
Toyota Cressida		Average	
Volvo DL		Good	Very Good
Volvo 760		Average	

Large	2 Door	4 Door	Station Wagon
Buick Electra		Very Good	Very Good
Cadillac Brougham		Very Good	
Cadillac DeVille	Average	Very Good	
Chevrolet Astro			Very Good
Chevrolet Caprice	Good	Very Good	Very Good
Chrysler 5th Ave		Good	
Dodge Caravan			Very Good
Dodge Diplomat		Very Good	
Ford Aerostar			Very Good
Ford LTD Crown Victoria	Good	Very Good	Very Good
Jaguar XJ-6		Very Good	
Lincoln Continental		Average	
Lincoln Mark VII		Good	
Lincoln Town Car		Very Good	
Mercury Grand Marquis	Very Good	Very Good	Very Good
Olds Custom Cruiser			Very Good
Oldsmobile 98	Good	Good	
Plymouth Gran Fury		Very Good	
Plymouth Voyager			Very Good
Pontiac Safari			Very Good
Toyota Van Wagon			Good
Volkswagen Vanagon			Good

* Based on data collected by the Highway Loss Data Institute, a non-profit, public service organization. HLDI is closely associated with the Insurance Institute for Highway Safety. For more information on this and other work, you may write to the IIHS, 600 Watergate, Washington, D.C. 20037

Bumpers

The main purpose of the bumper is to protect your car in low-speed collisions. Despite this intention, most of us have been victims of a $200 to $400 repair bill resulting from a seemingly minor impact. Because most bumpers offered little or no damage protection in low-speed crashes, for two years the federal government required auto makers to provide bumpers capable of withstanding up to 5 mph crashes with no damage.

Despite consumer satisfaction with these bumpers and despite repair statistics that demonstrated the savings for consumers, in 1983 the federal government rolled back the requirement to 2.5 mph. While this was done to make automobile manufacturers happy, consumers clearly preferred the stronger bumpers.

Some automobile manufacturers are betting that consumers still want better performing bumpers. Thankfully, companies such as Toyota are still offering crash-resistant bumpers.

Ironically, the federal government's own purchasing requirements specify that government cars come equipped with the 5 mph bumpers. There is good reason for this preference. Even if you do not have an accident, the new, weaker bumpers end up costing you more—many insurance companies have increased premiums on some of the cars with the new bumpers.

The Insurance Institute for Highway Safety conducts extensive tests of car bumpers to determine differences in the way bumpers perform their job. The results are rather startling when you consider that the sole purpose of a bumper is to protect a car from damage in low speed collisions. Only about one-third of the cars tested to date had bumpers which prevented damage in front and rear 5 mph collisions. As the Institute's figures show, there is no correlation between the price of the car and how well the bumper worked.

The following table lists the results of the IIHS bumper crashes from the best to the worst performers.

Bumper Bashing - Test Results
Damage Repair Costs in 5 MPH Crash Tests

Car (Year, Sticker Price)	Front Crash	Rear Crash	Total Cost
AMC Alliance (86, $5,999)	$0	$0	$0
Buick Skylark (87, $9,915)	$0	$0	$0
Chev. Chevette (86, $5,645)	$0	$0	$0
Ford Escort (86, $6,052)	$0	$0	$0
Ford Taurus (87, $11,622)	$0	$0	$0
Honda Accord (87, $10,625)	$0	$0	$0
Mazda 323 (86, $5,645)	$0	$0	$0
Mercury Sable (87, $12,340)	$0	$0	$0
Nissan 200SX (86, $9,549)	$0	$0	$0
Olds. Ciera (87, $10,940)	$0	$0	$0
Olds. Firenza (87, $8,449)	$0	$0	$0
Plymouth Colt (86, $5,633)	$0	$0	$0
Toyota Celica (86, $9,398)	$0	$0	$0
Toyota Corolla (86, $8,408)	$0	$0	$0
Toyota Tercel (86, $5,598)	$0	$0	$0
Pontiac Sunbird (87, $7,999)	$0	$13	$13
Chev. Corsica (87, $8,995)	$40	$0	$40
Mazda 626 (86, $9,245)	$0	$42	$42
Nissan Stanza (87, $10,449)	$0	$53	$53
Toyota Camry (87, $10,998)	$67	$0	$67
Nissan Pulsar (86, $8,749)	$97	$0	$97
Buick Skyhawk (87, $8,559)	$124	$0	$124
Mitsubishi Cordia (86, $8,949)	$125	$0	$125
Chry. LeBaron GTS (87, $10,152)	$19	$113	$132
Pontiac 6000 (87, $10,499)	$55	$88	$143
Honda Civic (86, $5,649)	$0	$155	$155
Subaru DL (86, $7,960)	$179	$0	$179
Pontiac Grand Am (87, $9,499)	$79	$120	$199
Dodge Charger (86, $6,787)	$113	$91	$204
Isuzu I-Mark (86, $7,149)	$72	$155	$227
Ford Tempo GL (87, $8,310)	$221	$12	$233
Olds. Calais (87, $9,741)	$216	$35	$251
Chev. Sprint (86, $5,380)	$92	$164	$256
Chev. Cavalier (87, $7,449)	$25	$248	$273
Buick Century (87, $10,989)	$204	$73	$277
Chrysler Laser (86, $9,364)	$175	$104	$279
VW Jetta (86, $8,325)	$135	$170	$305
VW Golf (86, $7,350)	$86	$269	$355
Plymouth Reliant (87, $8,364)	$127	$284	$411
Chrysler LeBaron (87, $10,707)	$208	$211	$419
Nissan Sentra (86, $5,649)	$147	$338	$485
Dodge 600 (87, $10,010)	$261	$332	$593
Chev. Celebrity (87, $10,265)	$350	$265	$615
Yugo GV (86, $3,990)	$256	$399	$655
VW Scirocco (86, $9,980)	$320	$348	$668

These tables are based on studies conducted by the Insurance Institute for Highway Safety. For more information on this work you may write to IIHS, 600 Watergate, Washington, D.C. 20037.

The **TIRE** Chapter

For most of us, buying tires has become an infrequent task. The reason is the widespread use of radials, which last longer than the bias and bias-belted tires of the past. However, when we do get around to buying tires, making an informed purchase is not easy. That is not surprising when you consider that the tire is the single most complex item on a car. It has to perform more functions than any other part of the car simultaneously. These functions include maintaining contact with the road to bear the load, steering the vehicle, transmitting power to the road, cushioning the ride, and stopping the vehicle. In addition, all of these functions have to be performed in all kinds of weather and on all kinds of roads.

Tires today last longer, ride smoother, and provide better fuel economy than ever before. The primary reason for these improvements has been the widespread acceptance of the radial tire. Ironically, the tire industry is partially responsible for the recent downturn in tire sales: with tires lasting longer, we are replacing them less frequently. Many new car owners will sell their cars before it's time to replace the tires.

Although the industry is offering better tires than ever before, the selection process is still difficult. At last count, there were nearly 1,800 tire lines to choose from. With only 10 major tire manufacturers selling tires, the difference in many tires may be only the brand name. Because it is so difficult to compare tires, it is easy to understand why many consumers tend to use price and brand name to determine quality. But there is help. The U.S. government has a rating program to help consumers comparison shop for this all-important automotive accessory.

Tire Registration

You may be missing out on free or low-cost replacement tires or, worse, driving on potentially hazardous ones, if you don't fill out the tire registration form when you buy tires. The law once required all tire sellers to submit your name automatically to the manufacturer, so the company could contact you if the tires were ever recalled. While this is still mandatory for tire dealers and distributors owned by tire manufacturers, it is not required for independent tire dealers. A recent government study found that 70% of independent tire dealers had not registered a single tire purchase. Ask for the tire registration card when you buy tires and remember to fill it out and send it in. This information will allow the company to get in touch with you if the tire is ever recalled. For information about auto tire care and safety, send a business-size, self-addressed stamped envelope to the Tire Industry Safety Council, Box 1801, Dept. CB, Washington, D.C. 20013. Ask for the "Consumer Tire Guide" or the "Recreational Vehicle Consumer Tire Guide."

There are three basic types of tires on the market today: Bias Ply, Belted Bias, and Radial.

Bias Ply tires (8 percent of sales) have been on the market since the 1920s. This type of tire is made with layers (or plies) of cords which crisscross each other. These cords may be arranged in two or more (even numbered) layers. The more layers, the stronger the tire.

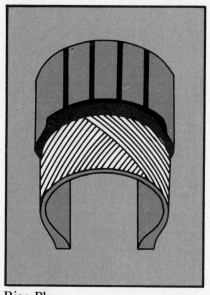

Bias Ply

Belted Bias tires (7 percent of sales) have cords arranged in a criss-cross pattern (like bias ply) as well as two or more layers of fabric or steel "belts" over the cords. This process increases the overall strength of the tire. Belted tires tend to run cooler and therefore last longer than bias ply tires.

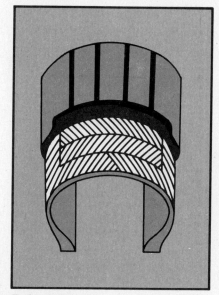

Belted Bias

Radial tires (85 percent of sales) are provided on most new cars sold in America. The cords in a radial tire run at right angles to the center line and may be in one to three layers (plies). Over this radial section is added a four-ply belt whose cords run at a slight angle to the center line of the tire. The result is a tire with a flexible sidewall (that's why radials often look like they need air) but with stiffness and strength in the tread. These characteristics add up to longer tread life and improved fuel efficiency.

Snow and **"all-season"** are two subcategories of tires. Snow tires have an open tread pattern with deep grooves. If you are in an area with intermittent snow, a deep-groove snow tire will wear out rapidly on dry roads. Because of this and the inconvenience of seasonally changing your tires, "all-season" tires are becoming popular. These tires are effective in occasional snow, have good traction on wet roads, and last longer than snow tires on dry roads.

Finally, there are **retreads.** In building a tire, adding the tread is the last step of the process. A retreader takes undamaged used tires, strips off the remaining tread and repeats the last step of the original manufacturing process. Retreads can save 30 to 50 percent over the price of a similar new tire and high-quality retreads perform nearly as well. The National Tire Dealers and Retreaders Association (NTDRA) rates retread plants on a scale of A to F. A and B are passing, with A being the best. When buying a retread, be sure to ask for the manufacturer's NTDRA rating.

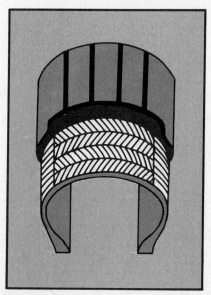

Radial

To select the best tire, there are three important considerations: 1. How long you plan to keep your car; 2. Whether the majority of your driving is highway or local; and, 3. Higher prices do not necessarily mean better tires.

If you often drive on wet roads, buy a tire with a high traction grade (see below). If you do a lot of high speed driving, a high heat resistance grade is best (see below).

Radial and belted bias tires give greater tread life than bias ply tires. For long-distance highway driving, radial tires generally give the most tread life.

Properly inflated radial tires will give you better fuel economy than other tires. Never mix radials with other tire types.

When to replace. If any part of Lincoln's head is visible when you insert the top of a penny into a tread grove, it's time to replace the tire. While this old rule of thumb is still valid, today's tires have a built-in wear indicator. A series of horizontal bars will appear across the surface of your tire when the tread depth reaches the danger zone.

Tread design. Look for a tread design that is made up of independent blocks arranged in a staggered fashion. These new designs have grooves that run from side to side in order to displace more water for better traction on wet roads. Most "all-season" tires have this tread pattern.

Load range. Check the tire's load range to ensure that the tires are adequate for your driving needs. The maximum load is printed on each tire. The higher the load range the more weight you can carry. To insure the tires are adequate, add your car's weight (in your owner's manual) and the weight of your average payload (passengers and baggage) and divide by four. This number should never exceed the maximum load printed on each tire.

Where to buy. Most tires are sold at one of four outlets: independent dealers (large national chains and small stores which carry a number of brands), department stores (Sears, K-Mart, Penney's), tire company stores (Goodyear, Uniroyal) and service stations.

The price of the same tire can vary depending on where you shop. It is not uncommon for competing stores on the same street to offer the same tire at different prices. Because of this, shopping around is vital to finding a good buy. This task is made somewhat easier by the fact that most tire ads are grouped together in the sports section of your daily newspaper on Wednesdays and Saturdays.

The most expensive place to buy tires is at a new car dealership, with service stations a close second. You are most likely to find your best prices at independent tire dealers who carry a variety of tire brands.

You can also buy tires by mail. For most consumers, buying by mail doesn't make sense. While you may save a little in the price of the tire, you have to pay shipping, and when they arrive, you have to take the tires to a service station and pay for mounting and balancing.

How to read a tire. Manufacturers are required by law to provide certain information on the sidewall of a tire. In addition to the tire grades and load range, you can find: maximum inflation in pounds per square inch, tire size, composition of the cord, number of plies (sidewall and tread), whether the tire is tubeless and the serial number. The serial number contains four parts. The "DOT" at the beginning indicates that the tire meets federal safety standards, the next two letters indicate who made the tire, and the last three numbers on the tire indicate when it was manufactured. (The number 107, for instance, would indicate the tire was made the tenth week of 1987.)

A New Way to Compare Tires

It is very difficult for most of us to tell the difference between one tire and another. This confusion is compounded by the advertising terminology that is used to describe tires. One company's definition of "first line" or "premium" may be entirely different from another's. As a way of helping consumers compare tires, the government now requires tires to have mileage and safety ratings. This little-known system grades tires according to treadwear, traction, and heat resistance. These grades are printed on the sidewall and attached to the tire on a paper label. In addition, every dealer can provide you with the grades of the tires he or she sells. The system works like this:

Treadwear: The treadwear grade gives you an idea of how much mileage to expect from a tire. It is shown in numbers—90, 100, 110, 120, and so forth. A tire graded 150 should give you 50 percent more mileage than one graded 100. In order to estimate the expected mileage, multiply the treadwear grade by 200. Under average conditions a tire graded 150 (times 200) should last 30,000 miles. Because individual driving habits vary considerably, it is best to use the treadwear as a relative basis of comparison rather than an absolute predictor of mileage. Also remember that tire wear is affected by regional differences in the level of abrasive material used in road surfaces. (See the following map.)

Traction: Traction is graded A, B, and C and describes the tire's ability to stop on wet surfaces. Tires graded A will stop on a wet road in a shorter distance than tires graded B or C. Tires rated C have poor traction. If you often drive on wet roads, buy a tire with a high traction grade.

Heat resistance: Heat resistance is also graded A, B, and C. This grading is important because hot-running tires can result in blowouts or tread separation. An A rating means the tire will run cooler than one rated B or C and is less likely to fail if driven over long distances at highway speeds. In addition, tires that run cooler tend to be more fuel efficient. If you do a lot of high-speed driving, a high-heat-resistance grade is best.

The tables at the end of this section list the highest rated tires on the market. For a complete listing of all the tires on the market, call the Auto Safety Hotline, toll free, at 800-424-9393. (In DC call 426-0123.)

Tire Pricing: Getting the Best Value

There are few consumer products on the market today that are as price competitive as tires. While this situation provides a buyer's market, it does require some price shopping.

The price of each tire is based on the size of the tire and each tire may come in up to nine sizes. For example, the list price of the same Goodyear Arriva tire can range from $74.20 to $134.35, depending on its size. In fact, some manufacturers do not provide list prices, leaving the appropriate markup to the individual retailer. Even when list prices are provided, dealers rarely use them. Instead, they offer tires at what is called an "everyday low price," which can range from 10 to 25 percent below list.

Here are some tips for getting the best buy:

1. Check to see which manufacturer makes the least expensive "off brand". Only ten major manufacturers produce the over 1,800 types of tires sold in the U.S. So you can save dollars and still get high quality.

2. Remember: generally, the wider the tire, the higher the price. (Tire width is described by the aspect ratio, which is the height-to-width ratio of a tire's cross section. The lower the profile number, the wider the tire.)

3. Don't forget to inquire about balancing and mounting costs when comparing tire prices. Inquire about the extra charges for balancing, mounting, and valve stems. In some stores these charges can add up to more than $25. Other stores may offer them as a customer service at little or no cost. That good buy in the newspaper may turn into a poor value when coupled with these extra costs. Also, compare warranties; they do vary from company to company.

4. Never pay list price for a tire. A good rule of thumb is to pay at least 30 to 40 percent off the suggested list price.

5. Use the treadwear grade the same way you would the "unit price" in a supermarket. It is the best way to ensure that you are getting the best tire value. The tire with the lowest cost per grade point is the best value. For example, if tire A costs $100 and has a treadwear grade of 300, and tire B costs $80 and has a treadwear grade of 200:

Tire A:
$100 ÷ 300 = $.33 per point

Tire B:
$80 ÷ 200 = $.40 per point

Since 33 cents is less than 40 cents, tire A is the better buy.

Which Tires Last the Longest?

For most of us, mileage is one of the most important qualities of a tire. However, few of us realize that where we live is a key factor in determining how long tires will last. In addition to construction and design, tire wear is affected by the level of abrasive material in the road surface. Generally, the West Coast, the Great Lakes region, and northern New England have road surfaces that are easiest on tires. The Appalachian and Rocky Mountain areas are hardest on tires.

To estimate a tire's treadlife, look at the accompanying map to determine whether you live in a high-, medium-, or low-mileage area. Then use the treadwear grade of the tires you are considering to estimate their treadlife for your area. For example, if you are considering tires with a treadwear grade of 150, you can expect those tires to get about 45,000 miles in a high-mileage area, 30,000 miles in a medium-mileage area, and 22,500 miles in a low-mileage area. *Of course, your actual mileage will depend not only on where you drive, but also on how you drive and whether you keep your tires properly inflated and your wheels aligned.*

What You Can Expect from Your Tires

Treadwear Grade	High-mileage Area	Medium-mileage Area	Low-mileage Area
50	15,000	10,000	7,500
60	18,000	12,000	9,000
70	21,000	14,000	10,500
80	24,000	16,000	12,000
90	27,000	18,000	13,500
100	30,000	20,000	15,000
110	33,000	22,000	16,500
120	36,000	24,000	18,000
130	39,000	26,000	19,500
140	42,000	28,000	21,000
150	45,000	30,000	22,500
160	48,000	32,000	24,000
170	51,000	34,000	25,500
180	54,000	36,000	27,000
190	57,000	38,000	28,500
200	60,000	40,000	30,000
210	63,000	42,000	31,500
220	66,000	44,000	33,000
230	69,000	46,000	34,500
240	72,000	48,000	36,000
250	75,000	50,000	37,500
260	78,000	52,000	39,000
270	81,000	54,000	40,500
280	84,000	56,000	42,000
290	87,000	58,000	43,500
300	90,000	60,000	45,000
310	93,000	62,000	46,500
320	96,000	64,000	48,000
330	99,000	66,000	49,500
340	102,000	68,000	51,000

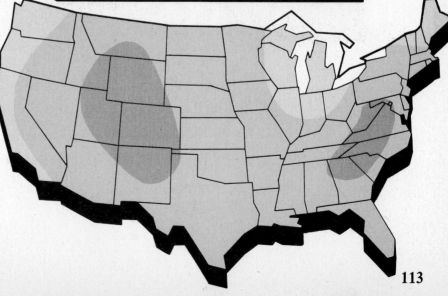

High-Mileage Area

Medium-Mileage Area

Low-Mileage Area

Tire Grades
Top Rated Radials

Brand Name	Model	Description	Grades			Expected Mileage		
			Tread.	Trac.	Heat	Low	Medium	High
Radial								
General	AmeriClassic	15	A	B	350	52,500	70,000	105,000
General	AmeriClassic	14	A	B	340	51,000	68,000	102,000
Michelin	XH	All	A	B	330	49,500	66,000	99,000
General	AmeriClassic	13	A	B	330	49,500	66,000	99,000
All American	Pacemaker SR	All	A	C	320	48,000	64,000	96,000
CBI	Cordovan	All	A	C	320	48,000	64,000	96,000
CBI	Multi Mile	All	A	C	320	48,000	64,000	96,000
Co-op	Pacemaker SR 60,70	All	A	C	320	48,000	64,000	96,000
Concorde	Trac Action	All	A	C	320	48,000	64,000	96,000
Cornell	SS G/T	All	A	C	320	48,000	64,000	96,000
Doral	Revenger HP	All	A	C	320	48,000	64,000	96,000
Douglas	Gran Trac	All	A	C	320	48,000	64,000	96,000
Gillette	Sprint G/T	All	A	C	320	48,000	64,000	96,000
Hallmark	Super GT Sport	All	A	C	320	48,000	64,000	96,000
Jetzon	Revenger	All	A	C	320	48,000	64,000	96,000
Kelly	Charger SR	All	A	C	320	48,000	64,000	96,000
Lee	Turbo Action	All	A	C	320	48,000	64,000	96,000
Monarch	Road Hugger	All	A	C	320	48,000	64,000	96,000
Montgomery Ward	Gas Miser 70	All	A	C	320	48,000	64,000	96,000
Multi-Mile	XL Glass/G/T/60	All	A	C	320	48,000	64,000	96,000
Patriot	Performance 60-70	All*	A	C	320	48,000	64,000	96,000
NTP	Pacemark	All	A	C	320	48,000	64,000	96,000
Peerless	Sprint	All	A	C	320	48,000	64,000	96,000
Ram	Invader	All	A	C	320	48,000	64,000	96,000
Republic	Road Rebel	All	A	C	320	48,000	64,000	96,000
Shell	70	All	A	C	320	48,000	64,000	96,000
Star	Super Star	All	A	C	320	48,000	64,000	96,000
Sigma	Grnd Spt G/T 60-70	All	A	C	320	48,000	64,000	96,000
Vanderbilt	Turbo Tech 60-70	All	A	C	320	48,000	64,000	96,000
Vogue	Custom	14&15	B	C	320	48,000	64,000	96,000
Winston	RWL 60,70	All	A	C	320	48,000	64,000	96,000
Winston	Signature-L	All	A	C	320	48,000	64,000	96,000
Michelin	XA4,X24	All	A	B	310	46,500	62,000	93,000
Sears	RD Handler	All	A	B	310	46,500	62,000	93,000

*All except p-metric

Tire Grades
Top Rated Radials

Brand Name	Model	Description	Grades			Expected Mileage		
			Tread.	Trac.	Heat	Low	Medium	High
Brigadier	B/G505	14&15	A	C	300	45,000	60,000	90,000
Cordovan	Grnd Prix G/T 60,70	All	B	C	300	45,000	60,000	90,000
Cornell	1000	All	A	C	300	45,000	60,000	90,000
Coronell	1000	14&15	A	C	300	45,000	60,000	90,000
Escort	Premium	14&15	B	C	300	45,000	60,000	90,000
Escort	Premium 5000	14&15	B	C	300	45,000	60,000	90,000
Empco	Supreme	14&15	B	C	300	45,000	60,000	90,000
Goodrich	Advantage	All*	A	C	300	45,000	60,000	90,000
Lee	Arizonian	All	A	C	300	45,000	60,000	90,000
Multi-Mile	Grand Am SE	All	A	C	300	45,000	60,000	90,000
Phillips	66xPR	14&15	B	C	300	45,000	60,000	90,000
Reynolds	VIP	14&15	B	C	300	45,000	60,000	90,000
Safemark	220 SX	14&15	B	C	300	45,000	60,000	90,000
Shell	2000	All	A	C	300	45,000	60,000	90,000
Sonic	Golden	14&15	B	C	300	45,000	60,000	90,000
Toyo	800	13&14	B	B	300	45,000	60,000	90,000
Toyo	800&P-70 Series	15	A	B	300	45,000	60,000	90,000
Winston	Classic Steel	All	A	C	300	45,000	60,000	90,000
Centennial	Constitution	14&15	A	B	290	43,500	58,000	87,000
Co-op	Golden Mark	All	A	C	290	43,500	58,000	87,000
Detroiter	Supreme 70 SBR	All*	A	C	290	43,500	58,000	87,000
Diamond	Supreme 70	All*	A	C	290	43,500	58,000	87,000
Dunlop	Elite	14&15	A	B	290	43,500	58,000	87,000
Medalist	Supreme 70 SBR	All**	A	C	290	43,500	58,000	87,000
Montgomery Ward	Grappler	All*	A	B	290	43,500	58,000	87,000
Regal	T/L Supra	All*	A	C	290	43,500	58,000	87,000
Remington	Society	14&15	A	B	290	43,500	58,000	87,000
Sears	All Season	All	A	B	290	43,500	58,000	87,000
Stratton	Super/Supreme	All*	A	C	290	43,500	58,000	87,000
Atlas	Conquest	14&15	B	C	280	42,000	56,000	84,000
Atlas	Pinnacle	15	B	C	280	42,000	56,000	84,000
Atlas	Radial A/W	14&15	B	C	280	42,000	56,000	84,000
Co-op	Co-operator	All	B	C	280	42,000	56,000	84,000
Co-op	Golden Mark P195	14	A	C	280	42,000	56,000	84,000
Continental	CS75	14&15	B	B	280	42,000	56,000	84,000
Cooper	Discoverer	All	B	C	280	42,000	56,000	84,000
Cooper	Lifeliner	15	B	C	280	42,000	56,000	84,000
Cordovan	Bonneville Gr Prix	All	B	C	280	42,000	56,000	84,000
Cornell	1000	13	A	C	280	42,000	56,000	84,000
Cornell	900	14&15	A	C	280	42,000	56,000	84,000

*All except p-metric
**All except 205,7 or 14

Americans spend billions of dollars on auto repairs every year. While most of those repairs are done to customers' satisfaction, there are times when getting a car fixed is a very difficult process. In fact, automobile defects and repairs are the number-one cause of consumer complaints in the U.S., according to the Federal Trade Commission. This section is designed to help you resolve your complaint, whether it involves a car you have had for years or a new car still under warranty.

No matter what your problem, keep accurate records. Copies of the following items are nearly indispensable in helping to resolve your problems:

- Your service invoices
- Bills you have paid
- Letters you have written to the manufacturer or the repair facility owner
- Written repair estimates from independent mechanics

Complaint Checklist

If you are having trouble you may want to take the following steps:

1

Return your car to the repair facility that did the work. Bring a written list of the problems.

Keep a copy of the list. Give the repair facility a reasonable opportunity to fix your car. Speak directly to the service manager (not the service writer who wrote up your original repair order). Ask the manager to test-drive the car with you so you can point out the problem.

2

If you can't get the problem resolved, take the car to a mechanic you trust for an independent examination. This may cost $25 to $30. Get a written statement defining the problem and telling how it may be fixed. Give your repair shop a copy. If your car is under warranty, do not allow any warranty repair by an independent mechanic; you may not be able to receive reimbursement from the manufacturer.

3

If your repair shop does not respond to the independent assessment, present your problem to a complaint-handling panel. If the problem is with a new-car dealer or you feel the manufacturer is responsible, you may be able to use one of the automobile arbitration programs discussed on the following pages.

If the problem is solely with an independent dealer, a local

Better Business Bureau may be able to mediate your complaint. It may also be able to offer an arbitration hearing. In any case the BBB should enter your complaint into its files on that particular establishment.

When contacting any complaint-handling program, determine how long it takes, who makes the final decision, whether you are bound by that decision, and whether the panel handles all problems or only warranty complaints.

4

If there are no mediation panels, contact private consumer groups or local government agencies. A phone call or letter from them may persuade a repair facility to take action. Or call or write to your local "action line" newspaper columnist, newspaper editor, or radio or TV broadcaster. Send a copy of your letter to the repair shop.

5

Bring suit against the dealer, manufacturer, or repair facility in small claims court. The fee for filing an action in such a court is usually small, and you generally act as your own attorney, saving attorney's fees. There is a monetary limit on the amount you can claim, which varies from state to state. Your local consumer affairs office, state attorney general's office, or the clerk of the court should be able to tell you how to file such a suit.

6

Talk with an attorney. It's best to select an attorney who is familiar with handling automotive problems. If you don't know of one, call the lawyer referral service listed in the telephone directory and ask for the names of attorneys who deal with automobile problems. If you can't afford an attorney, contact your Legal Aid society.

Warranty Complaints

If your car is under warranty or you are having problems with a factory-authorized dealership, there are some special steps you can take:

1

Have the warranty available to show the dealer if the problem comes up during the warranty period. Make sure you call the problem to the

dealer's attention before the end of the warranty period.

2

If you are still unsatisfied after giving the dealer a reasonable opportunity to fix your car, contact the manufacturer's representative (also called the zone representative) in your area. This person can authorize the dealer to make repairs or take other steps to resolve the dispute. Your dealer will have your zone representative's name and telephone number. Explain the problem and ask for a meeting and a personal inspection of your car.

3

If you can't get satisfaction from the zone representative, call or write the manufacturer's owner relations department. Your owner's manual contains the phone number and address.

4

Present your problem to a complaint-handling panel or the arbitration program in which the manufacturer of your car participates. See the

following pages for information.

5

If you complain of a problem during the warranty period, you have a right to have the problem fixed even after the warranty runs out. If your warranty has not been honored, you may be able to "revoke acceptance"—that is, return the car to the dealer. If you are successful, you may be entitled to a replacement car or a full refund of the purchase price and reimbursement of legal fees under the Magnuson-Moss Warranty Act. Or, if you are covered by one of the state Lemon Laws, you may be able to return the car and receive a refund or replacement from the manufacturer. For more information on Lemon Laws see the following pages.

You may also contact the Center for Auto Safety, 2001 S St., NW, Washington, DC 20009. The Center can provide the names of lawyers in your area who have handled automobile consumer problems. The Center also has published *The Lemon Book*, a detailed, 236-page guide to resolving automobile complaints. The book is available for $8.60 from the Center.

With the passage of the new Lemon Laws, one of the most popular methods of resolving automobile repair problems is through arbitration. In most cases, both parties present their cases to a mediator or arbitration panel which decides on the merits of the complaint.

In general, arbitration panels can be an effective means of resolving disputes. They are somewhat informal and relatively speedy, and you do not need a lawyer to present your case. If you can remedy a problem through arbitration, you can avoid the time and expense of going to court.

Almost all manufacturers now have, or subscribe to, arbitration programs. Ford and Chrysler have their own systems; others subscribe to programs set up by the Better Business Bureau (BBB) or the National Automobile Dealers Association's AUTOCAP program. (See the next page for the name of the program in which each manufacturer participates.) Look in your owner's manual and warranty for more information on programs you may be entitled to use.

You may seek repairs, reimbursement for expenses, a refund or replacement of your car through these programs.

Upon receiving your complaint, the arbitration program will attempt to mediate a resolution between you and the manufacturer or dealer. If you are not satisfied with the proposed solution, you have the right to have your case heard at an arbitration hearing.

These hearings vary among the programs. In the BBB program, you will get the chance to present your case, in person, to a volunteer arbitrator. The other programs, generally, will decide your case based on written submissions by you and the manufacturer.

If an arbitration program is incorporated into your warranty (see The Warranty Chapter), you may have to use the program before filing a legal claim. (Note: You may always go to small claims court instead of arbitration.) Federal law requires that arbitration programs incorporated in a warranty be non-binding on the consumer. That is, if you do not like the result, you can seek other remedies.

Different arbitration programs have different eligibility requirements, so be sure you are eligible for the program you are considering. Remember, you do not have to have a Lemon Law in your state in order to participate in arbitration programs.

Let the Federal Trade Commission, the Center for Auto

Ford Appeals Board: This was one of the first panels established by a manufacturer. Each case is considered by a five-person panel which includes two dealers. The dealers have no vote in warranty cases. A recent review of the cases turned up the following statistics on the panel's decisions: about half of the consumers did not receive what they asked for, about one-quarter received something less than what they asked for, and the remaining quarter got the resolution that they asked for. For more information call 800-241-8450, toll-free.

Chrysler Customer Satisfaction Board: No oral presentations are given under this program. All decisions are based on written submissions by each party. A Chrysler zone representative and dealer are on the panel but they cannot vote. The promotional material describing the program indicates the panel will hear only cases under warranty. If pressed, however, in certain states (Alabama, Connecticut, District of Columbia, Kansas, Safety (their addresses are on the following pages) and your state Attorney General (c/o your state capitol) know of your experience with arbitration. It is particularly important to contact these offices if you have a complaint about how your case was handled.

Maine, Maryland, Massachusetts, Minnesota, Mississippi, New Hampshire, Vermont, Washington and West Virginia), Chrysler will sometimes hear cases beyond the warranty.

Generally, just under half of the cases are settled to the satisfaction of the consumer. For more information, contact Chrysler Customer Satisfaction Board, Box 1919, Detroit, MI 48288.

Better Business Bureau Arbitration Program: The BBB always tries to mediate a dispute before recommending arbitration. Less than 10 percent of the disputes actually go to arbitration. Theoretically, each party receives a list of potential arbitrators with a background description of each person and ranks them according to preference. The arbitrator with the most votes handles the case. In fact, the consumer rarely has a voice in the selection of an arbitrator.

The arbitrators are volunteers from the local community and sometimes are not automobile experts. This can both help and harm your case. As a result, it is important to be well prepared when participating in the BBB program. If not, the potential exists for the dealer or manufacturer to appear as the "expert" on automobiles.

Of the people who actually go to arbitration in the BBB program, surveys show that approximately one-third of the cases are settled in favor of the consumer, one-third split and one-third in favor of the manufacturer. For more information, contact your local BBB.

Automobile Consumer Action Program (AUTOCAP): Currently, most AUTOCAPs do not operate under the FTC guidelines required for warranty cases. Seventy-two percent of the cases that AUTOCAP considers are resolved in mediation. Of those that actually go to arbitration, 52 percent are resolved in favor of the consumer, 19 percent are a compromise and 29 percent are in favor of the company. For more information and the name of your local AUTOCAP, contact: AUTOCAP, 8400 Westpark Drive, McLean, Virginia 22102; 703-821-7144.

Arbitration Programs

Alfa Romeo – AUTOCAP	Mitsubishi – AUTOCAP
AMC/Renault – BBB	Nissan – AUTOCAP and BBB
Audi – BBB	Peugeot – AUTOCAP and BBB
BMW – AUTOCAP	Porsche – BBB
Chrysler – Chrysler Customer Satisfaction Board	Rolls-Royce – AUTOCAP
	Saab-Scania – AUTOCAP and BBB
Fiat – AUTOCAP	Sterling – AUTOCAP
Ford – Ford Appeals Board	Subaru – AUTOCAP
General Motors – BBB	Toyota – AUTOCAP
Honda – AUTOCAP and BBB	Volkswagen – BBB
Isuzu – AUTOCAP	Volvo – AUTOCAP
Jaguar – AUTOCAP	Yugo – AUTOCAP
Mazda – AUTOCAP	

Ten Tips for Arbitration

1. Before deciding to go to arbitration, get a written description of how the program works and make sure you understand the details. If you have any questions, do not hesitate to contact the local representatives of the program. Remember, the manufacturer or dealer most likely has more experience with this than you do.

2. Make sure the final decision is nonbinding on you. If the decision is binding on you, you give up your right to appeal the decision.

3. Determine if the program allows you to appear at the hearing. If not, make sure your written statement is complete and contains all the appropriate receipts and documentation. If you think of something that you want considered after you have sent your material in, send it in and request that the additional information be considered.

4. Make sure the program follows required procedures. If the arbitration program is incorporated into the car's warranty, for example, the panel must make a decision on your case within 40 days of receiving your complaint.

5. Contact the manufacturer's zone manager and request copies of any technical service bulletins that apply to your car. (See "Secret Warranties," in The Warranty Chapter, for a description of technical service bulletins and how to get them.) Service bulletins may help you prove your car is defective.

6. Well before the actual hearing or panel meeting, ask the program representative to send you copies of all material submitted by the other party. You may want to respond to this information.

7. Make sure all your documents are in chronological order, including a brief outline of the events. Submit copies of all material associated with your problem as well as a copy of your warranty.

8. Even though you may be very angry about the situation, try to present your case in a calm, logical manner.

9. If you are asking the program to award you a refund or replacement of your car in accordance with your state Lemon Law, do not assume that the panel or arbitrator is completely familiar with the law. You should be prepared to make clear how the Lemon Law and basic fairness entitle you to what you are asking for.

10. In most programs, you have to reject the decision in order to go to court or pursue other action. Accepting the decision may limit your rights to pursue further action. You will, however, have additional claims if the manufacturer or dealer does not properly perform the decision or if your car breaks down again.

Attention: GM Owners

Have you had problems with your GM engine or transmission that the repair shop cannot seem to fix? If so, General Motors must make arbitration available through the Better Business Bureau for any current owner with an engine or transmission defect, regardless of the age or mileage of the vehicle. Note: If you had problems with a THM 200 transmission, 350 V-8 diesel fuel injection system or the cam shaft or valve lifters in Chevrolet 305 or 350 V-8 gas engines(made before April 27, 1983), you have a right to arbitrate for repair costs *even if you no longer own your car*.

For more information call GM at 800-824-5109 and ask for their information packet and call your local office of the BBB. If you have problems getting help through your local BBB or GM, you can call or write to the FTC Enforcement Division, Washington, DC 20580 (202-326-2996).

A Note on Arbitration

Many times state-run arbitration programs can be more fair to the consumer than national programs. In fact, in five states — Connecticut, District of Columbia, Massachusetts, New York, Texas and Vermont — the Attorney General has set up state-run programs which are far better than their national counterparts. If you live in one of these states, be sure to contact your Attorney General's office for information on using your local arbitration program. Other states often have information on the local arbitration programs and advice on going to arbitration. Again, contact your state Attorney General's office, (in care of your state capitol), and ask for any advice or information they may have on going to arbitration.

Consumer Groups

Aid for Lemon Owners
21711 West Ten Mile Road
Suite 210
Southfield, MI 48075
313-354-1760
Focus: Arbitration, reimbursement of repairs, buy backs

American Lemon Club
205 East Southern Avenue
Covington, KY 41015
606-431-5393
Focus: General problems

Audi Victims Network
777 Old Country Road #2
Plainview, NY 11803
516-933-1922
Focus: Provides assistance to owners of Audis with sudden acceleration problems.

Auto Protection Association
292 St. Joseph Blvd., W.
Montreal, Quebec H2V 2N7
514-273-1366
Focus: General problems

Consumer Action
693 Mission Street
San Francisco, CA 94105
415-777-9635
Focus: General problems

Lemon On Wheels
4044 Connecticut Avenue
Island Park, NY 11558
516-431-6597
Focus: Assistance with Lemon Law and GM Diesel arbitration.

LemonAid
6929 Race Horse Lane
Rockville, MD 20852
301-231-5243
Focus: Arbitration

Motor Voters
Box 3163
Falls Church, VA 22043
703-448-0002
Focus: Auto safety and air bags

Consumers United to Reform BBB
P.O. Box 7228
Washington, D.C. 20004
Focus: Assistance with BBB arbitration programs.

Legal Aid

If you find you need legal assistance with your repair problem, the Center for Auto Safety has compiled a list of lawyers who specialize in helping consumers with auto repair problems. For the names of some attorneys in your area, send a stamped, self-addressed envelope to: Center for Auto Safety, 2001 S Street, NW, Washington, D.C. 20009.

Attorneys Take Note: If you would like information on litigation assistance provided by the Center for Auto Safety, including *The Lemon Law Litigation Manual*, please contact the Center for Auto Safety at the above address.

Center for Auto Safety

Every year the automobile manufacturers spend millions of dollars to ensure that their voices are heard in government decision-making. For example, General Motors and Ford have large staffs in Detroit and Washington whose sole job is to attempt to influence government activity. But who looks out for the consumer?

For eighteen years, the nonprofit Center for Auto Safety has been the consumer's representative in Washington. During this time the Center has told the "consumer's side of the story" to government agencies, the federal government, Congress, and the courts. Its efforts are directed at the broad base of consumers rather than individual complaints.

The Center for Auto Safety was established in 1970 by Ralph Nader and Consumers' Union. As consumer concerns about automobile safety issues expanded, so did the work of the Center. It became an independent consumer group in 1973, and its original staff of two has increased to fourteen attorneys, researchers, and engineers.

The Center's activities include:

Initiating Safety Recalls: The Center analyzes more than 20,000 consumer complaints each year. By following problems as they develop, the Center can request government investigations and recalls of defective vehicles. The Center was responsible for the Ford Pinto faulty gas tank recall and for the Firestone 500 steel-belted radial tire recall.

The Center continues to publicize other defects and push for recalls. The largest pending recall effort involves 1970-1980 Ford vehicles with automatic transmissions that jump from park to reverse, often causing extensive damage, injury, and deaths.

Representing the Consumer in Washington: The Center follows the activities of federal agencies and Congress to ensure that they carry out their responsibilities to the American taxpayer. The Center also brings a consumer's point of view to vehicle safety policies and rule-making activities. Since 1970 the Center has submitted more than 200 petitions and comments on federal safety standards.

One major effort in this area has been the fight for adoption of automatic crash protection in passenger cars. The Center feels strongly that these systems (such as air bags) are a more effective and less intrusive alternative to crash protection than mandatory safety belt laws or safety belts that must be buckled in order to start the car.

Exposing Secret Warranties: The Center played a prominent role in the disclosure of secret warranties, or "policy adjustments," as they are called by the auto manufacturers. These occur when an auto company quietly agrees to pay for repair of defects beyond the warranty period but refuses to notify the consumer.

Improving Rust Warranties: Rust and corrosion cost the American consumer up to $14 billion annually. The Center has been successful in its efforts to get almost all domestic and foreign auto companies to lengthen these all-important rust warranties.

Lemon Laws: The Center's work on Lemon Laws played a major role in the enactment of state laws which now make it easier to return a defective new automobile and get your money back.

Tire Ratings: After a two-year gap, consumers once again have reliable treadwear ratings to help them buy new tires that will get the most miles for their dollar. A Center lawsuit overturned a Department of Transportation revocation of this valuable consumer information program.

Initiating Legal Action: When the Center has exhausted other means of obtaining relief for consumer problems, it will initiate legal action. For example, in 1978 when the Department of Energy attempted to raise the price of gasoline 4 cents per gallon without notice or comment, the Center succeeded in stopping this illegal move through a lawsuit, thus saving consumers $2 billion for the six-month period that the action was delayed.

Another Center lawsuit against the Environmental Protection Agency in 1985 forced the agency to order the recall of polluting cars rather than let car companies get away with promises to make new cars cleaner in the future. As part of the settlement, GM (which was responsible for the polluting cars) agreed to fund a $7 million program to make clean-fuel buses.

Monitoring Highway Safety: The Center plays a major role in highway safety by providing the Federal Highway Administration, Congress, and the public with the only independent critique of federal regulations and policies that determine the quality of roadway safety.

Publications: The Center has many publications on automobiles, motor homes, recreational vehicles, and highway safety. These publications include a number of free information packets. For *each* of the packets listed below or a complete description of all of the Center's publications, send a separate, stamped, self-addressed, business-sized envelope with 39 cents postage to the Center at the address below.

Audi 5000S, 4000 & Coupe, and VW Quantum: *Sudden Acceleration (1978-87 models)*

Chrysler: *Stalling and Fires (1981-87 model front-wheel-drive cars and minivans)*

Ford Econoline Vans and Ambulances: *Fuel-spurting and Fires (1984-87 models)*

Ford Escort/Mercury Lynx: *Fires and Stalling (1981-87 models)*

Ford: *Sudden Acceleration & Stalling (1983-87 models)*

Ford Tempo/Topaz: *Problems with 1981-87 models*

GM Celebrity, Century, Cutlass Ciera, Custom Cruiser (A-cars): *Problems with 1982-85 models*

GM Diesels: *Class Action Update (1981-85 models)*

GM Diesels: *Class Action Settlement Information (1978-80 models)*

GM Camaro, Firebird, Z28 & Trans Am (F-cars): *Problems with 1982-85 models*

GM Cavalier/Z24, Cimarron, Firenza, Skyhawk, Sunbird/ J2000 (J-cars): *Problems with 1982-87 models*

GM: *Sudden Acceleration (1977-87 models)*

GM THM 200 Transmission: *Class Action Update (1976-80 models)*

GM THM 440 Transmission: *Problems with Large GM Transmissions*

GM Tire Warranty: *Premature Tire Wear (1985-86 models)*

GM Citation, Omega, Phoenix, Skylark (X-cars): *Problems with 1980-85 models*

Honda Civic, Accord, Prelude: *Sudden Acceleration (1979-87 models)*

The Center for Auto Safety depends on the public for its support. Annual consumer membership in the Center is $15. Because the Center is a nonprofit organization, all contributions are tax-deductible. Annual membership includes a quarterly newsletter called "Lemon Times." If you would like to join the Center, send a check to:

Center for Auto Safety
2001 S St., N.W.
Suite 410
Washington, DC 20009

Identifying automobile safety defects is the responsibility of the U.S. Department of Transportation. Thousands of letters and calls are received by the department's National Highway Traffic Safety Administration (NHTSA) and are used as the basis of safety defect investigations. Often, those letters lead to recall campaigns.

To receive consumer calls, NHTSA operates a toll-free Auto Safety Hotline. The Hotline operators can provide information on recalls, record information about safety problems, and refer you to the appropriate government experts on other automobile problems.

If you need recall information on a particular automobile, you need to tell the Hotline operator the make, model, and year of the car, or the type of equipment involved. You will receive any recall information that NHTSA has about that car or item. This information can be very important if you are not sure whether your car has ever been recalled. If you want a printed copy of the recall information, it will be mailed within 24 hours at no charge.

You also can use the Hotline to report a safety problem. You will be mailed a questionnaire asking for the information the agency's technical staff will need to evaluate the problem. After you fill out and return the questionnaire, the following things will happen:

1. A copy will go to NHTSA's safety defect investigators.

2. A copy will be sent to the manufacturer of the car or equipment, with a request for help in resolving the problem.

3. You will be notified that your questionnaire has been received.

If you have other car-related problems, the Hotline operators can refer you to the appropriate federal, state, and local government agencies. If you need information about federal safety standards and regulations, you will be referred to the appropriate experts.

You may call the Hotline day or night, seven days a week. If you call at a time when no operators are available, you will receive a recorded message asking you to leave your name and address and a description of the information you are seeking. The appropriate materials will be mailed to you. Operators are available from 7:45 a.m. to 4:15 p.m. (Eastern time), Monday through Friday.

NHTSA Toll-Free Hotline

800-424-9393

(in Washington, D.C.: 366-0123)

TTY for hearing impaired:

800-424-9153

(in Washington, D.C.: 755-8919)

127

Here are names and addresses of the top executive of each of the major automobile companies doing business in the United States.

Mr. Gunter Kramer
President and Chairman
BMW of North America, Inc.
BMW Plaza
Montvale, NJ 07645

Mr. Lee A. Iacocca
Chairman of the Board
Chrysler Corporation
P.O. Box 1919
Detroit, MI 48288

Mr. Marik Bosia
President
Fiat Auto U.S.A., Inc.
777 Terrace Avenue
Hasbrouck Heights, NJ 07604

Mr. Donald E. Petersen
Chairman of the Board
Ford Motor Company
The American Road
Dearborn, MI 48121

Mr. Roger B. Smith
Chairman of the Board
General Motors Corporation
General Motors Building
Detroit, MI 48202

Mr. Soichiro Irimajiri
President
American Honda Motor Co.
100 West Alondra Blvd.
Gardena, CA 90247

Mr. H.W. Baik
President
Hyundai Motor America
7373 Hunt Ave.
Garden Grove, CA 92642

Mr. Masashi Suzuki
President
American Isuzu Motors, Inc.
2300 Pellissier Place
Whittier, CA 90601

Mr. Graham W. Whitehead
President
Jaguar Cars Inc.
600 Willow Tree Rd.
Leona, NJ 07605

Mr. Hisao Kaide
President
Mazda of North America
1444 McGaw Avenue
Irvine, CA 92714

Mr. Walter Bodack
President
Mercedes-Benz
1 Mercedes Drive
Montvale, NJ 07645

Mr. Kazue Naganuma
President
Mitsubishi of America
10540 Talbert Street
Fountain Valley, CA 92708

Mr. Kazutoshi Hagiwara
President
Nissan Motor Corp.
18501 Figueroa Street
Carson, CA 90248

Mr. Pascal Henault
President
Peugeot Motors of America
1 Peugeot Plaza
Lyndhurst, NJ 07071

Mr. John A. Cook
President
Porsche Cars North America
200 S. Virginia Street
Reno, NV 89501

Mr. P. Henry Mueller
Chairman of the Board
Saab-Scania of America, Inc.
Saab Drive, P.O. Box 697
Orange, CT 06477

Mr. Raymond Ketchledge
President
Sterling Motor Cars
8325 N.W. 53rd Street
Miami, FL 33166

Mr. Harvey Lamm
Chairman of the Board
Subaru of America, Inc.
7040 Central Highway
Pennsauken, NJ 08109

Mr. Toshiyuki Aray
President
Suzuki of America
3251 E. Imperial Hwy.
Brea, CA 92621-6722

Mr. Yukiyasu Togo
President
Toyota Motors Sales-USA
19001 S. Western Avenue
Torrance, CA 90509

Mr. Noel Phillips
Chairman of the Board
Volkswagen/Audi
888 West Big Beaver Road
Troy, MI 48099

Mr. Bjorn Ahlstrom
Chairman of the Board
Volvo of America Corp.
1 Volvo Drive
Rockleigh, NJ 07647

Mr. William Prior
President
Yugo America, Inc.
28 Park Way
Upper Saddle River, NJ 07458

Federal Government Agencies

Below are the federal agencies that conduct automobile-related programs. Listed with each agency is a description of the type of work they perform plus an address and phone number of each agency's headquarters in Washington, D.C.

National Highway Traffic Safety Adminstration
400 7th Street, S.W.
Washington, D.C. 20590
202-366-5972

Issues safety and fuel economy standards for new motor vehicles; investigates safety defects and enforces recall of defective vehicles and equipment. Conducts research and demonstration programs on vehicle safety and fuel economy, driver safety, and automobile inspection and repair; provides grants for state highway safety programs in areas such as police traffic services, driver education and licensing, emergency medical services, pedestrian safety, and alcohol abuse.

Office of Highway Safety Federal Highway Adminstration
400 7th Street, S.W.
Washington, D.C. 20590
202-366-1153

Develops standards to ensure that highways are constructed to reduce the occurrence and severity of accidents.

Federal Trade Commission Pennsylvania Avenue and 6th Street, N.W.
Washington, D.C. 20580
202-326-2000

Regulates advertising and credit practices, marketing abuses, and professional services and ensures that products are properly labeled (as in fuel economy ratings). The commission covers unfair or deceptive trade practices in motor vehicle sales and repairs, as well as in non-safety defects.

Environmental Protection Agency
401 M Street, S.W.
Washington, D.C. 20460
202-382-2090

Responsible for the control and abatement of air, noise, and toxic substance pollution. This includes setting and enforcing air and noise emission standards for motor vehicles and measuring the fuel economy in new vehicles (*EPA Gas Mileage Guide*).

Office of Consumer Litigation Civil Division
U.S. Dept. of Justice
Washington, D.C. 20530
202-724-6786

Enforces the federal law requiring manufacturers to label each new automobile and forbidding removal or alteration of such labels before delivery to the consumer. The label must contain the make, model, vehicle identification number, dealer's name, basic suggested price, cost for all options installed by the manufacturer, and manufacturer's suggested retail price.

Sometimes, despite our best efforts, we buy a car that just doesn't work properly. There may be little problem after little problem, or perhaps one big problem that never seems to be fixed. Because of the bad taste that such cars leave in the mouths of consumers who buy them, these cars are know as "lemons." In the past, it has been very difficult to obtain a refund if a car turned out to be a lemon. The burden of proof was left to consumers. Because it is hard to define exactly what constitutes a lemon, many lemon owners have not been able to win a case against a manufacturer. But things are changing. Already most states have passed "Lemon Laws" and the rest are considering them. Although there are some important state-to-state variations, all of the laws have similarities: They establish a period of coverage, usually one year from delivery or the written warranty period, whichever is shorter; they may require some form of noncourt arbitration; and, most important, they define a lemon. In most states a lemon is defined as a new car, truck or van that has been taken back to the shop at least 4 times for the same repair (each repair unsatisfactory) or is out of service for a total of 30 days.

The following table outlines the Lemon Laws passed to date. There are generally two ways to be sure your car qualifies as a lemon: Repeated attempts to repair the same problem, or being out of service due to repairs for a certain amount of time. This time does not mean consecutive days. In most states it can be based on different repair problems.

Specific information about the laws in your state can be obtained from your State Attorney General's office (c/o your state house) or your local consumer protection office.

Lemon Laws — State by State

State	Lemon Law Description
Alaska	**Vehicles covered:** All except tractors, farm or off-road vehicles. **Qualification for a lemon:** 3 unsuccessful repairs or 30 business days, (manufacturer has another 30 calendar days to repair after notice) within the shorter of 1 year or warranty. **Who must be notified:** Written notice by certified mail to manufacturer and dealer (or repair agent) that problem has not been corrected in reasonable number of attempts and refund or replacement demanded within 60 days.
Arizona	**Vehicles covered:** All under 10,000 lbs. except the living portion of motor homes. **Qualification for a lemon:** 4 unsuccessful repairs or 30 calendar days within shorter of 1 year or warranty period. **Who must be notified:** Written notice and opportunity to repair to manufacturer.
California	**Vehicles covered:** All except motorcycles, motor homes or off-road vehicles. **Qualification for a lemon:** 4 unsuccessful repairs or 31 calendar days within shorter of 1 year or 12,000 miles. **Who must be notified:** Direct notice to manufacturer of need for repair.

State	Lemon Law Description
Colorado	**Vehicles covered:** Private passenger motor vehicles except motor homes and those with fewer than 4 wheels. **Qualification for a lemon:** 4 unsuccessful repairs or 30 business days within shorter of 1 year or warranty. **Who must be notified:** Certified mail written notice and opportunity to repair to manufacturer.
Connecticut	**Vehicles covered:** Passenger vehicles. **Qualification for a lemon:** 4 unsuccessful repairs or 30 calendar days within shorter of 2 years or 18,000 miles or 2 repairs of problem likely to cause serious bodily injury within shorter of one year of warranty. **Who must be notified:** Report to manufacturer, agent or authorized dealer. Written notice to manufacturer only if required in owner's manual or warranty.
Delaware	**Vehicles covered:** All except motorcycles and living facilities of motor homes. **Qualification for a lemon:** 4 unsuccessful repairs or 31 calendar days within shorter of 1 year or warranty. **Who must be notified:** Written notice and opportunity to repair to manufacturer.
District of Columbia	**Vehicles covered:** All except buses motorcycles, motor homes and RVs. **Qualification for a lemon:** 4 unsuccessful repairs or 30 calendar days within shorter of 2 years or 18,000 miles or one unsuccessful repair of a safety-related defect. **Who must be notified:** Report to manufacturer, agent or authorized dealer.
Florida	**Vehicles covered:** All except off-road vehicles and mopeds. **Qualification for a lemon:** 3 unsuccessful repairs or 15 working days within shorter of 1 year or warranty. **Who must be notified:** Written notice to manufacturer who has 10 business days to repair after delivery to designated dealer.
Hawaii	**Vehicles covered:** All. **Qualification for a lemon:** 3 unsuccessful repairs or 30 business days within warranty on repaired components. **Who must be notified:** Written notice & opportunity to repair to manufacturer.
Illinois	**Vehicles covered:** All passenger cars except motor homes and van campers. **Qualification for a lemon:** 4 unsuccessful repairs or 30 business days within shorter of 1 year or 12,000 miles. **Who must be notified:** Written notice and opportunity to repair to manufacturer.
Iowa	**Vehicles covered:** Cars and pickups. **Qualification for a lemon:** 4 unsuccessful repairs or 30 calendar days within shorter of 1 year or warranty. **Who must be notified:** Direct notice and opportunity to repair to manufacturer.
Kansas	**Vehicles covered:** All under 12,000 lbs. except parts added or modified by converters. **Qualification for a lemon:** 4 unsuccessful repairs or 30 calendar days or 10 total repairs within shorter of 1 year or warranty. **Who must be notified:** Actual notice to manufacturer.
Kentucky	**Vehicles covered:** All except conversion vans, motor homes, motorcycles, mopeds, farm machines and those with more than two axles. **Qualification for a lemon:** 4 unsuccessful repairs or 30 calendar days within shorter of 1 year or 12,000 miles. **Who must be notified:** Written notice to manufacturer.

State	Lemon Law Description
Louisiana	**Vehicles covered:** All under 10,000 lbs. except those used only for commercial purposes. **Qualification for a lemon:** 4 unsuccessful repairs or 30 calendar days within shorter of 1 year or warranty. **Who must be notified:** Report to manufacturer or authorized dealer.
Maine	**Vehicles covered:** All except commercial vehicles over 8,500 pounds. **Qualification for a lemon:** 3 unsuccessful repairs or 15 business days within shorter of 2 years or 18,000 miles. **Who must be notified:** Written notice to manufacturer or authorized dealer only if required in warranty or owner's manual. Manufacturer has 7 business days after receipt to repair.
Maryland	**Vehicles covered:** Passenger vehicles and trucks with 3/4 ton or less rated capacity, except motor homes. **Qualification for a lemon:** 4 unsuccessful repairs or 30 days or 1 unsuccessful repair or failure of braking or steering system within shorter of 15 months or 15,000 miles. **Who must be notified:** Certified mail notice, return receipt requested and opportunity to repair to manufacturer or factory branch.
Massachusetts	**Vehicles covered:** All except motor homes and off-road or commercial vehicles. **Qualification for a lemon:** 3 unsuccessful repairs or 15 business days within shorter of 15,000 miles or 1 year. **Who must be notified:** Report to authorized dealer or manufacturer, who has 7 additional business days to repair.
Michigan	**Vehicles covered:** Passenger vehicles except motor homes, buses, motorcycles and large trucks. **Qualification for a lemon:** 4 unsuccessful repairs or 30 calendar days within shorter of 1 year or warranty. **Who must be notified:** Certified mail notice, return receipt requested, to manufacturer who has 5 business days to repair after delivery.
Minnesota	**Vehicles covered:** Passenger cars, pickups, vans and chassis of RVs. **Qualification for a lemon:** 4 unsuccessful repairs or 30 business days or 1 unsuccessful repair of total braking or steering loss likely to cause accident within shorter of 2 years or warranty. **Who must be notified:** Written notice and opportunity to repair to manufacturer, agent or authorized dealer.
Mississippi	**Vehicles covered:** All except off-road vehicles, motorcycles, mopeds and portions added by motor home manufacturers. **Qualification for a lemon:** 3 unsuccessful repairs or 15 business days within shorter of 1 year or warranty. **Who must be notified:** Written notice to manufacturer who has 10 business days to repair after delivery to designated dealer.
Missouri	**Vehicles covered:** All except commercial and off-road vehicles, mopeds and motorcycles. Includes the chassis, engine and powertrain of RVs. **Qualification for a lemon:** 4 unsuccessful repairs or 30 business days within shorter of 1 year or warranty. **Who must be notified:** Written notice to manufacturer who has 10 calendar days to repair after delivery to designated dealer.
Montana	**Vehicles covered:** All except motor homes, motorcycles and trucks over 10,000 pounds. **Qualification for a lemon:** 4 unsuccessful repairs or 30 business days after notice within shorter of 2 years or 18,000 miles. **Who must be notified:** Written notice and opportunity to repair to manufacturer.
Nebraska	**Vehicles covered:** All except motor homes. **Qualification for a lemon:** 4 unsuccessful repairs or 40 days within shorter of 1 year or warranty. **Who must be notified:** Certified mail notice and opportunity to repair to manufacturer.

State	Lemon Law Description
Nevada	**Vehicles covered:** All except off-road vehicles and motor homes. **Qualification for a lemon:** 4 unsuccessful repairs or 30 calendar days within shorter of 1 year or warranty. **Who must be notified:** Written notice to manufacturer.
New Hampshire	**Vehicles covered:** All under 9,000 pounds except tractors, off highway RVs and mopeds. **Qualification for a lemon:** 4 unsuccessful repairs or 30 business days within shorter of 1 year or warranty. **Who must be notified:** Report to manufacturer, distributor, agent or authorized dealer.
New Jersey	**Vehicles covered:** All passenger vehicles except motorcycles and living portion of motor homes. **Qualification for a lemon:** 4 unsuccessful repairs or 31 business days within shorter of 1 year or warranty. **Who must be notified:** Written notice and opportunity to repair to manufacturer.
New Mexico	**Vehicles covered:** Passenger vehicles under 10,000 pounds. **Qualification for a lemon:** 4 unsuccessful repairs or 30 business days within shorter of 1 year or warranty. **Who must be notified:** Written notice and opportunity to repair to manufacturer.
New York	**Vehicles covered:** Passenger vehicles except motor homes, motorcycles and off-road vehicles. **Qualification for a lemon:** 4 unsuccessful repairs or 30 days within shorter of 2 years or 18,000 miles. **Who must be notified:** Report to manufacturer, agent or authorized dealer.
North Carolina	**Vehicles covered:** All motor vehicles under 10,000 pounds. **Qualifications for a lemon:** 4 unsuccessful repairs for a problem that occurred within the shorter of 24 months, 24,000 miles or the car's warranty or 20 business days during any 12 month period of the warranty. **Who must be notified:** Written notice and opportunity to repair (not more than 15 calendar days) to manufacturer only if required in warranty or owner's manual.
North Dakota*	**Vehicles covered:** Passenger vehicles and trucks under 10,000 lbs. **Qualification for a lemon:** 4 unsuccessful repairs or 30 business days within shorter of 1 year or warranty. **Who must be notified:** Direct notice and opportunity to repair to manufacturer.
Ohio	**Vehicles covered:** Passenger cars and non commercial motor vehicles except RVs and living facilities or motor homes. **Qualifications for a lemon:** 3 unsuccessful repairs, 30 days, 8 total repairs, or 1 unsuccessful repair of problem likely to cause serious bodily injury within shorter of 1 year or 18,000 miles. **Who must be notified:** Report to manufacturer, its agent or authorized dealer.
Oklahoma	**Vehicles covered:** All under 10,000 lbs. except living facilities of motor homes. **Qualification for a lemon:** 4 unsuccessful repairs or 45 calendar days within shorter of 1 year or warranty. **Who must be notified:** Written notice and opportunity to repair to manufacturer.
Oregon	**Vehicles covered:** All passenger vehicles except motorcycles. **Qualification for a lemon:** 4 unsuccessful repairs or 30 business days within shorter of 1 year or 12,000 miles. **Who must be notified:** Direct written notice and opportunity to repair to manufacturer.

* WARNING: Consumers who seek a refund or replacement under the North Dakota lemon law may lose other important legal rights against the dealer and manufacturer.

State	Lemon Law Description
Pennsylvania	**Vehicles covered:** All except motorcycles, motor homes and off-road vehicles. **Qualification for a lemon:** 3 unsuccessful repairs or 30 calendar days for problem that first occurred within shorter of warranty or 12,000 miles. **Who must be notified:** Delivery to authorized service and repair facility. If delivery impossible, written notice to manufacturer or its repair facility obligates them to pay for delivery.
Rhode Island	**Vehicles covered:** Autos, trucks or vans under 10,000 lbs. except motorized campers. **Qualification for a lemon:** 4 unsuccessful repairs or 30 calendar days within shorter of 1 year or 15,000 miles. **Who must be notified:** Report to authorized dealer or manufacturer who has 7 additional days to repair.
Tennessee	**Vehicles covered:** All motor vehicles under 10,000 pounds except motorbikes, lawnmowers, garden tractors and RVs and off-road vehicles. **Qualification for a lemon:** 4 unsuccessful repairs of problem reported within shorter of 1 year or warranty or 30 business days within shorter of 1 year or warranty. **Who must be notified:** Certified mail notice to manufacturer. If 4 unsuccessful repairs or 30 days exhausted before notice manufacturer has additional 10 days to repair.
Texas	**Vehicles covered:** All. **Qualification for a lemon:** 4 unsuccessful repairs or 30 days within shorter of 1 year or warranty. **Who must be notified:** Written notice and opportunity to repair to manufacturer.
Utah	**Vehicles covered:** All under 12,000 lbs. except motorcycles, tractors, motor and mobile homes. **Qualification for a lemon:** 4 unsuccessful repairs or 30 business days within shorter of 1 year or warranty. **Who must be notified:** Report to manufacturer, agent or authorized dealer.
Vermont	**Vehicles covered:** All passenger vehicles except tractors, motorized highway or road-making equipment, snowmobiles, motorcycles, mopeds, trucks over 6,000 lbs., or living portion of RVs. **Qualification for a lemon:** 3 unsuccessful repairs or 30 calendar days within warranty on repaired component. Manufacturer has 1 more opportunity to repair within 30 days after notice. **Who must be notified:** Notice to manufacturer (on provided forms) of 3 unsuccessful repairs or 30 days starts arbitration process.
Virginia	**Vehicles covered:** Passenger cars, pickup or panel trucks, motorcycles, mopeds and chassis of motor homes. **Qualification for a lemon:** 4 unsuccessful repairs or 30 calendar days within 1 year. **Who must be notified:** Written notice to manufacturer of need for repair. If 4 unsuccessful repairs or 30 days already exhausted before this notice, manufacturer has 1 more repair attempt not to exceed 15 days.
Washington	**Vehicles covered:** All motor vehicles except motorcycles, trucks with more than 19,000 pounds GVWR, and living portions of motor homes. **Qualification for a lemon:** 4 unsuccessful repairs, 30 calendar days (15 during warranty period), 2 repairs for serious safety defects, first reported within the shorter of the warranty or 24 months or 24,000 miles. **Who must be notified:** Written notice to manufacturer.
West Virginia	**Vehicles covered:** All passenger automobiles, including pickup trucks, vans and chassis of motor homes. **Qualification for a lemon:** 3 unsuccessful repairs or 30 calendar days or 1 unsuccessful repair of problem likely to cause death or serious bodily injury within shorter of 1 year or warranty. **Who must be notified:** Written notice and opportunity to repair to manufacturer.
Wisconsin	**Vehicles covered:** All. **Qualification for a lemon:** 4 unsuccessful repairs or 30 days within shorter of 1 year or warranty. **Who must be notified:** Report to manufacturer or any authorized dealer.
Wyoming	**Vehicles covered:** All under 10,000 lbs. **Qualification for a lemon:** 4 unsuccessful repairs or 30 business days within 1 year. **Who must be notified:** Direct written notice and opportunity to repair to manufacturer.

SHOPPING GUIDE

For most of us, buying a car can be an intimidating experience. Not only is it an infrequent and expensive purchase, but the process requires us to match negotiating talents with a seasoned professional.

This section offers some practical advice on buying a car, tips on getting the lowest price and some additional information to make you a smarter shopper. The last three pages contain a guide to help you comparison shop.

While you may think the odds are against your getting the best deal, remember that you have the most important weapon in the bargaining process, the 180-degree turn. If you are prepared to walk away from a deal, and exhibit this attitude to the salesperson, even at the risk of losing the "very best deal your salesperson has ever offered," you will be in the best position to get the very best deal. The bottom line is that dealerships need you, the buyer, to survive.

Showroom Strategies

Avoid new models: Any new-model vehicle in its very first year of production usually turns out to have a lot of defects. Often, the manufacturer isn't able to remedy the defects until the second, third, or even fourth year of production. If the manufacturer has not been able to work out a new car's problems by the third model year, the car will likely be a lemon forever. Classic examples of these lemons are the GM X-body and diesel engine cars, both now phased out.

Avoid the first cars off the line: Most car companies close down their assembly lines every year to make annual style changes. In addition to adding hundreds of dollars to the price of a new car, these annual style changes can introduce new defects. It takes a few months to iron out these bugs. Ask the dealer when the car you are interested in was manufactured.

Buy last year's model: The majority of new cars, with the exception of minor cosmetic changes, are the same as the previous year's model. You can save considerably by buying your new car in the early fall when the dealers are clearing the way for the "new" models.

Don't trade in: Although it is more work, you can almost always do better by selling your car yourself than trading it in. To determine what you'll gain by selling your car yourself, check the NADA "Blue Book" at your bank or library. The difference between the wholesale price (what the dealer will give you) and the retail price (what you typically can sell it for) is your extra payment for selling it yourself.

If you do decide to trade your car in at the dealership—*keep the buying and selling separate.* First, negotiate the best price for your new car, *then*, find out how much the dealer will give you for your old car. Keeping the two deals separate will ensure that you know exactly what you're paying for your new car and greatly uncomplicates the transaction.

Shop around: Once you have determined the make, model, and options for the car you want, call as many dealers as possible within a 50 or 60 mile radius of your home for the best price. Do not hesitate to tell the salesperson that you have determined exactly what you want and that you are price shopping. If you find a substantial savings at a dealership far from your home, call your local dealer and tell him or her the price. He or she may very well match it. If not, pick up the car from the distant dealer knowing your trip has saved you hundreds of dollars. Remember: No matter where you purchase the car, you can still bring it to your local dealer for warranty work and repairs.

Buying from stock: You can often get a better deal by buying one of the cars that the dealer has on the lot. However, many times these cars have expensive or flashy options that you do not want or need. For example: Fabric protector—instead of paying the dealer $79.95, go out and buy a can of Scotchguard. Do not hesitate to ask the dealer to remove the option (and its accompanying charge) or sell you the car without charging for the option. Another advantage of buying from stock is that the longer the car sits there the more interest the dealer pays on the car. This can increase the dealer's incentive to sell.

Ordering a car: Domestic cars can be ordered from the manufacturer. One benefit of ordering a car is that once you have decided on a model and options, all the salesperson has to do is take your order. Simply offering the salesperson a fixed amount over invoice may be attractive because it's a sure sale and the dealership has not invested anything in the car. If you do order a car, make sure when it arrives that it includes only the options you requested. Sometimes the car will arrive with additional options on which "because it was a mistake and you didn't order them" the dealer will make a special deal. Remember: If you didn't order it, you don't have to take it.

Avoid delicate options: Delicate options have the highest frequency-of-repair records. Power seats, power windows, power antennas and special roofs are all fun to have—until they break down. Of all the items on the car, they tend to be the most expensive to repair. An internal list of warranty repairs on 1978 model Fords obtained by Ralph Nader listed moon roofs, manual sun roofs, electric sun roofs, and power windows as first, third, fifth, and sixth in frequency of repair.

Inspect the dealer's checklist: Request a copy of the dealer's predelivery service and adjustment checklist (also called a "make-ready list") at the time your new car is delivered. Write the request directly on the new-car order. This request informs the dealer that you are aware of the dealer's responsibility to check your new car for defects.

Examine the car on delivery: Most of us are very excited when it comes time to take the car home. This is the time where a few minutes of careful inspection can save hours of aggravation later. Carefully look over the body for any damage, check for the spare tire and jack equipment, make sure all electrical items work, make sure all the hubcaps and body molding are on. You may want to take a short test drive. Finally, make sure you have the owner's manual, warranty forms, and all the legal documents.

Getting the Best Price

Clearly, the most difficult aspect of buying a new car is getting the best price. While most of us try to get a good price, we are often at a disadvantage because we attempt to negotiate without knowing how much the car actually cost the dealer. The difference between what the dealer paid for the car and the sticker price represents the amount that is negotiable. The general rule of thumb for dealer profit on domestic cars is 15 to 20 percent. The markup on popular imports is usually less. But the actual markup will vary significantly among different models. Lower priced cars have a lower markup. Luxury cars offer the most room for negotiation, subcompacts the least.

The key to getting the best price is to find out what the dealer paid for the car. One source of dealer costs is *Edmund's New Car Prices* available in book stores. The prices in *Edmund's* are not the most precise, but the book does give you a good starting point and is very inexpensive. *Consumer Reports* also offers a computerized pricing service which gives more accurate and up-to-date dealer costs, but can cost up to $27 for the information on three cars.

Because many savvy shoppers demand to see the factory invoice, some dealers have begun to promote cars by offering to sell a car at $49 or $99 dollars over factory invoice. While this may sound like a good deal, these cars are often equipped with expensive options you may not want, and most wholesale prices include an additional 3 percent profit for the dealer.

While every dealer is entitled to a fair profit, every consumer is entitled to negotiate with the best possible price. Following are some pointers to remember when negotiating the price of your new car.

Don't talk price until you're ready to buy. Your first trips to the show room should be to look over the cars, determine what options you want and do your test driving.

Shop the corporate twins. This chapter contains a list of corporate twins—different name plates on nearly identical cars. Check the price and options of the corporate twins of the car you are interested in. You may find that a higher-priced twin may have more options and thus be a better deal than buying the lower-priced car and paying extra for the options you want.

Never narrow your choice to one car. Settling on two or three options gives you the flexibility to be able to walk away from an unfavorable deal.

Negotiate from the invoice price. Rather than see how much you can get off the sticker price, ask the salesperson to tell you the minimum profit, in dollars, that the dealership will accept. Clearly, the dealership has to make a profit. On most cars, however, the markup should fall between $200 and $500. Markups on sporty cars and luxury models are likely to be higher. While advertisements that offer $1000 off the sticker price may sound impressive, that price may still include a $1000 markup for the dealer. If the sales person says that your offer is too low to make a profit, then ask to see the factory invoice.

Watch out for dealer preparation overcharges. Before paying up to $200 for the dealer to clean your new $12,000 car, make sure that dealer preparation has not already been included in the basic price. The price sticker on the car will state: "Manufacturer's suggested retail price of this model includes dealer preparation."

Another item to watch for on the price sticker of some Japanese cars is ADM or ADP. This stands for "additional dealer markup" and "additional dealer profit." This additional profit is the result of the tremendous popularity of some Japanese cars. As import restrictions are lifted and Japanese production in the U.S. increases, these markups should disappear.

Deposits. Make sure anything you sign includes a statement that you can get your deposit back if something goes wrong with the deal.

Price Guide

The following tables contain price information on many of the 1988 cars. When available, we used the basic sedan version of the car with power brakes, power steering, automatic transmission and air conditioning. Keep in mind that a particular model may have many different versions and a variety of different prices. In addition, some manufacturers try to sell popular options as part of a package. For example, in order to get air conditioning you may have to buy power steering and deluxe seats.

You can use this information to get an idea of the price range for many of the popular cars. Be prepared for higher prices when you get to the showroom. Manufacturers like to load their cars with factory options and dealers like to add their own items such as fabric protection, paint sealant and service contracts. *Remember, prices and dealer costs can change during the year. Use these figures for general reference and comparisons, not as a precise indication of exactly how much the car you are interested in will cost.*

The key to getting the best price is to know the dealer cost before beginning your negotiating and work *up* from that cost rather than down from the retail price. One source of dealer cost information is *Edmund's New Car Prices*. You can usually find a copy in your library or bookstore. A more accurate and complete listing of the dealer cost for both the car and the options can be obtained from *Consumer Reports*. The service costs $11 per car, ($20 for 2 and $7 for each additional car), and is available by sending a check to:

Consumer Reports
Auto Price Service
Box 570
Dept. CB
Lathrup Village, MI 48076.

Please indicate the make, model and exact style of the car (or cars) you are interested in.

Subcompacts	Price
Chevrolet Nova	$10,325
Chevrolet Spectrum	$9,587
Chevrolet Sprint	$8,086
Dodge Colt	$8,341
Honda Civic	$8,515
Honda Prelude	$17,345
Hyundai Excel	$8,100
Izuzu I-Mark	$9,874
Mazda 323	$9,313
Mitsubishi Cordia	$11,725
Mitsubishi Mirage	$9,746
Mitsubishi Precis	$8,454
Mitsubishi Tredia	$11,205
Nissan Pulsar	$13,429
Nissan Sentra	$10,059
Pontiac LeMans	$8,405
Subaru DL/GL	$11,274
Subaru Hatchback	$7,866
Subaru Justy	$6,466
Subaru XT	$11,926
Toyota Corolla	$10,788
Toyota Corolla SR-5 (RWD)	$10,538
Toyota FX16	$10,668
Toyota MR-2	$13,528
Toyota Tercel	$8,498
Volkswagen Fox	$7,575
Volkswagen Golf	$10,015
Volkswagen Jetta	$10,490
Yugo GVL	$5,498

Compacts	Price
BMW 325i Conv.	$32,500
BMW 535i	$36,000
BMW 735i	$53,000
Buick Skyhawk	$8,884
Buick Skylark	$11,074
Buick Regal	$12,449
Cadillac Cimarron	$16,071
Chevrolet Cavalier	$8,997
Chevrolet Corsica/Beretta	$11,712
Chrysler Conquest	$19,741
Chrysler LeBaron	$11,286
Chrysler LeBaron GTS	$12,151
Dodge Aries	$8,364
Dodge Daytona	$13,394
Dodge Lancer	$12,715
Dodge Shadow	$9,337
Ford Mustang	$9,221
Isuzu Impulse	$14,209
Mazda RX-7	$19,830
Mazda 626	$13,918
Mitsubishi Starion	$19,899
Nissan 200 SX	$13,659
Oldsmobile Firenza	$9,934
Plymouth Reliant	$8,364
Plymouth Sundance	$8,891
Pontiac Sunbird	$8,599
Pontiac Fiero	$12,264
Pontiac Grand Am	$11,934
Renault Medallion	$11,714
Toyota Camry	$11,538
Toyota Celica	$15,618

Intermediates	Price
Acura Legend	$21,760
Audi 5000S	$22,180
Buick Century	$11,793
Buick LeSabre	$15,910
Buick Regal	$12,449
Buick Riviera	$21,615
Cadillac Eldorado	$24,891
Cadillac Seville	$27,627
Chevrolet Celebrity	$12,799
Chevrolet Corvette	$30,580
Chrysler New Yorker	$17,416
Dodge 600	$10,659
Honda Accord	$11,745
Mazda 929	$18,950
Mitsubishi Galant	$16,549
Nissan Maxima GL	$16,949
Oldsmobile Cutlass Ciera	$12,447
Oldsmobile Delta 88	$15,818
Peugeot 505 T	$24,615
Plymouth Caravelle	$10,659
Pontiac Bonneville	$16,229
Pontiac Firebird	$15,834
Pontiac 6000	$12,823
Porsche 924 S	$25,970
Porsche 928 S4	$66,439
Saab 900	$15,441
Saab 9000 Turbo	$23,928
Sterling 825 SL	$25,238
Toyota Cressida	$20,250
Volvo DL	$17,130
Volvo 740	$23,570
Volvo 760	$31,200

Large Cars	Price
Cadillac Allante	$56,533
Cadillac Brougham	$28,846
Cadillac Fleetwood Sixty Special	$34,750
Chevrolet Caprice	$14,834
Chrysler 5th Ave	$17,243
Dodge Diplomat	$14,221
Jaguar XJ6	$43,500
Lincoln Mark VII	$25,068
Lincoln Town Car	$26,179
Mercury Grand Marquis	$16,612
Oldsmobile 98	$20,119
Plymouth Gran Fury	$12,127
Pontiac Safari Wagon	$14,519
Rolls-Royce Corniche II	$183,500

Trucks	Price
Dodge B 150 Van	$10,195
Dodge Caravan	$16,069
Dodge Dakota	$12,553
Jeep Cherokee 4x4	$13,027
Jeep Comanche	$11,541
Jeep Wagoneer	$21,962
Jeep Wrangler	$12,856
Mitsubushi Montero	$12,325
Plymouth Voyager	$15,509
Raider	$12,443
Ram 50	$9,672
Suzuki Samurai	$9,520
Toyota 4-Runner 4x4	$15,738
Toyota Truck	$9,178

Options: The Good and The Bad

The following are some items to consider when selecting the options for your new car:

Extra Safety in the Rear Seat: Since 1972, automakers have been required to install the mounting points for rear shoulder belts. There is no question that shoulder and lap belts are better than single lap belts but most cars have only lap belts in the rear. You may want to have the dealer install shoulder belts in the rear before you take delivery. Tip: The charge for this installation may vary considerably, so request the installation when you are negotiating for price. Note: In some cases, the shoulder belt may be separate from the lap belt, unlike the continuous three point belts in the front seat.

Safer Windshields Are Coming: Today's windshields are one of the few items on the car that must meet certain crash test standards. The safety glass used in windshields is essentially a sheet of plastic sandwiched between two sheets of glass. The plastic sheet keeps the glass from shattering. Although the glass is held in place by the sandwiched plastic, the smashed surface, with its thousands of jagged edges, is extremely hazardous. Each year more than 200,000 people suffer facial cuts and injuries when their heads hit this jagged glass.

In Europe, these injuries are prevented with an additional safety feature—a plastic coating on the inner surface of the windshield. The plastic provides a protective barrier between the sharp edges of a smashed windshield and your face. In fact, even after the windshield has been smashed, you can run your hand over the glass and it will feel smooth. These new windshields, which represent a major step forward in the quest for safer cars, are now available on a limited number of luxury cars.

High Tech Safety Belts: Some European cars now have "crash-sensitive pretensioners" on the front seat belts. In the event of a frontal crash, these devices take up any slack in your safety belt and reduce your forward movement. Saab and Mercedes-Benz are currently offering these devices but other manufacturers are expected to follow. Find out if the cars you are considering have these devices as they represent an important advancement in safety belt technology.

Antilock Braking System: Many manufacturers are offering a new safety feature called antilock braking or ABS. ABS can shorten your stopping distance on dry, wet and even icy roads. By helping to prevent brake lockup, ABS ensures steering control even under severe emergency braking.

ABS works by sensing the speed of each wheel. If one or more of the wheels begins to lock up or skid, it automatically reduces hydraulic pressure to that (or those) wheels' brakes, allowing them to roll normally again, stopping the skid. When the wheel stops skidding, the hydraulic pressure is instantly reapplied. This cycle can be repeated up to several times per second, keeping each wheel at its optimum braking performance even though the driver keeps pushing on the brake pedal.

Cruise Control Problems: A properly functioning cruise control system can be an added convenience and even contribute to improvements in fuel efficiency on long trips. Unfortunately, in investigating the growing problem of sudden acceleration (when your car suddenly lurches out of control), the Center for Auto Safety has noticed that a sudden acceleration is often related to a failure in the cruise control system. If you do not regularly use cruise control, you may consider deleting it from the options on your next car.

Factory Sound?

Buying a factory-equipped or dealer-supplied sound system will cost you 20 to 50 percent more than having one installed by a company that specializes in car stereos. Unfortunately, manufacturers are making it very difficult to buy a car with no sound system.

The option to delete a standard radio is not being offered to most consumers. Instead, most manufacturers make the option available on a limited basis only to car dealers and to those few consumers who special-order their cars and know enough to ask for radio deletion.

Car dealers are caught in the middle of the sales transaction between the consumer and the car manufacturer. The radio might be removed in the dealership at the consumer's request, but then the car maker denies the dealer full credit for the return, demands purchase of another radio to replace the return, or prohibits return and credit of any kind.

Consumers allowed to delete a standard radio are often awarded only a nominal credit, not the full credit that should be allowed for any audio equipment removed from the car. The difference between the credit and the actual cost of the radio is a gap which car makers may attribute to the price of such things as speakers,

wiring, and noise suppression equipment that remain on the car. The credit may not be equitable in all cases.

Consumers are being misled on the actual price of upgraded, factory-installed radios. For example, the quoted price (1985) for the General Motors Delco/Bose sound system is $895. But the actual cost to the consumer is $895 plus at least $275 which is buried in the base price of the car—a total of $1,170.

As you shop for a new car, read each brochure carefully. If the list of standard equipment includes a sound system, look for an asterisk that may refer you to a fine-print footnote on the availability and terms of a delete option.

Look for delete option information on the window stickers of the cars at the dealership. Look for almost hidden references in the advertisements for the car. If you can't find information anywhere—ask the dealer.

If the vehicle you're interested in is one that offers a radio deletion "for credit," with no qualifying language tacked on to the description, the implication is that deletion is possible at the dealership.

But, no matter what the sales brochures say, talk with your dealer. Almost everything in a car purchase agreement is

negotiable. And remember: the car maker is banking on the fact that you won't ask about radio delete options.

If you choose to buy upgraded sound equipment offered by the car dealer, ask for full disclosure of the actual cost of upgraded equipment, and make sure you're given a fair credit for the original radio that comes with the car. That credit should be either subtracted from the price of the car, or applied toward the suggested list price of the upgraded equipment. Familiarity with prices of comparable equipment in the car audio aftermarket will enable you to know whether you're being quoted a fair list price.

If you choose to buy an upgraded system from the car maker, with the system pre-installed at the factory, the cost of the upgrade portion should be listed on the car's window sticker.

But don't forget the "buried" cost of the standard sound system, which the car maker includes in the base price of the car. Ask your dealer about any cost not itemized on the window sticker. Don't be misled if the dealer tells you that the sound system is "free," because it is included in the base price of the car.

Operating Costs

Buying a 1987 luxury car rather than a 1987 economy model will cost considerably more, not only in up-front costs, but also during the life of the vehicle.

According to an analysis by Runzheimer International, a Rochester, Wisconsin management consulting firm, a 1987 Cadillac DeVille will cost $6,968 in annual ownership and operating costs while a Ford Escort will cost only $4,174. That's a $2,794 annual cost difference. The higher cost of the Cadillac is due not only to the higher initial cost, but to higher fuel, maintenance, tire replacement, insurance and finance costs. Also, higher-priced cars are more likely to depreciate (decrease in value) faster.

The table below compares the complete operating costs for ten popular domestic cars. For the purposes of this comparison all the cars were four door models and equipped with automatic transmission, power steering, power disc brakes, air conditioning, tinted glass, AM-FM radio, body side modeling, cruise control, and left-hand remote control mirror. The costs include operating expenses (fuel, oil, maintenance and tires), ownership expenses (insurance, depreciation, financing, taxes and licensing) and are based on keeping the car for 3 years and driving 20,000 miles per year.

Operating Costs: Comparing Some Popular 1987 Domestic Cars

Car	Annual Costs*		
	Operating	Ownership	Total
Cadillac DeVille	$1,390	$5,578	$6,968
Chevrolet Caprice CL	$1,370	$3,945	$5,315
Olds Cutlass Supreme	$1,230	$3,736	$4,966
Ford Taurus L	$1,200	$3,764	$4,964
Chevrolet Celebrity	$1,270	$3,630	$4,900
Dodge Caravan	$1,170	$3,552	$4,722
Ford Tempo GL	$1,040	$3,431	$4,471
Chevrolet Cavalier	$1,050	$3,352	$4,402
Plymouth Reliant K	$1,030	$3,370	$4,400
Ford Escort GL	$1,000	$3,174	$4,174

* Based on data collected by Runzheimer International, Rochester, Wisconsin. See the text above for an explanation of the costs.

Leasing Vs. Buying

As car prices continue to rise and dealer ads scream out the virtues of leasing, many car buyers are wondering whether they should lease rather than buy. Here is some basic information to help you make the right decision for your needs. In a typical lease situation, you agree to pay a monthly fee for a set period of time in exchange for the use of a car. In some cases, the fee covers all expenses (except gas and oil) associated with the car. In most cases, however, you pay for maintenance, insurance, and repairs as if the car were your own.

There are two types of leases—*closed-* and *open-ended*. Most consumer leases are *closed-ended* which means you simply return the car to the leasing company. The amount you pay depends on the purchase price and what the company thinks it can sell the car for after the lease is up. An *open-ended* lease is riskier because you have to pay the difference between the expected value of the car and its actual resale value when the lease expires. If the lessor underestimated the resale value of the car when figuring your monthly payments, you will end up paying a lump sum at the end of the lease. While the terms *open* and *closed* describe the two general types of leases, within those categories leases will vary considerably.

Generally speaking, leasing will cost you more than either buying outright or financing. Still, there are some reasons why you might consider a lease.

Do I use the car for business? While it is more expensive for a business to lease than to buy, leasing ties up less capital and makes record keeping easier.

Do I want a more luxurious car than I can currently afford? Leasing offers lower upfront costs because there is no downpayment (except for a security deposit). In addition, your monthly leasing costs will be less than monthly finance payments.

Can I put the cash I save by not making a down payment to better use? Unless you have an urgent need for the cash, your down payment would have to offer a return of 12%-24% in order to pay off.

When shopping for a lease:
- Know the make and model of the vehicle you want to lease. Tell the agent exactly how you want the car equipped. You don't have to pay for options you don't want. Decide in advance how long you want to keep the car.
- Find out how much cash you are required to pay at the time of delivery. Most leases require at least the first month's payment. Others have a security deposit, registration fees, or other "hidden" costs. When shopping around, make sure price quotes include taxes—sales tax, a monthly use tax, or gross receipt tax.
- Find out the annual mileage limit. Don't accept a contract with a lower mileage limit than you realistically think you will need. Most standard contracts allow 15,000 to 18,000 miles per year. If you go under the allowance one year, you can go over the allowance the next year.
- Ask about early termination. If you have to terminate the lease before it is up, what are the financial penalties?
- Avoid maintenance contracts. Getting work done privately is cheaper in the long run—and don't forget, this is a new car with a standard new car warranty.
- Arrange for your own insurance; you can usually get it cheaper than programs offered by the lessor.
- Make sure you understand the service charges at the end of your lease. They are usually around $100 but can be as high as $250.
- Make sure you retain your option to buy the car at the end of the lease and that the price is predetermined. The price should equal the residual value; if it is more, then the lessor is trying to make additional profit on the car.

Below is a comparison of the cost of leasing a $14,000 car vs. buying one. These figures represent typical prices. Your actual costs may vary slightly but you can use this format to make the comparison for the car you are considering.

Lease prices are generally fixed and based on the manufacturer's suggested retail price of the car, less a predetermined *residual* value. The residual value is what the leasing company expects the car to be worth at the end of the lease. In order to protect themselves, they tend to underestimate the car's residual value, but there is little you can do about this estimate. Generally speaking, there is little or no negotiation when leasing a car.

Here are some typical residual values for a few 1987 cars from GE Credit Auto Leasing:

Audi 5000 CS Turbo	21%
Plymouth Reliant	24%
Chrysler 5th Avenue	34%
Toyota Cressida Wagon	38%
Ford Taurus	41%
Pontiac Grand Am	44%
Toyota Camry	47%
Honda Prelude	51%
BMW 325i Convertible	57%

Our example assumes that the leased car has a residual value of 40%. Because leasing companies tend to underestimate their cars' residual value, we estimate the residual value of a purchased car to be 50%. While leasing costs are usually not negotiable, when buying, you can nearly always negotiate a price lower than the suggested retail price. Our example below assumes (conservatively) that you will be able to get a $14,000 car for $13,300, or 5% less than the retail price.

We did not consider the tax benefits of financing a car because these would be off-set by the interest you could make if you saved the difference between the monthly cost of leasing vs. buying. In our example, this would be $357 - $276 or $81 per month.

A note about taxes: There has been a lot of talk about the effect of the new tax laws on leasing. Tax reform did not make leasing more attractive, it simply made buying a car somewhat less attractive. In 1987 only 65% of the interest on a car loan was deductible. That figure falls to 40% in 1988, 20% in 1989, and 10% in 1990. In 1991 you will not be able to deduct the interest on car loans. In addition, the sales tax on a new car is no longer deductible.

Finally, keep in mind that at the end of a lease period you have nothing—at the end of your finance period you will own a car.

Buying vs. Leasing

Buying

Retail Price of Car	$14,000
Negotiated Discount	-$700
	$13,300
Sales Tax	+ $780
	$14,080
Financing 100% at 10%; $357 Per Month for 4 Years - Total Cost:	$17,136
Less Car's Value at the End of Loan	-$7,040
Actual Cost	$10,096

Leasing

Up Front Costs	$500
Payments 48 x $276 (4 Year Lease):	+$13,248
Total Cost	$13,748

Difference

Actual Cost of Leasing	$13,748
Actual Cost of Buying	-$10,096
Difference:	$3,152

Corporate Twins

"Corporate twin" is a term used to indicate similar cars that are sold under different names. It is mainly an American phenomenon. In many cases, the cars are virtually identical, such as Dodge's Omni and Plymouth's Horizon. Sometimes, the difference is in the body style and luxury options, as with the Chevrolet Celebrity and the Buick Century. For the most part, corporate twins have the same mechanics, engine, drive train, size, weight, and internal workings.

Chrysler	Ford	General Motors	
Chrysler 5th Avenue Dodge Diplomat Plymouth Gran Fury	Ford Crown Victoria Mercury Gr. Marquis	**"A" cars** Buick Century Chevrolet Celebrity Olds Cutlass Ciera Pontiac 6000	**"G" cars** Chevy Monte Carlo Olds Cut. Sup. Classic
Chrysler LeBaron GTS Dodge Lancer	Ford Taurus Mercury Sable		**"H" cars** Buick LeSabre Oldsmobile Delta 88 Pontiac Bonneville
Chrysler N Y Landau Dodge Dynasty	Ford Tempo Mercury Topaz	**"B" cars** Chevrolet Caprice Pontiac Safari Buick Estate Wagon Oldsmobile Custom Cruiser	**"J" cars** Buick Skyhawk Cadillac Cimarron Chevrolet Cavalier Oldsmobile Firenza Pontiac Sunbird
Dodge Aries Plymouth Reliant	Ford Thunderbird Mercury Cougar		
Dodge Caravan Plymouth Voyager		**"C" cars** Buick Electra Cadillac DeVille Cadillac Fleetwood Oldsmobile 98	**"N" cars** Buick Skylark Oldsmobile Cutlass Calais Pontiac Grand Am
Dodge 600 Plymouth Caravelle			
Dodge Colt Plymouth Colt		**"E" cars** Buick Riviera Cadillac Eldorado Olds Toronado	**"W" cars** Buick Regal Olds Cutlass Supreme Pontiac Grand Prix
Dodge Shadow Plymouth Sundance			
Dodge Omni Plymouth Horizon		**"F" cars** Chevrolet Camaro Pontiac Firebird	

Japanese Cousins

In addition to corporate twins, we also have "Japanese cousins." These are essentially Japanese cars marketed under a U.S. name. In most cases the only difference is the name plate.

Chevrolet Nova – *Toyota Corolla*
Chevrolet Spectrum – *Isuzu I-Mark*
Chevrolet Sprint – *Suzuki*
Chrysler Conquest – *Mitsubishi Starion*

Dodge Colt – *Mitsubishi Mirage*
Mercury Tracer – *Mazda 323*
Plymouth Colt – *Mitsubishi Mirage*

Some of the best values in new cars can be obtained at the end of the model year. Because auto dealers are desperately trying to rid their lots of last year's overstock, you will often be able to save considerably by buying last year's models. In addition to saving money, you may even save on your insurance costs because you will be insuring an "older" car. Remember that most cars really don't change that much from year to year, so you are probably not missing much by buying last year's model.

The "Purchasing Guides" on the following pages will provide you with an overall comparison of last year's cars in terms of safety, fuel economy, maintenance, and insurance costs. The cars are put into size classes based on weight. We used weight because currently the relative safety of automobiles is dependent on weight. The U.S. Environmental Protection Agency (EPA) uses interior volume to categorize automobiles. Because of this, our list of subcompacts may not exactly match the EPA's list. For example, the EPA lists the Mercedes as a compact car.

To fully understand these summary charts, it is important to read the appropriate section in the book. You will note that here and throughout the book some of the charts contain empty boxes. Empty boxes appear where the data were unavailable at the time of printing.

1983 Cars with the Best and Worst Resale Value

In general, cars are a very poor investment in terms of retaining their value. There are some exceptions, however, and the following table indicates which of the top 100 selling 1983 cars held their value the best and which did not. Most new cars are traded in within four years and are then available on the used car market. The highest priced used cars may not necessarily be the best or highest quality. Supply and demand, as well as appearance, are extremely important factors in determining used car prices.

The Best

Model	1983 Price	1987 Price	Retained Value
Volvo DL	$10,650	$ 8,500	80%
Honda Civic CRX	$ 6,592	$ 5,120	78%
Porsche 944	$18,980	$14,625	77%
Honda Prelude	$ 9,645	$ 7,325	76%
Toyota Camry	$ 7,798	$ 5,925	76%
Pontiac Parisienne	$10,256	$ 7,750	75%
Chevrolet Corvette*	$21,800	$15,950	73%
Toyota Celica	$ 8,599	$ 6,100	71%
Toyota Corolla	$ 6,138	$ 4,325	70%
Chevrolet Camaro	$ 8,186	$ 5,625	69%

The Worst

Model	1983 Price	1987 Price	Retained Value
Renault Fuego	$ 8,695	$ 2,775	32%
Renault LeCar	$ 5,295	$ 1,875	35%
Ford EXP	$ 5,462	$ 2,025	37%
Mercury Zephyr	$ 6,624	$ 2,700	41%
Dodge Omni	$ 5,841	$ 2,475	42%
Chevrolet Chevette	$ 5,333	$ 2,300	43%
Plymouth Horizon	$ 5,841	$ 2,550	44%
Dodge Charger/024	$ 6,379	$ 2,800	44%
Dodge Sap./Chall.	$ 8,043	$ 3,575	44%
Audi 5000S Wagon	$14,355	$ 6,450	45%

Table is based on 1987 statistics compiled by the National Automobile Dealers Association and applied to the top 100 selling cars.

* 1984 model introduced in 1983

Purchasing Guide - 1987 Models
Subcompact

Car	Crash Test Performance	Fuel Economy mpg	Preventive Maintenance Cost	Repair Cost	Insurance Rate
Acura Integra	Good	25	Medium	High	Regular
AMC/Renault Alliance		24	High	Low	Regular
Chevrolet Chevette	Poor	25	Low	Low	Regular
Chevrolet Nova	Good	28	Medium	High	Regular
Chevrolet Spectrum	Poor	31	Medium	High	Regular
Chevrolet Sprint	Poor	44	Medium	High	Regular
Dodge Charger/Ply. Turis.		25	Low	Low	Surcharge
Dodge/Plymouth Colt	Good	29	Low	High	Surcharge
Dodge Omni/Ply. Horizon	Poor	23	Low	Medium	Regular
Ford Escort	Good	26	Low	Medium	Regular
Honda Civic	Good	27	Medium	Low	Regular
Honda CRX-Si	Poor	29	Medium	Medium	Surcharge
Honda Prelude	Good	25	Medium	Medium	Surcharge
Hyundai Excel	Moderate	27	Medium	High	Regular
Isuzu I-Mark	Poor	31	Medium	High	Regular
Mazda 323	Moderate	25	Medium	High	Surcharge
Mercury Lynx	Good	26	Low	Medium	Regular
Mitsubishi Cordia	Good	24	High	High	Surcharge
Mitsubishi Mirage	Good	29	High	High	Surcharge
Mitsubishi Tredia	Poor	24	High	High	Surcharge
Nissan Sentra		26	Medium	High	Regular
Nissan Stanza		21	Low	High	Regular
Pontiac 1000	Poor	25	Low	Low	Regular
Subaru GL	Poor	25	Low	High	Surcharge
Toyota Corolla	Good	28	High	High	Regular
Toyota MR-2	Good	25	High	High	Surcharge
Toyota Tercel		36	High	High	Surcharge
Volkswagen Golf	Good*	23	High	Low	Surcharge
Volkswagen Jetta	Moderate	23	High	Medium	Surcharge
Volkswagen Scirroco	Moderate	23	High	High	Surcharge
Yugo GV	Poor	29	Medium	Low	Surcharge

* Model tested had automatic crash protection.

Purchasing Guide - 1987 Models
Compact

Car	Crash Test Performance	Fuel Economy mpg	Preventive Maintenance Cost	Repair Cost	Insurance Rate
BMW 325 e		21	High	Medium	Surcharge
Buick Skyhawk	Good	24	Low	High	Regular
Buick Skylark	2 dr. Good 4 dr. Poor	22	Low	Medium	Discount
Buick Somerset	2 dr. Good 4 dr. Poor	22	Low	Medium	Surcharge
Cadillac Cimarron	Good	23	Medium	High	Discount
Chevrolet Cavalier	Good	24	Medium	High	Regular
Chrysler LeBaron	Poor	22	Low	Low	Discount
Chrysler LeBaron GTS	Poor	22	Low	Low	Regular
Dodge Aries	Good	23	Low	Low	Discount
Dodge Daytona	Good	22	Low	Low	Surcharge
Dodge Lancer	Poor	22	Low	Low	Regular
Ford Mustang	Good	18	Low	Low	Surcharge
Ford Tempo	Moderate*	22	Low	Medium	Regular
Honda Accord	Good	24	Medium	High	Regular
Isuzu Impulse	Poor	23	Medium	Medium	Surcharge
Mazda RX-7		17	Medium	Low	Surcharge
Mazda 626	Good	23	Medium	Low	Regular
Mercury Topaz	Moderate*	22	Low	Medium	Regular
Nissan 200 SX		21	Medium	Low	Surcharge
Oldsmobile Calais	2 dr. Good 4 dr. Poor	22	Low	Medium	Regular
Oldsmobile Firenza	Good	24	Low	High	Regular
Plymouth Colt Vista	Poor	23	Low	High	Regular
Plymouth Reliant	Good	23	Low	Low	Discount
Pontiac Fiero	Good	25	Medium	Medium	Surcharge
Pontiac Grand Am	2 dr. Good 4 dr. Poor	20	Low	Medium	Regular
Pontiac Sunbird	Good	25	Low	High	Regular
Toyota Camry	Good	25	High	High	Discount
Toyota Celica	Good	26	High	High	Surcharge
VW Quantum	Poor	18	High	High	Regular

* Model tested had automatic crash protection.

Purchasing Guide - 1987 Models
Intermediate

Car	Crash Test Performance	Fuel Economy mpg	Preventive Maintenance Cost	Repair Cost	Insurance Rate
Acura Legend		19	Medium	Low	Regular
Audi 5000S	Poor	18	High	High	Surcharge
Buick Century	Good	22	Medium	Medium	Regular
Buick LeSabre	Good	18	Medium	Medium	Discount
Buick Regal	Moderate	19	High	Medium	Regular
Buick Riviera	Good	19	Medium	Medium	Regular
Cadillac Eldorado	Good	17	Medium	Medium	Surcharge
Chevrolet Camaro	Good	19	High	Low	Surcharge
Chevrolet Celebrity	Good	22	Medium	Medium	Regular
Chevrolet Monte Carlo	Moderate	19	High	Medium	Surcharge
Chrysler NY/Dodge 600	Good	22	Low	Low	Discount
Ford Taurus/Merc. Sable	Poor	20	Low	Medium	Regular
Ford Thunderbird	Poor	18	Low	Medium	Surcharge
Mercedes 190E		19	High	High	Regular
Mercury Cougar	Good	18	Low	Medium	Surcharge
Mitsubishi Galant	Good	20	High	High	Regular
Nissan Maxima GL	Poor	18	Medium	High	Regular
Nissan 300 ZX T	Moderate	18	Low	High	Surcharge
Oldsmobile Cutlass Ciera	Good	20	Medium	Medium	Regular
Oldsmobile Cut. Supreme	Moderate	19	High	Medium	Regular
Oldsmobile Delta 88	Good	19	Medium	Medium	Discount
Oldsmobile Toronado	Good	19	Medium	High	Regular
Peugeot 505 T	Poor	18	High	High	Surcharge
Plymouth Caravelle	Good	22	Low	Low	Regular
Pontiac Bonneville	Good	18	High	Medium	Discount
Pontiac Firebird	Good	17	High	Low	Surcharge
Pontiac Grand Prix	Moderate	19	High	High	Regular
Pontiac 6000	Good	22	Medium	Medium	Regular
Saab 9000T	Good	21	High	High	Surcharge
Toyota Cressida	Good	18	High	High	Regular
Volvo DL	Good	21	High	Low	Discount
Volvo 760	Good	22	High	Medium	Discount

Purchasing Guide - 1987 Models
Large

Car	Crash Test Performance	Fuel Economy mpg	Preventive Maintenance Cost	Repair Cost	Insurance Rate
Buick Electra	Poor	18	Medium	High	Discount
Cadillac Brougham		18	Medium	Medium	Discount
Cad. DeVille/Fleetwood	Poor	17	Medium	High	Discount
Chevrolet Caprice	Moderate	18	Medium	Low	Discount
Chrysler 5th Ave		16	Medium	Low	Discount
Dodge Diplomat		16	Medium	Low	Discount
Ford LTD Crown Victoria	Moderate	17	Low	Medium	Discount
Lincoln Mark VII		17	Low	Medium	Regular
Lincoln Town Car		17	Low	Medium	Discount
Mercury Grand Marquis	Moderate	17	Low	Medium	Discount
Oldsmobile 98	Poor	19	Medium	High	Discount
Plymouth Gran Fury		16	Medium	Low	Discount
Pontiac Safari (SW)	Moderate	16	Medium	Low	Discount

Purchasing Guide - 1987 Models
Minivans, Pickups and 4x4s

Car	Crash Test Performance	Fuel Economy mpg	Preventive Maintenance Cost	Repair Cost	Insurance Rate
AMC Jeep Cherokee 4x4	Poor	16	High	Low	Regular
AMC Jeep Comanche	Poor	16	High	Low	Regular
AMC Jeep Wrangler	Poor	18	High	Low	Regular
Chevrolet Astro	Poor	17	High	Low	Discount
Chevrolet C-10 Pickup	Good	14	High	Low	Regular
Chevrolet S-10 Blazer	Poor	21	High	Low	Regular
Dodge B 150 Van	Poor	16	Medium	Low	Discount
Dodge Caravan	Good	19	Low	Low	Discount
Ford Aerostar	Poor	18	Low	Low	Regular
Ford Bronco II	Moderate	17	Low	Medium	Regular
Ford E-150 Club Wagon	Poor	13	Low	Low	Regular
Ford F-150 Pickup	Poor	14	Low	Low	Regular
Ford Ranger		23	Low	Low	Surcharge
Isuzu Trooper II 4x4	Poor	19	Medium	Low	Regular
Mazda B-2000 Pick-up	Poor	22	Medium	Low	Regular
Nissan Pickup		17	Low	Medium	Surcharge
Plymouth Voyager	Good	19	Low	Low	Discount
Toyota 4-Runner 4x4	Poor	19	High	Medium	Surcharge
Toyota Van	Moderate	21	High	High	Regular
Volkswagen Vanagon	Poor	14	High	High	Regular

	CAR 1	CAR 2	CAR 3
Dealer Name and Location:	_____	_____	_____
Make and Model of Car:	_____	_____	_____
Optional Equipment:	_____	_____	_____
When will the car be ready?	_____	_____	_____
How long is the warranty? (Be sure to compare coverage and your responsibilities)	_____	_____	_____

Safety and Convenience

General

Is the passenger capacity and number of seat belts adequate?

Is the baggage/cargo capacity adequate?

Can you easily load or unload items from the trunk or other cargo area?

Are you satisfied with the quality and design of the car? (Do the doors fit well, for example?)

Does the dealer have a good reputation for customer service?

Occupant Protection

How did the car fare in the NHTSA crash-test program?

If adjustable, can the headrests be set so the center of the headrest is just above the center of your head?

Does the steering wheel have a large padded hub?

Is the fuel tank located forward or above the rear axle, minimizing the chance of leakage in a rear-end collision? (Ask dealer)

	CAR 1	CAR 2	CAR 3
Dashboard Features			
Can you easily identify, locate and operate the car controls in the daylight and at night?			
Is the dashboard free of sharply protruding knobs and controls?			
Is the dashboard well padded in the areas where your face, knees, or chest would hit in an accident?			
Is the car equipped with visual dashboard displays to monitor:			
• brake wear			
• door ajar			
• exterior lights			
• fluid levels			
Seats and Doors			
Are the doors free from hard protrusions or sharp edges?			
Are the doors and roof pillars padded? (Pillars are the metal structures which support the roof)			
Visibility			
Is your vision free from obstructions or blind spots when you use the rearview mirror or when you turn your head in either direction?			
Is a right side-view mirror available?			
Is a rear window defogger available?			
Do the side marker lights flash when the turn signals are on?			

	CAR 1	CAR 2	CAR 3
Maintenance			
Is the preventive maintenance cost acceptable?			
Is the cost of the nine repair items acceptable?			
Are the tire changing tools easy to find?			
Fuel Economy			
Is the estimated mpg acceptable?			
Will the options you want decrease fuel economy?			
Miscellaneous			
Are the tire grades satisfactory?			
Does the car have adequate towing capability if you need it?			
Can you quickly move your foot from the accelerator to the brake pedal?			
After a test drive, were you satisfied with the following:			
Ease of entering and exiting the car			
Seat belt comfort and ease of use			
Starting			
Acceleration			
Braking			
Cornering			
Turning radius			
Steering effort			
Ride comfort			
Noise level			
Visibility, including from mirrors			
Parking			

About the Author

Jack Gillis spent three years as a marketing analyst with the U.S. Department of Transportation's National Highway Traffic Safety Administration. While at NHTSA, he was responsible for preparing the first edition of *The Car Book*, in 1981. Since then, over two million consumers have received copies of the book. In 1982 he began developing the guide independently.

Gillis is frequently called upon by the national media to comment on consumer issues. He has testified before both the Senate and House at the invitation of Republicans as well as Democrats. He has addressed consumer groups, business schools and professional societies on a number of marketing and consumer issues. Gillis is a member of the faculty of The George Washington University, where he teaches Marketing and Public Policy, is Director of Public Affairs for the Consumer Federation of America, and is a member of the Consumer Advisory Board of the National Futures Association.

He is author of *The Used Car Book* and *How to Make Your Car Last (Almost) Forever*, co-author of *The Childwise Catalog: A Consumer Guide to Buying the Safest and Best Products for Your Children* and *The Armchair Mechanic*, editor of *The Bank Book* and *The Product Safety Book*, and writes two monthly columns for *Good Housekeeping*. He is currently preparing consumer guides on air travel and home safety.

As an expert on consumer issues, he is a regular guest on the *Today Show*. He has appeared on all three network evening news programs as well as on local and national talk shows, including *Donahue, Late Night America, CBS Morning News* and *The Larry King Show*. He is frequently quoted in *The Wall Street Journal, The New York Times, Business Week, Money Magazine* and *USA Today*.

He received his MBA from The George Washington University and his BA from the University of Notre Dame. He currently lives in Washington, D.C., with his wife and two children.

If you cannot find additional copies of *The Car Book* in a local bookstore, you may obtain them by mail from the Center for Auto Safety. Send a check for $10.95 ($9.95 plus $1 postage and handling) for each copy to:

The Car Book
Center for Auto Safety
2001 S Street, N.W.
Washington, D.C. 20009

Make check payable to "The Car Book" and allow three to four weeks for delivery. *Sales of the book by mail benefit the non-profit Center for Auto Safety.*